Forever 17

ETHNOGRAPHIC ENCOUNTERS AND DISCOVERIES
A series edited by Stefan Timmermans

Forever 17

Coming of Age in the German Asylum System

ULRIKE BIALAS

The University of Chicago Press   Chicago and London

The University of Chicago Press, Chicago 60637
The University of Chicago Press, Ltd., London
© 2023 by The University of Chicago
Published 2023
Printed in the United States of America

32 31 30 29 28 27 26 25 24 23   1 2 3 4 5

ISBN-13: 978-0-226-83006-3 (cloth)
ISBN-13: 978-0-226-83008-7 (paper)
ISBN-13: 978-0-226-83007-0 (e-book)
DOI: https://doi.org/10.7208/chicago/9780226830070.001.0001

Library of Congress Cataloging-in-Publication Data

Names: Bialas, Ulrike, author.
Title: Forever 17 : coming of age in the German asylum system / Ulrike
    Bialas.
Other titles: Ethnographic encounters and discoveries.
Description: Chicago : The University of Chicago Press, 2023. | Series:
    Ethnographic encounters and discoveries | Includes bibliographical
    references and index.
Identifiers: LCCN 2023020234 | ISBN 9780226830063 (cloth) |
    ISBN 9780226830087 (paperback) | ISBN 9780226830070 (ebook)
Subjects: LCSH: Immigrants—Germany—Social conditions. | Refugees—
    Germany—Social conditions. | Germany—Emigration and immigration.
Classification: LCC JV8020 .B54 2023 | DDC 305.9/069140943—
    dc23/eng/20230427
LC record available at https://lccn.loc.gov/2023020234

♾ This paper meets the requirements of ANSI/NISO Z39.48-1992
(Permanence of Paper).

Our passion for categorization, life neatly fitted into pegs, has led to an unforeseen, paradoxical distress; confusion, a breakdown of meaning. Those categories which were meant to define and control the world for us have boomeranged us into chaos; in which limbo we whirl, clutching the straws of our definitions.

James Baldwin, *Notes of a Native Son*

CONTENTS

PREFACE * *Age and the False Binary of Vulnerability*

In late summer 2017, almost exactly two years after Germany had opened its borders to hundreds of thousands of refugees, I joined Paul, a young man from Guinea, to Berlin's university hospital, Charité, where adult asylum seekers could receive basic mental health care. After a general anamnesis, the psychiatrist asked: "Paul, what would you say your main problem is?" Paul hesitated for a few seconds, then decided: "My age. It's not correct on my identity card." The psychiatrist seemed confused and tried to clarify: "But I don't understand. Why is that such a problem for you? It's just paper. *C'est la même vie.* It's the same life." Paul answered, this time without hesitation: "*Non, ce n'est pas la même vie.* It's not the same life." Over the next several years of studying the lives of young unaccompanied asylum seekers in Berlin, I became convinced that Paul was right. For adult and minor asylum seekers in Germany, life was decidedly not the same.

The control of people's movements within and across countries has involved categorization for centuries, and bureaucratic categories still shape the context of reception for migrants, particularly those seeking asylum, today. These categories include minority age, unaccompaniment, trauma, or the particularly contested distinction between refugees and so-called economic migrants. Yet our knowledge of migrants' own experience of bureaucratic categories, how they negotiate the categorization of their bodies and biographies, and how they live with its outcome, is insufficient. It is important, however, to think about bureaucratic structures and the lived experience of migrants together, not only to get a fuller sense of migrants' lives, but to understand better how social categories such as age really work.

Social scientists are inherently interested in categorization. Their scholarship has helped to reveal that categories such as race and gender, which once appeared natural, are socially constructed. They have shown how categorization differs across time and space, how categories are imbued with norms and are often used with political intentions, and how they *strabbrushen* —

intersect with one another. We know that <u>categorization has profound consequences for the people who fall inside or outside its grids</u>, or who <u>defy a particular categorization altogether</u>. Categorization is a central aspect of social stratification, particularly that of migrants (Massey 2007; Menjívar 2023; Vertovec 2023). Douglas Massey even writes: "All <u>strati-fication</u> processes boil down to a combination of <u>two simple but power-ful mechanisms:</u> <u>the allocation</u> of people to social categories, and the institutionalization of practices that allocate resources unequally across these categories [. . .], producing what Charles Tilly (1998) referred to as 'categorical inequality'" (2007, 5).

The categorization of asylum seekers in Germany takes place at the interface of Global North and South, revealing discordant documentation practices and cultural notions of age—and other categories—between the two. This clash provides a unique opportunity for examining not only an important category shaping migrants' lives, but indeed one that affects us all, albeit not always as overtly. In the <u>Global North, nearly everyone knows and is able to provide evidence of their</u> date of birth, making the <u>application of age-based legal distinctions straightforward and unobtru-sive</u>. Even if a particular age threshold occasionally becomes the subject of debate, children—in present-day Germany, people under eighteen—are generally considered vulnerable. Moreover, the chronological objectivity of age, the undeniable truth that <u>everyone was in fact born on a specific day, has abetted the misunderstanding that age as a social category</u> is natural. Perhaps age also seems like a fair arbiter for the differential treat-ment of people because everyone will presumably inhabit the same age brackets over the course of their life, not the case with other category sys-tems such as race and gender. The problem is that <u>for migrants from coun-tries where an exact age has little legal</u> or cultural importance, neither the first point (that <u>age is universally known and easy to measure</u>) <u>nor the second</u> (that <u>the burdens and benefits</u> associated with specific age groups are, when viewed over the course of a lifetime, <u>equally distributed</u>) <u>holds</u> true. On the contrary, many migrants from Sub-Saharan Africa and the greater Middle East who have sought asylum in Germany since 2015 do not know their date of birth, let alone own official documentation of it, and have not had the kind of childhood and adolescence that their peers in the Global North rely on to prepare them for adulthood.

This book evolved from my interest in age as a category. In fall 2015, at the peak of that refugee crisis, I first learned about the age determination exams my home country, Germany, was conducting to classify the many young asylum seekers who claimed to be minors but had no identity docu-ments with which to substantiate these claims. This was not a peripheral phenomenon; the German state estimates that <u>only 40 percent of asylum</u>

seekers show identifying documents (Tangermann 2017). Among asylum seekers from Afghanistan, Somalia, and Guinea—unaccompanied minors' most common countries of origin—almost none do (Deutscher Bundestag 2021, 26). I initially shadowed forensic medical examiners at a hospital to understand how they estimated young migrants' ages with the help of radiological images, then volunteered with an organization for unaccompanied minors to learn how these exams impacted their legal status. I eventually decided that I would devote the bulk of my fieldwork to the young asylum seekers themselves. My earliest encounters with them had shown me that the significance of age extended far beyond forensic labs and legal counseling offices, into the daily lives and self-reflections of those whose ages were in question.

I conducted more than three years of daily ethnographic fieldwork with young male asylum seekers in Berlin, as well as with the volunteers, social workers, and other "helpers" they encountered as they navigated their new life, and the state workers charged with verifying their identities. I decided to focus on male asylum seekers because they make up the vast majority of young asylum seekers in Germany, and because their masculinity exacerbates suspicions about their age and their own sensitivity to feeling belittled.[1] I did, of course, encounter young women over the course of my fieldwork, and I include some of their stories as foils to sharpen my portrayal of the men's experiences, or in instances where gender seemed to me less salient than a more general point I wanted to make.

My goal is to offer an intimate look at how young asylum seekers in Germany negotiate their official identities, particularly their age, as well as the consequences of these negotiations: the emotional costs of having to fabricate parts of their identity so as to be considered vulnerable, and the practical costs of being classified as not vulnerable. The stakes of age classification are tremendous. To give just one example of the differential treatment of minors and adults: while minors can choose the country in which they want to file for asylum, adults fall under the Dublin III Regulation, which stipulates that the country through which they entered the European Union (EU) is responsible for their asylum case and that Germany may forcibly return them there.

Yet the state's difficulty in classifying young asylum seekers, and the shared struggles of asylum seekers classified on opposite sides of the minority-adulthood binary, reveal this category system to be culturally contingent, politically charged, and largely inadequate as a proxy for vulnerability. I show three particularly taxing consequences of binary classification. First, the rigidity of allocating youth welfare based on determinations of age and the granting of asylum based on national origin create incentives for asylum seekers to fabricate parts of their identity, accompanied by shame for having lied and fear of being found out. Young asylum seekers find it difficult to trust even their close friends, because confiding always bears the risk of exposure. Their relationships with Germans are often fraught with tension and mistrust—seriously hampering their social integration into German society. Second, official demands for vulnerability are at odds with young men's age-based personal growth, including independence and self-actualization, and are therefore experienced as infantilizing and emasculating. Finally, binary determinations of vulnerability leave many highly vulnerable asylum seekers outside vital state support systems: a rigid focus on the age of seventeen or younger obscures the vulnerabilities of young adults, and posits healthy desires for independence as incompatible with deserving state protection.

The term "refugee" was originally codified to protect the vulnerable, but, as Rebecca Hamlin argues, it is a legal fiction—a concept that does not accurately depict reality but is treated as if it did, "for purposes of bureaucratic expediency and convenience" (2021, 3). The binary of which it is necessarily only one side has often achieved just the opposite, disqualifying vulnerable migrants who do not fit its narrow definition from receiving protection. Likewise, I argue, the category of minor, intended to protect the vulnerable, is frequently used to deny protection and support to young adults who need both. Dates of birth, too, are often just a legal fiction, and the malleability of age changes at different stages of the construction, application, and experience of the category. Although age determination is highly ambiguous, once a date of birth has been assigned, it begins to signify fixed characteristics, and to produce effects that are nearly impossible to resist. This paradox is central to the stories I tell in the coming chapters.

While in chapters 2 and 3 I show that in the absence of documented dates of birth the social category age is not straightforward, in chapters 4, 5, and 6 I show that even if the category of age is successfully applied to differentiate asylum seekers, it may still not be indicative of the needs it is intended to assess. In chapter 7 I ask whether, in the eyes of my interlocutors, coming to Europe was worth the great personal sacrifices. I also propose that renewed arguments over how to define vulnerability might be the only way to address some of the dilemmas encountered in determining it. Finally, in the epilogue I offer some methodological reflections. Although throughout the book I give more than just cursory accounts of social workers, age examiners, and volunteers—particularly in chapters 1 and 3—the primary purpose of those accounts is to contextualize the experiences of the young asylum seekers, who remain at the heart of this book.

The seemingly outlandish circumstance of being without a date of birth in an age-obsessed society actually has wider theoretical significance. Asylum seekers with contested identities are noteworthy not only because of their large numbers, but because they disrupt the alleged clarity of certain identity categories. Those who do not fit a category system presumed to encompass everyone can, in fact, often say something profound about the system to which they remain alien. This is as true of young migrants whose age is contested as it is, for example, of people whose citizenship is "in question" (Lawrance and Stevens 2017). Though we believe the minor/adult, or citizen/noncitizen, binary accurately captures everyone, and that it is just a matter of individuals honestly claiming or states correctly assigning such status, the realities of age and national belonging are actually more complicated, and there are individuals who do not fit their respective parameters. As Cecilia Menjívar argues, "Classification systems assign people to categories into which they either do or do not fall, but peoples' experiences can also fall *between* categories" (2023, 13). Categories like age also rely so heavily on state documents for their verification that no "non-circular account" (Stevens 2017, 221) exists of how their boundaries emerged. Circularity marks both the German state's accounts of the supposed coherence between vulnerability and minority age, and the attempts of young migrants to fit this mold. To explore binaries such as the migrant/refugee one, Hamlin calls on us to "move beyond positivist frameworks that take definitions at face value and instead examine the ways in which various terms are deployed discursively, particularly by people who wield the authority of the state, or who seek to appeal to that authority" (2021, 9). I want to turn our attention precisely to the difficulties of determining who is a minor and who is an adult, and to the dilemma of deciding who should receive the benefits of minority and who the burdens of adulthood—rather than merely joining in the left's critiques of the inadequate treatment of minors, or the right's critique of undue protections afforded to adults. Both children and citizens have special rights, but they may only claim them if they can prove these identities.

Individuals whose age, citizenship, or other category membership is "in question" unwittingly expose covert norms and standards by violating them. The migration of youth without documented dates of birth therefore constitutes what Robert Merton called a "strategic research site" (1987, 15), where common and important phenomena which, in Jack Katz's words, "exist widely but in a more diluted form elsewhere" (2012, 259)—in this case, our dependence on exact chronological age in judgments of vulnerability—become uniquely evident. The arrival of ageless people in a society steeped in age-based legal boundaries provides the conditions for an "infrastructural inversion," to use a phrase coined by the science and technology scholars Geoffrey C. Bowker and Susan Leigh Star (2000): a rendering visible of an infrastructure that normally is so ubiquitous and works so smoothly that it all but disappears. The historical moment of the 2015–16 refugee crisis and Germany's response to it thus provide a rare gateway to questions of greater magnitude.

In the absence of birth certificates, how do we define and measure age? Why does an age still seem natural and straightforward even as many other social categories have lost their self-evidence, or even have come to be seen as fluid? Why do we care about someone's chronological age, and for what do we imagine it is a proxy? What price do we ask young migrants to pay in exchange for help and hope? How do they live with the identities they feel compelled to adopt in order to fit our legal and cultural notions of vulnerability? Have we succeeded in creating a system that identifies the most vulnerable and empowers them to thrive?

To be "forever seventeen"—as in the title of this book—seems like a panacea, but it can turn out to be a curse, especially as it stands in contrast to young asylum seekers' dreams of migration as a rite of passage to adulthood. "Forever seventeen" is the sarcastic allegation made by those suspicious of young asylum seekers' identities. And indeed, many asylum seekers, who see no other chance for making it in Germany, place all their hopes in being classified as seventeen, and would choose to be seventeen for much longer than is plausible. Yet being seventeen, let alone *forever* seventeen, is also a burden. Being seventeen means being supervised, dependent, and other-directed. It means that former peers outpace you. To be forever seventeen is life come to a standstill, a setback in stark contrast to the leap toward dignity and self-actualization that crossing the ocean was meant to be.

1 * *The Long Summer of Migration*

When Idris's boat—carrying about two hundred Egyptian and East African men, along with some women and children—finally reached Italian waters, one of the three captains called the Italian coast guard, who assured them they would be there within the hour. "What did you do, that last hour on the boat?" I asked Idris. After eight days on an overcrowded, understocked timber fishing boat—with pants turned colorless and stiff from constant submersion in salt water, limbs weak from sitting and fasting, a mind numb from prayer, and a throat sore from vomiting—what does a person do when rescue is suddenly near? Idris said: "Someone opened a plastic bag with disposable razors and handed them out, and most of the men—maybe 150 men—started shaving. I didn't understand why at first, but someone handed me a razor and said that we needed to look as young as possible when we got to Europe."

Young men from the Global South follow their dreams of independence and self-actualization to the Global North, only to find that appearing young and vulnerable offers them a much better chance at a successful and safe existence in Europe.[1] Unlike adult asylum seekers, unaccompanied minors receive special protections and resources regarding their residence status, housing, education, and medical care, among other spheres of life. While these benefits cannot be claimed by legal adults, those who have obtained them as minors are often able to carry them into adulthood. Young migrants learn about this legal distinction and its far-reaching consequences from friends who have moved before them, from other migrants they meet during the journey, or only upon arriving in Europe. Although they often come from countries where dates of birth have little cultural or legal significance, and sometimes do not even know their exact age, once they arrive in Germany their age becomes—both in the eyes of the state and in their own—possibly their most important distinction. Some know they are not actually minors, but believe that minority age is their only path to living and thriving in Europe. Others do not know their exact age, so that claiming to be minors feels not like a lie but like the natural corollary of moving to an age-stratified society. Aside from the bizarre activity of shaving on the migration trail, young asylum seekers agree to radiation exposure in forensic age exams, belittle themselves in youth welfare interviews, ask for supporting documents from the embassies of the countries they have fled, and slip into the role of adolescent in their interactions with Germans and even with other migrants. In pursuit of help and hope, they thus resort to the cumbersome process of establishing their minority age, and to the often infantilizing reality of living in Europe as a minor.

A Perfect Storm: Germany in 2015 and 2016

The year 2015 marked a unique moment in German migration history. The Syrian civil war had forced several million Syrians to leave their country. Chancellor Angela Merkel opened Germany's borders to them in August 2015 and suspended the Dublin agreement for Syrians, so that they no longer had to file for asylum in the EU country of their first arrival, but could do so in Germany. Humanitarian crises in the greater Middle East and Sub-Saharan Africa, and extremely high levels of global inequality—as well as news and rumors of Germany's open borders and *Willkommenskultur*, the collective public euphoria and readiness to help that at least initially accompanied Merkel's policies—especially propelled young men, including many who had been stuck in transit in Iran or Libya, to also make their way to Germany. Between 2015 and 2019 nearly 1.8 million people filed for asylum in Germany, and 600,000 of them were men under the age of twenty-five (BAMF 2015–19). In 2018, my first full year of fieldwork with asylum seekers, 74 percent of asylum seekers in Germany were under thirty years of age and 48.3 percent under eighteen.[2] Among unaccompanied minors, 17.5 percent were from Afghanistan, 14.1 percent from Somalia, 12.8 percent from Guinea, and 11.7 percent from Eritrea, and 80.1 percent of them were male (BAMF 2018).

The European refugee crisis was widely reported across European and even international media.[3] Most know the images of capsized or flaming boats and drowned children, of thousands walking through Europe, and, in the German case, of a stunning cheer welcoming the new arrivals. Germans waved to those who reached their cities by bus or train, and walked alongside those who came by foot. The jubilation, however, waned soon. Representative surveys from 2018–19 show that 56 percent of Germans thought their country had taken in too many refugees, and that 68 percent thought the federal government had no viable plan for dealing with them (Faus and Storks 2019). It became obvious that Germany could not register, house, and provide for every asylum seeker so quickly. In Berlin, makeshift shelters were built, and school gymnasiums and a former airport were turned into camps. These were meant to accommodate asylum seekers for a few weeks, but ended up being home to many for the next several years. Social workers, translators, and asylum case adjudicators were hired in a hurry, often with few qualifications and no experience. Volunteer groups organized to avert catastrophe. At the same time, new right-wing groups and parties mobilized around the claim that asylum seekers were undeserving of the social benefits they received, and that they presented a cultural-religious, or even criminal, infiltration of German society.

Several high-profile crimes, in the wake of which the official identity of the perpetrator came under doubt, fueled public suspicion over the identity of young male asylum seekers, even culminating in significant changes to German migration policy in summer 2019: the Law of Orderly Return (*Geordnete-Rückkehr-Gesetz*). This law explicitly addressed the problem of so-called "persistent identity resisters" (*hartnäckige Identitätsverweigerer*), people who obstruct the clarification of their identity. These people now received an even more precarious residence permit than before, and were entitled to even fewer resources. In addition to visual and forensic age determination exams, asylum interviews, language analyses for the determination of national origin, phone readouts, and document verification, the sanctioning of people without personal documents had become another cornerstone in Germany's frenetic but ultimately futile efforts to determine the identities of asylum seekers.

Although Syrians dominated media coverage of the refugee crisis, they only account for about a third of asylum applications submitted in Germany since 2015 (BAMF 2019), and for only a fraction of unaccompanied minors. African and Afghan youths encountered problems of age classification that Syrians largely did not, for at least three reasons. First, Syrians usually move with their families, whereas teenagers from those other regions do so alone (FitzGerald and Arar 2018), making age more consequential for them than for Syrians accompanied by relatives. Second, Syrians usually know their date of birth, and own identity documents that the German state accepts as valid, making alternative methods of age determination unnecessary. Third, Syrians received protection with relative ease—often even without asylum interviews—and could thus receive permanent residence without the circuitous route through minority, whereas other migrants' traumatic experiences rarely fit European definitions of persecution. Asylum seekers who will likely have their requests for asylum rejected because they are from countries considered safe may then, in a sense, use the protections of minority age to compensate for their lack of other protections.

Thus, while Syrian families left their war-torn country with very good prospects of asylum or other forms of protection, and were often well educated and in possession of identity documents, young men from the greater Middle East and Sub-Saharan Africa left their homes without the consent or often even the knowledge of their families, and were unhappy with their economically and socially stifled lives, yet had no identity documents and almost no prospect of receiving protection in Europe. There are several reasons for asylum applications being submitted without documents: migrants come from countries without extensive civil registration systems and have never owned documents; they have lost documents while en route to Europe; their documents have been taken by traffickers; or they have deliberately gotten rid of documents so as to conceal their identity. These concurrent circumstances have created a large population of young men living in Germany with contested identities and bleak prospects of residence, let alone asylum. Their struggles are at the heart of this book.

Paradise within Reach

Almost three years had passed since Idris had been advised to shave on the boat. We were in Dessau for the weekend to visit his friend Aman. Idris and Aman had lived together in Berlin, but Aman had been classified as an adult and forced to relocate to Dessau, a town in the former East of Germany. "Why did you even come?" Idris asked Aman, who had just told us about growing up well-off in Ethiopia.

Aman grinned. "You know why we all came here, brother. Because when you live in Africa, you think there is more life in Europe."

"Paradise," Idris added.

"Yeah," Aman nodded.

Aman and seven other young Ethiopian men occupied two adjacent run-down apartments provided by Dessau's Refugee Office. The prefabricated high-rise building stood at the former industrial outskirts, a fifteen-minute walk from the nearest tram stop, past swampy meadows and a defunct gas station. The men had not dealt out the four bedrooms among the eight of them, though for our visit I was assigned my own; usually, everyone just slept wherever. Anyway, there was no furniture besides a few mattresses and a table with chairs. The front doors of both apartments were kept ajar so that everyone could come and go at will. In the kitchen, names scribbled on pieces of tape indicated which foodstuffs belonged to whom, though the young men usually ate together and everyone seemed to own the same groceries: packs of spaghetti, cans of chickpeas and tomato paste, onions, potatoes, Maggi instant seasoning, and safflower seed oil. The fridge was nearly empty, and the only frying pan had no handle. "Like our boat," Idris remarked—a comparison he often made when having to make do with something unsound. He burned his hand trying to scramble eggs for us all in the morning. The bathroom floor was dank from a chronic leak, and the sink needed all night to drain after being used in the evening. It was February, and the heat had been out of order all winter. I did not take my coat off that weekend, not even to sleep.

We spent Friday night indoors, crowded around the only table in the slightly warmer of the two apartments. The young men switched seamlessly between Amharic, Oromo, Tigrinya, and Somali, and Idris's reminders to the group to speak German so that I would not be excluded became something of a running gag, met with apologetic laughter: "Forgive us for using the only wealth we have—languages." Everyone but Idris, Eba, and I drank beer, and when Abdi began slurring his words, Eba seized the bottle from his hand.

"Hey, *habibi*," Abdi protested. "This is my life. I can drink a hundred beers if I want to."

"He's right," Idris seconded, "This is Germany, bro; leave him alone."

A few of the men began teasing Eba, who, they said, was in love with his former caseworker. He had whispered her name in his sleep, and Abdi had seen Eba's diary—which, as Abdi recounted, read, "I missed her today, 31st January, blah blah blah." Abdi said Eba shouldn't be afraid to admit his feelings. Idris agreed that this was Germany and that love here knew no religion, age, or color. Abdi pointed out that Eba had not been eating much for weeks, a sure sign of love sickness. When Eba countered that he had simply been trying to lose weight, the group burst into laughter. "He was on the boat for seventeen days, that's why he is crazy," Abdi roared.

"Seventeen days? Really?" Idris asked incredulously, suddenly serious. Conversations among young asylum seekers often oscillated between playful banter and the most somber of topics, so rapidly that the line between different moods became blurry.

One of the young men started playing music by the popular Ethiopian singer Teddy Afro on his phone. Aman said he hated Teddy Afro because of his song about Menelik II, the Ethiopian emperor who had heroically parried Italy's attempts to colonize Ethiopia, but had also brutally killed people of Oromo ethnicity, Aman's own ethnic group. An argument ensued about whether it was OK to sing about Menelik, and whether he could be considered the Hitler of Ethiopia. Idris, who always tried to appease the conflicts that arose between Ethiopians of different ethnicities, insisted that the past was the past and that now they were all brothers, all Ethiopians. Yet, he announced to no one in particular, he would never go back to Ethiopia, not for a million euros. He had risked his life to come to Germany, and no one could make him leave now. A few minutes later, however, he remembered aloud the lush greenery of the coffee plants in Jimma, the traditional Ethiopian dishes that never turned out quite right in Germany, and the spontaneous folk dancing that everybody knew. He turned to me and said, "If you ever go to Ethiopia, you will love it so much that you will never want to come back."

Idris was an athletic young man whose demeanor fluctuated between outgoing and sweet, when things were going well, and withdrawn, when he made his own hardships even harder by mercilessly admonishing himself for neglecting his duties as a Muslim. In good times his hair quickly grew into a high Afro, he helped strangers on the street to the point where I almost expected him to be late to our meetings, he entertained whomever was around with his impressive moonwalking, and he cooked generous Ethiopian meals for friends and acquaintances while singing along to Ethiopian pop songs. He even went to the disco and sometimes drank alcohol; and when on these occasions he said, "*Ya Allah*, forgive me!" there was no fear or self-contempt in his voice—just amused astonishment about where life had taken him. When things were not going well, however—due to difficulties in school, conflicts with his caseworkers, or the rejection of his request for asylum—he resorted to the explanation that it must be God's punishment for his life in Germany, which in those moments he viewed as impious. He then cropped his hair so close to his head that its kink was no longer visible, canceled social commitments in order to observe the correct prayer times, and spoke in contempt of Germany, a country he otherwise showered in words of admiration and gratitude. He cycled through these phases over the years, struggling to reconcile faith and piety with his irrefutable thirst for a new life in Berlin.

We spent the rest of the weekend with Aman and his roommates, sitting around wrapped in blankets, clutching cups of tea, watching Bollywood movies, and talking. None of the men worked or went to school. The group decided against going to a disco because German girls, they sensed, either snubbed or exoticized Black men; and they did not want to go for walks either, because they felt that locals looked at them contemptuously. Whereas the young refugees I knew in Berlin blended into a varicolored cityscape of tourists, international students, and children and grandchildren of former guest workers, here in Dessau, as in many smaller, ethnically homogenous eastern German towns, the refugees stood out. The young men typically spent their days using the local mall's free wi-fi, filling out sports bets, and keeping appointments with the refugee or social welfare offices and the evenings drinking beer and smoking cannabis, despite considering both those things *haram*. When Idris asked how everyone's asylum cases were going, Aman was the first to reply, "Reject, *habibi*," as the others nodded in assent. Abdi added, almost bitterly, "Because there's democracy in Ethiopia now." The election of Abiy Ahmed—soon to receive the Nobel Peace Prize, and celebrated internationally as a progressive reformer—had made Ethiopians' prospects for asylum even more dismal.[4] This was paradise?

The Concurrence of Force and Aspiration in Refugee Migration

Young men like Idris leave home because their countries seem without prospects. Yet their dreams for the future exceed mere escape. Migrants often share a hierarchical view of the world as consisting of more and less attractive places—what in anthropology has been called a "cosmology" (Belloni 2019, 3). Refugee studies scholars, afraid of undermining their interlocutors' chances of asylum, sometimes hesitate to acknowledge aspiration within forced migration. Milena Belloni, for instance, frequently found audiences unsettled when she presented her findings on Eritrean refugees' desires and aspirations; some attendees claimed she was hurting vulnerable refugees, while others thought she had inadvertently exposed the illegitimacy of her interlocutors' requests for asylum (2019, 9). The idea that real, vulnerable refugees must only be fleeing from something, and could not also be moving in search of something, also manifests in the narrow demands of the asylum system, which I will discuss in later chapters. This implied mutual exclusion of vulnerability and the desire for a better life is unrealistic, however, and in international migration scholarship, a field that has been curiously separate from refugee studies (FitzGerald and Arar 2018), such coexisting dynamics have long been known as the interplay of push and pull factors (Massey et al. 1999). There is simply no contradiction between leaving your homeland for safety reasons and being excited to start a new life elsewhere—between fleeing from and aspiring toward. As Hamlin puts it, so-called mixed flows should not just be understood as "people with differing but pure motivations migrating together in the same boat. [. . .] Rather, individual border crossers often embody mixed motivations that combine to inspire migration" (Hamlin 2021, 66). Even Eritrean refugees, who have high protection rates internationally precisely because of their undeniably oppressive government, are motivated by "desires for modernity" (Belloni 2019, 43), which do not in any way delegitimize their claims to protection.

Especially for men, migrating can also be a coming-of-age experience—a rite of passage to adulthood (Boehm 2012). Migration is particularly auspicious in regions where the ambitions of youth are systematically stifled, and when young people are "caught in a seemingly unbridgeable schism between the culturally expected and the socially possible" (Vigh 2009, 95). Besides economic difficulties, political disenfranchisement impedes the aspirations and dignity of youth. Nowhere, for example, is the discrepancy between the share of young people in the population and their political influence greater than in Sub-Saharan Africa (Smith 2018). The transition to adulthood is difficult in such economically depressed countries with generationally very unequal access to resources and power (Thorsen 2006; Vigh 2009; Waage 2006). Millions of young Africans have virtually no political power, as African politics privileges seniority, essentially excluding the bulk of the electorate from any real influence. Many young Africans also have little chance of vocational self-actualization, and are constantly confronted with digital images of the alleged solution to their problems: Europe. The Cameroonian journalist Eric Chinje has called migration a "natural movement" for Africans, "an integral part of life" (*Die Zeit* 2019). Africa's future— its youth—is sitting on packed bags, as the German-Ethiopian writer Asfa-Wossen Asserate (2018) puts it. Eventually picking up those bags, moreover, is made progressively easier by a growing African diaspora in Europe that can assist with the journey and settlement. It is unsurprising, then, that in Sub-Saharan Africa, international migration constitutes "the most vital and promising social sphere, in which a better, more prosperous and more secure life can be imagined" (Drotbohm 2017, 22).

The scope of the migration of unaccompanied youth without identity documents is already enormous, and will only increase as more young people from the Global South head north. Various reports (including McKinsey 2016 and Pew Research Center 2018) suggest that millions of young Africans are still hoping to come to Europe. Whatever one thinks of the sometimes populist wielding of such prognoses, there is solid empirical evidence that migration of young men from Africa to Western Europe will continue to increase—constituting what Saskia Sassen (2016) has called one of the "emergent migrations."

The longing for Europe, particularly by young men, is one of the defining sentiments between the Global South and North. In Somali, this hunger is called *buufi* (Horst 2006). Gambian youth lost in thought about Europe have, in vernacular parlance, "the nerves syndrome" (Suso 2019). In *Atlantique* (Diop 2019), a film about young men from Dakar who decide to canoe to Europe, one young man's girlfriend says at the beach, as the waves pull his gaze toward Europe like aquatic magnets: "You never look at me. You only have eyes for the ocean." And for what presumably lies beyond. The writer Chimamanda Ngozi Adichie describes her Nigerian protagonists as "conditioned from birth to look towards somewhere else, eternally convinced that real lives happened in that somewhere else" (2013, 276). Former German President Horst Köhler observed in an op-ed that "in Africa, a generation is coming of age whose ambitions look to the affluence of developed countries, which has become the global benchmark" (2017).

Migration dreams are born from the "interpretation of local realities versus global possibilities" (Bal and Willems 2014, 256). Globalization generates the knowledge of the existence of a different life and, to an extent, the ability to reach its geographic locus—often followed by the realization that this coveted life is more than a trek away. On Facebook and Instagram, young people from the Global South see images of compatriots who have already made it to Europe: expensive clothes, shopping malls, apartments, sometimes European girlfriends and babies. Before coming to Europe, my interlocutors assumed that everyone who got there had become rich. So as not to be the only failure in a supposedly unbroken line of success stories, asylum seekers, once in Europe, often themselves begin producing images like the ones that initially lured them. Browsing through my interlocutors' social media accounts, I barely recognized the lives of young men who I knew did not own cars or spend their days clad in expensive clothes, promenading on villa-lined streets. The German embassy in Afghanistan even ran a campaign using the hashtag #RumoursAboutGermany to dissuade Afghans from coming (*Die Zeit* 2015). The Danish government placed ads in Lebanese newspapers warning would-be migrants of Denmark's reduced benefits and stricter deportation enforcements (BBC 2015), and Eritrean National Television purposely broadcasts news about struggling refugees in Europe (Belloni 2019).

The young men I got to know left their home countries—Afghanistan, Cameroon, Eritrea, Ethiopia, Guinea, Nigeria, Somalia, and Sudan—for complex reasons that also changed in hindsight and over time, as justifications for life decisions tend to do. Samir's story is typical. Having grown up in an Eritrean refugee settlement in Sudan, he had wanted to go to Europe as long as he could remember. Not only was life in Sudan marked by poverty and futility, but as undocumented Eritrean refugees his family also faced arbitrary arrests, police brutality, and systematic exclusion from education and work, as well as hostility and discrimination in the streets. Samir first announced that he would go to Europe as a preteen, but his parents forbade it. In 2013 two of his cousins died in one of the deadliest migrant shipwrecks in the Mediterranean near Lampedusa. This made his mother even more adamant to keep her son from following the same path. His uncle, too, warned, "Do you want to end up like your cousins?" But Samir told me he replied: "I don't want to end up like *you*. What have *you* done with your life?"

Samir was scrawny and squirrelly, made a few inches taller by a tuft of disheveled dreads on top of his head, usually adorned with small white or silver beads. He wore the same pair of sneakers most of the time I knew him, and combined them with a variety of matching tracksuits and hoodies, as well as a black pouch that seemed to contain everything he needed. A teacher once said of him that he didn't go through life; he danced through it. He was quick-witted and quick-moving, and I often marveled at how well he knew my home city after only a few years. He could show me, a native-born Berliner, the fastest shortcuts, the cleanest public restrooms and reliable free wi-fi, the most secluded benches from which to gaze at the moon in the middle of the night, and the waterfronts from which to watch it fade again at daybreak. He could be charming and funny when he wanted to get his way or genuinely liked someone, or combative and rude when he sensed someone's disrespect or was simply in a bad mood, disheartened by a life that never quite seemed to go his way. Samir's "street German," as he called it, was literal and full of poetry. He had the ability to make his point in words so simple and poignant that they stuck with me. Once, at a coffeeshop, the barista asked if he took his coffee with milk or sugar. Samir grabbed the paper cup and said "with sun," as he stepped out into the golden hour. Before lighting up a joint or preparing a line of coke, he would habitually switch his phone to airplane mode so as not to be disturbed. Half an hour later, when he was high, he would say, "I'm flying!" and spread his arms as if he were about to take off. He would only switch the airplane mode off during the comedown.

Determined not to repeat the disappointing lives of their parents, Samir and other young men believe Europe to be the place where their dreams of adulthood still stand a chance. When Samir and his friend Asim left Sudan in 2016, they did not tell anyone. Had Samir told his mother he was going, she would have said, "If you leave, you're no longer my son," and then he would not have left. Had he told his girlfriend, she would have cried, and then he would not have left. Had he told his friends, they might have told his mother or his girlfriend. While the migration of minors has commonly been portrayed as a family project (see, for example, Hopkins and Hill 2008), my interlocutors left without the approval or even the knowledge of their parents. Perhaps migration more easily serves as a rite of passage to adulthood when arranged by the adult-to-be himself. Many young men also told me they did not want to worry their parents or make them feel guilty if they consented to a journey that turned out to be fatal. So Samir and Asim went to sleep one night, and by morning their rooms were empty. Samir called his mother from Libya, and she cried and begged him not to get on a boat; but, after working and saving money for several months, he did. Asim got on one boat and Samir on another, so as to minimize the chance that they would both die. Their families were close, and Samir and Asim had promised each other that whoever made it would help out the other's family financially as well.

From Italy, Samir had called his mother for the first time in two months. "*Kifek?* How are you?" he said.

"Who is this?" replied his mother.

"It's me, Samir."

"Samir, I thought you had died. I prayed that you had gone to paradise." But he had not. Samir had made it to Europe.

Despite the dangerous journey, countless adolescents remain willing to take the risk, thinking like others before them of Europe as a paradise within reach. Samir regularly received calls and messages from teenagers in his Sudanese hometown who asked him for tips on how to make it to Germany. He would get angry and yell at them not to involve him in the possibility of their death. If he knew their parents, he would call and warn them about their children's plans. I interpreted this as his attempt to make amends for how he had hurt his own family when he left without saying goodbye.

In defiance of the complexity and changeability of motivations, asylum seekers need to present a coherent story of their decision to leave, often centering an event—actual or invented—that precipitated their departure. Even if the event they describe in their asylum interview has actually occurred, however, it is often not the one that primarily caused them to leave. To transform their departure into flight, they reach into a box of memories and draw from their many terrible experiences that fit— they imagine—European expectations of forced migration: child labor, judiciary arbitrariness, police brutality, corruption, interethnic conflict. They do not necessarily invent these experiences, but inflate their impact on the decision to leave—thereby molding the truth in a way that is common among immigration lawyers' and immigrants' accounts of their own life histories (Lakhani 2013). These experiences may have provided confirmation that leaving was the right decision, but the more pertinent reasons for leaving—the triggers, if you will—are often much more personal: disappointed love, family feuds, and the sense that the best version of themselves lives elsewhere. As Idris once put it: "There is your *reason* for why you came to Europe. And then there are your *reasons.*"

Idris himself had given the imprisonment resulting from his relationship with the daughter of his town's most powerful family as his reason for leaving Ethiopia, but he had actually stayed there for two years after being released from incarceration. He had initially joined friends headed toward Europe in 2014, but turned around after half a day because he could not bear the thought of abandoning his mother, who depended on him to help raise her younger children. He later applied for resettlement to North America through the United Nations—a Somali family living in Ethiopia while waiting for their resettlement had agreed to say he was their son—but he eventually grew tired of waiting for a decision. So in 2016, he followed his friends to Germany. With reports of open borders and *Willkommenskultur*, the moment seemed opportune.

The Boat Journey and the Institutional Invisibilization of Trauma

Asylum seekers from all countries, religions, legal statuses, and age groups are united by the common experience of having survived but not forgotten the horrors of their journey to Europe. Thus, when videos surfaced in late 2017 of Sub-Saharan African migrants being sold on a Libyan slave market, I joined a few hundred protesters—including Idris, his best friend Yakob, and Paul from Guinea—outside the Libyan embassy in the sleet, fists raised in silent protest. Occasions like this gathering offered glimpses of an unspoken solidarity among young asylum seekers, even as their factual knowledge of each other's journeys was scarce. The harrowing journey to Europe actually often seemed more prominent in the minds of young asylum seekers than did the difficulties they had escaped in their home countries. Unprompted, they would tell me about being driven through the Sahara by smugglers and beaten by camp guards in Libya, and about praying to God on ramshackle boats in the Mediterranean. In the desert, they sped past skeletons on overcrowded Jeeps, and when someone fell off a vehicle, the smugglers just drove on. The smugglers also continuously separated and regrouped migrants so that they could not form friendships and ally against their smugglers.[5] Paul had exchanged Facebook names with other migrants, and he drily remarked that those who had not accepted his friend requests must have died. Yakob and Idris showed me pictures of their days in the Sahara: young men in mismatched tracksuits and sandals, showing thumbs-up and victory signs. In these photos they looked out of breath, squinting, their hair and faces covered in fine sand. "I was as white as you then," Yakob joked. After crossing the desert, Libyan smugglers detained migrants in camps near Sabha and Bani Walid, and called their families to tell them their children were being held for ransom. At night, the camp guards came and collected the women, whom they returned the next morning, except for the ones they liked best. Samir and his friend Asim worked in a house where female migrants were held as sex workers; they were in charge of making sure the girls did not run away. Paul was responsible for burying migrants who had died. Others just collected building materials, or earned their boat fare through other menial jobs.

Many of the two million people who have filed for asylum in Germany since 2015 reached Europe by boat. They paid smugglers who herded together as many hopefuls as would fit, equipped with too little water and food and an insufficient sense of direction or nautical knowledge. Some later said they had expected the journey to be as horrid as it was; others were caught unaware. All remembered the boat, the water, and the other passengers for years afterward. The moment you stepped onto the boat, an "either-or life" began, Idris recapitulated; you either died or lived, now ever aware of those two possibilities. Had Idris known what the crossing would be like, he would not have come. I asked what one does for days on a boat. You vomit, he said. You pray. You pray even if you do not believe in God. A young man sitting near Idris would not stop wailing, "Mama, what have I done to you?" The children cried and screamed. When food and water ran out, fights erupted over the reserves that passengers assumed the captains still had—conflicts made worse by lack of a common language. Some drank seawater and became sicker. Sometimes you fell asleep for a bit, but then a wave came and washed over you. Everyone told me about the water, water like they had never seen before. Samir remembered: "Water to the left, to the right, behind you, in front of you." Blue when you gazed into the distance, black and white when you looked straight down. Stuff floated in the water: things that presumably belonged to people who had set out for Europe earlier.

Guled, Paul's Somali classmate, used his phone to show me a video another man had taken of their crossing. For minutes, one saw nothing but water foaming and undulating behind the boat. The hum of the Yamaha motor nearly drowned out the man's invocation: "*Ya Allah! Ya Allah*, I am so afraid of the ocean. So afraid. I pray that God brings us to Malta safely." Guled pointed to the motor on his phone screen and remarked matter-of-factly: "If that had stopped, we would all be gone now." The camera panned to the inside of the small boat, where about eighty people were packed body to body. The video ended with the man pointing the camera at himself and raising his fist to the sky, like a victorious athlete.

Asylum seekers also joked about even more ludicrous attempts to reach Europe. Over dinner with Idris, me, and his girlfriend, Masarat, Yakob told us that some Africans have themselves sewn into mattresses and transported to Europe that way. He pantomimed the police cutting open mattresses and finding one African after another. Idris, Masarat, and I laughed at his performance, but Yakob said: "Just to have a good life. It seems funny, but it actually isn't."

Idris had initially told his family he was going to Egypt to study religion, and had withheld his plans to take a boat to Europe. Idris's brother Ahmed, who was living in Munich, had never heard him talk about the journey, and shook his head in disbelief when Idris recounted it over dinner. "You could have died, and we wouldn't have known," Ahmed kept saying. Idris said he was lucky. He showed Ahmed and me a video another passenger had later sent him, of their arrival in Italy. In it, men in rubber boats, wearing full-body suits and face masks, approached a ragged-looking fishing boat. They lifted children out of the boat, to safety. In one shot, Idris sat on the floor of the boat, staring into the camera. In another shot, he stood and gestured for people to let the children through to be taken off the boat. Two years after the crossing, Idris ran into yet another fellow passenger by chance, in Berlin. When they realized how they knew each other, they began reminiscing, their memories vivid despite the intervening years. They both shook their heads in retrospective horror. The other man said, "If Germans knew what we did to come to Europe, that we gave our life as a wager, if they had felt the feeling you have on that boat, they would give all of us papers."

The danger of the journey can actually contribute to migrants' view of it as a rite of passage (Aguilar 1999; Sheridan 2009; Suso 2019), a traumatic initiation into a new life (Van Gennep [1909] 2019). The boat crossing also became a source of solidarity among asylum seekers: a symbol of their unrestrainable yearning for a new life, a reference point for their break with the old, a beacon of personal accomplishment, and a handy signpost in times both good and bad to gauge whether coming to Europe had been worth it. It became the subject of darkly humorous remarks, and a response to Germany's ignorance of the true trauma of flight. "The boat" became shorthand for the absurdity of wanting to be in Europe at all costs, an easy reference all asylum seekers understood. Other traumas of the past must be invented, or at least reinvented, to meet the asylum system's narrow focus on specific kinds of experiences. Those stories are charged with guilt and fear, and therefore are unsuitable as a source of solidarity among strangers. The frightening journey to Europe, however—especially the boat crossing—needs no embellishment, and unites asylum seekers across nationalities and ethnicities, official ages, and legal statuses. To explain Eba's romance with a caseworker, his friends in Dessau teased: "He spent seventeen days on the boat. That's why he's crazy." Whenever Idris wanted to express that something had a fifty-fifty chance of success, he simply said, "Like our boat"—and, to my amazement, other asylum seekers immediately understood what he meant.

Just as complex causes of migration eventually get reduced to choice versus compulsion in the asylum procedure, and the vulnerability of young adults is disguised by the rigid age boundaries used in youth welfare and the many other realms of German law that rely on dates of birth, the trauma of the journey to Europe—the days in the Sahara, the weeks on the boat—also becomes administratively invisible. In an asylum case, only trauma incurred in the country of origin—not during the attempt to escape it—counts. In asylum counseling workshops and in attempts to convince volunteers of their exceptional need for help, asylum seekers often begin by narrating what they witnessed en route to Europe, intuiting that this is, in large part, the root of their nightmares, flashbacks, and depression—only to be reminded that while regrettable, these incidents are irrelevant to their prospects of being allowed to stay in Germany. Talk of the Sahara, Libya, and the boat becomes the stuff of private conversations and therapy, while being eliminated from official settings such as the asylum interview or court hearing. Just as the notion of Europe as paradise continues to unite asylum seekers, however, so the boat remains an important common reference point and a source of solidarity. The boat experience affiliates asylum seekers, and sets them apart from Germans who cannot, and German bureaucrats who will not, understand.

Volunteering in the "Wild West"

As Idris and Samir were leaving Africa, a perfect storm was already beginning to brew in Germany, sweeping toward "the long summer of migration" of 2015. Given its position between southern and northern Europe, Bavaria, Germany's southernmost state, had attracted thousands of asylum seekers even before 2015. The situation at Bayernkaserne, a complex of former barracks in Munich that had been turned into a refugee shelter, foreshadowed what awaited the rest of the country. One social worker who worked in the part of Bayernkaserne reserved for unaccompanied minors (before they were accommodated through the youth welfare office) described the situation as a "Wild West" and a "blatant defiance of the rights of the child." He entrusted me with the files in which he and his colleagues had secretly documented the state of Bayernkaserne's minors tract, where about two hundred minors lived under the supervision of just eight social workers. The minors tract was not closed off from the rest of the barracks, and residents from other parts came and went freely. "Adult men, two or three together, walked through the hallways and picked out the prettiest boys, took them with them, and returned them after three or four hours. There was nothing we could do, we couldn't retain them."

The files show about a hundred occurrences daily of "slander," "threats," "spitting," "power games," and "ethnic conflicts"—and, on average, two suicide attempts per week, matter-of-factly listed as either "strangulation," "jumping," "self-harm knife," or "overdose pills." The social worker said, "To me, this shows what happens to children when you keep them in camps for adults." He founded a therapeutic group in which minors living at Bayernkaserne could share their problems and support one another; but, he confessed, "we were working against windmills because the circumstances were simply brutal." In 2013, several riots destroyed much of the facility. The pictures I viewed showed doors kicked out of their frames, broken windows and lamps, and floors covered in splinters of glass. Following the riot and several hunger strikes, minors in Bavaria were eventually housed in designated youth welfare facilities. The reception of unaccompanied minors was formalized throughout Germany—perhaps due in part to conditions like those at Bayernkaserne—and the minors came to live separately from adult asylum seekers.[6]

By 2015 the chaos had reached the rest of Germany. Local government officials I spoke to made no secret of the fact that the influx of asylum seekers would have been impossible to handle without the countless volunteer-run organizations that had mushroomed in Berlin and other places. Notwithstanding international observers' nearly unanimous applause over Germany's "dignity and efficiency" (Balibar 2015) in receiving the newcomers, volunteers involved in this reception largely remember a pandemonium that was neither dignified nor efficient. Their memories also diverge sharply from Germany's image as that of a well-functioning bureaucracy—perhaps a testament to our tendency to generalize the state, especially in a supposedly well-organized country like Germany, and to overlook the huge amount of fragmentation across various state agencies, including in the matter of immigration control (Eule 2016). The significance of volunteers can be read not only as an encouraging example of civil society; their indispensability and the "windmills" against which they had to work also laid bare considerable state failures.

Reminiscing about the chaotic first year after the 2015 "long summer of migration" became a genre of conversation and collective ritual among the German volunteers, making up, as they saw it, for the state's inability to care for all the asylum seekers that had arrived. At a legal guardian and volunteer regulars' table I attended each month, a young woman told me how she had moved in with her sister in fall 2015 so that asylum seekers could stay at her apartment. The near-strangers who lived there for several months broke the appliances and left the place a mess; but because she did not want to seem xenophobic, it took her almost a year to tell anyone about the experience and to admit to herself that vacating her apartment had been a mistake. In the last months of 2015, she and some friends had also walked around Berlin with a spreadsheet list of names and addresses of Germans willing to host someone. They approached people who looked like asylum seekers, and accommodated them without any screening or identification—something, she says, she would not do again.[7]

Social worker Franka, a resolute woman in her late thirties whom I befriended when she was Paul's caseworker, frequently told me about the nights she had spent helping out at LAGeSo (Landesamt für Gesundheit und Soziales, or State Office for Health and Social Issues), Berlin's infamous registration center for newly arrived adult asylum seekers. In fall 2015, on her way home from work one evening, Franka had noticed the crowds outside LAGeSo from the bus window. She decided to get off early and see what was going on. Franka started talking to the only volunteer on-site, who seemed hopelessly overwhelmed, and asked her what she needed. Food and blankets, the volunteer said. Franka went to her apartment nearby, and returned with granola bars and sheets. At 10 p.m. the other volunteer left to put her children to bed, and Franka found herself alone at the center. That's how her eight months of volunteering at LAGeSo started.

Asylum seekers spent all night outside LAGeSo's premises, trying to increase their chance of getting a turn in the morning. When the gates opened, everyone would run toward the building entrance, and often an ambulance had to come for people who had been trampled. Every night, new people showed up, and their faces and stories blurred into one another when Franka tried to remember them several years later. Some were more memorable because of their names, such as Saddam Hussein, Mohammed Ali, and Ali Baba. When people told her their names, Franka often thought, "You're kidding me." She laughs now when she remembers them.

LAGeSo was when you smelled people before you saw them, as Franka put it. One of the volunteers who drove people to their shelters said he was never able to clear his car of that smell again. There were discussions among volunteers in which some insisted they should all wear gloves. Franka thought this insolent: "What people needed most was trust, and you can't trust someone with gloves." To make her point, Franka finished eating bananas that others had bitten into before. Besides minding the physical closeness, many volunteers were simply scared: so many men, so many foreigners. They were scared, too, of the stories they might hear and be unable to forget. This, Franka says, was bullshit, because no one who has just arrived—dirty, hungry, overtired—starts by telling their life story. Yet she remembers that some Germans at LAGeSo were in tears, saying, "If I just imagine what happened to these poor people!"

"OK, then why don't you go home?" Franka would retort. "Yeah, they look awful, but you're not crying about every homeless person you see on the street."

Even when people did tell her sad stories, Franka did not cry: "It's not real empathy when it paralyzes you," she said. And she did not have time for pity, plain and simple. There was too much to do, problems to solve in the here and now, all while trying to fend off "vultures": bored housewives longing for purpose, pedophiles offering rooms, Lebanese drug clans in need of dealers, ISIS members looking to recruit. Volunteers publicly celebrated their burnout, and bragged about how many asylum seekers they had taken in, how many were sleeping on their balcony. "I saved something again today," one volunteer said, mocking the self-praise of another.

Donations came largely from private individuals. Sometimes a kebab shop would bring some meat leftovers. A church near LAGeSo never offered to help, and refused when LAGeSo volunteers asked if they could at least use the church's wi-fi and toilets.[8] Wide-eyed people brought organic cucumbers, declaring that the asylum seekers should eat something healthful. When they asked where they could wash the produce, and Franka told them that there was neither a bathroom nor a kitchen, they were flabbergasted. The district mayor once dropped by and asked Franka why everyone was out in the cold and not in one of the shelters. Franka could not believe his ignorance, and explained to him that people had been holding out for days before they even had the chance to register and be assigned a shelter. The district mayor offered to accommodate people temporarily, but preferred families. Exasperated, Franka asked him: "Look around, do you see families? These are all single men. I can find you groups of four with the same last name."

There were people who collected donations for cases that did not exist, and one volunteer invented a story about an asylum seeker having died in front of LAGeSo from standing in the cold. The local station featured the story, and volunteers erected a memorial site before the tale was exposed. Even Anis Amri—who would drive a truck onto a Christmas market the following winter, killing twelve people and injuring five dozen—roamed the LAGeSo premises. A really strange guy, Franka thought even then, who seemed drunk or drugged or crazy. Franka remembers him attacking volunteers with a knife and generally seeming aggressive. She filed charges against him twice for assault, but the police did nothing.

There were heartening examples, too, however. A tango dance studio allowed twenty-five people to sleep in the ballroom every night. Workers at the studio organized everything themselves, picked up everyone in the evening by car, and prepared the ballroom with tea, sandwiches, and fresh flowers. In the mornings they woke the sleepers by softly playing the piano, and gave everyone public transportation tickets to return to LAGeSo.

During that fall and winter, Franka never slept more than four hours a night. She went to work in the morning, napped in the early evening, spent all night at LAGeSo, came home at four in the morning, slept for a few more hours, and then went back to work. Despite the exhaustion, Franka and other former volunteers later agreed that they rather missed the LAGeSo days. At least they had a real sense of achievement then, they said. At the end of a night, people had been fed, clothed, and housed. The next day, new problems and concrete solutions would turn up.

In the years to come, the issues that asylum seekers and those trying to help them faced would become much more complex. The last names Franka had joked about matching became the object of serious suspicion and contestation. While those who might harm asylum seekers had been easy to recognize at LAGeSo, the ill will of bureaucrats and "helpers" turned out to be much harder to pinpoint. Rather than sleep deprivation and cold, asylum seekers would have to learn to live with extreme uncertainty and intractable predicaments. Volunteers had been able to find them food, blankets, and places to spend the night when hundreds of thousands arrived, but could do little to reconcile young migrants' dreams of adulthood with a society's preference for minors, the state's demand for birth date documentation with the migrants' lack of such knowledge, or the diversity of migrants with residence and welfare laws that hinged on unrealistic binary distinctions among them. These highly complex issues—particularly the often circuitous routes asylum seekers had to take to prove their identities—are the subject of the next chapter. Before describing young migrants' attempts to attain particular identities, however, it is first necessary to provide a brief overview of the German asylum system and the many points at which an applicant's age makes a difference.

German Residence Law and the Effects of Minority Age on Asylum

Although minority has a different meaning—related to race and ethnicity—for most sociologists, I use it to refer to minority age, defined in Germany as being less than eighteen years old. This threshold legally separates childhood and adulthood for everyone living in Germany, but it does so for unaccompanied asylum seekers in particularly consequential ways. Not only can minors choose the EU country in which they file for asylum, as the Dublin III agreement does not apply to them; they also do not have to file for asylum at all until they turn eighteen, and they have more options for alternative residence titles should their asylum application be rejected, as I will now explain.

Although open borders and *Willkommenskultur* made Germany a particularly attractive destination for migrants in 2015 and 2016, they belied the harsh bureaucratic reality that awaited the migrants after arrival—a jumble of sometimes contradictory residence and other laws stemming from international agreements such as the 1951 UN Convention Relating to the Status of Refugees (UNHCR 2010) or the 1990 UN Convention on the Rights of the Child (UN 1990); European ones such as the Dublin III agreement; national laws such as Germany's Residence Act, Asylum Law, and Social Code VIII; and, finally, local laws passed in the sixteen federal states (*Bundesländer*) and their often even more devolved interpretation and application.[9]

In accordance with the Dublin III agreement, the country through which an adult asylum seeker has entered the EU is responsible for handling their asylum application. The Dublin Regulation, first passed in 2013, was upheld by the European Court of Justice in 2017 despite the unprecedented numbers of recent asylum seekers. Nearly all asylum seekers enter the EU through one of its southern border states, but many soon move on to countries in northern and western Europe.[10] For six months—or eighteen, if an asylum seeker is thought to have gone into hiding—these countries can return them to the country of their first entry into the EU. In Germany, "having Dublin," as asylum seekers refer to this period, means having only a GÜB (*Grenzübertrittsbescheinigung*, or certificate of having crossed a border) as an ID. A GÜB has to be renewed with the Foreigner Registration Office every three days to six weeks, depending on the whim of the person working that day. Having such a short-term ID means spending up to two days a week in the Foreigner Registration Office's notoriously slow-moving waiting rooms—a time distraction unacceptable to teachers and employers—and being ineligible for contracts and commitments that require someone to be more permanently settled.

When Dublin is over, the migrant can file for asylum in Germany. They are then interviewed at BAMF (Bundesamt für Migration und Flüchtlinge, or Federal Office for Migration and Refugees) and they wait for the result—sometimes for weeks, sometimes for years. Some are invited for second or even third interviews for clarification of open questions, or for speech and cell phone evaluations to help determine their country of origin. When BAMF finally decides on their asylum application, they may be granted refugee status, asylum, or subsidiary protection for one or three years; may be issued a prohibition of deportation (*Abschiebungsverbot*); or may receive a rejection, which can include a deportation impediment (*Abschiebungshindernis*) if, for example, they are a minor or are psychologically unstable. While refugee status is granted on the basis of the criteria established in the Geneva Refugee Convention, asylum is granted on the basis of German constitutional law. The Geneva Refugee Convention considers someone a refugee who is "unable or unwilling to return to their country of origin owing to a well-founded fear of being persecuted for reasons of race, religion, nationality, membership of a particular social group, or political opinion" (UNHCR 2010, 3).[11] The Refugee Convention criteria thus also include individuals who are persecuted by nonstate actors, whereas German constitutional law only grants asylum to those who are persecuted by their state. Asylum, moreover, may be granted only to applicants who have not entered Germany through a safe state, which is rare given Germany's location in the center of Europe. Subsidiary protection, for its part, is a Europe-wide status granted to those who do not fulfill the criteria for refugee status but whose lives would nonetheless be threatened by a return to their home country, for instance because of a civil war. Those with subsidiary protection are severely disadvantaged in comparison to those with refugee status or asylum, as this title rarely leads to more permanent residence; such persons may not travel outside Germany, and do not have a general right to family reunification. Finally, a deportation prohibition—not to be confused with a deportation impediment—is granted to those who do not formally qualify for either refugee status, asylum, or subsidiary protection but who nonetheless might be seriously harmed by a return to their home country, for example because of a medical condition that cannot be properly treated there. Notwithstanding the terminological similarity, then, a prohibition of deportation is issued on the basis of conditions in the applicant's country of origin, while a deportation impediment is issued in response to circumstances in Germany.

Depending on the outcome of their asylum applications and on factors such as that of being a minor, asylum seekers are issued one of several residence titles by the Foreigner Registration Office: an *Aufenthaltserlaubnis* (residence permit), an *Aufenthaltsgestattung* (residence permit for specific purposes, such as the asylum procedure), one of several *Duldungen* (literally, "status of being tolerated"), or a GÜB (certificate of having crossed a border). Each residence title is further differentiated by whether employment is always allowed, is allowed only in consultation with the Foreigner Registration Office, or is not allowed at all. Although new in-between outcomes of asylum applications, such as subsidiary protection, are intended to acknowledge that "movement takes place on a continuum of compulsion" (FitzGerald and Arar 2018, 393), continuous reality is thus still fit into a few discrete protection categories. This simplification occurs analogously to that of age or nationality, so that multiple such reductive systems operate simultaneously.

Asylum seekers have a statutory period of two weeks to appeal BAMF's decision, and 75 percent of those who have received a rejection do appeal

(BAMF 2020). During the appeals process, which is of no officially limited duration and often takes several years, an asylum seeker may not be deported. This gives young people, in particular, valuable time to learn German, work toward a high school degree, and eventually start an apprenticeship before their appeal is decided in the negative. According to section 60c of the German Residence Act, an apprenticeship, if begun before the termination of the asylum procedure, can secure one's residence in Germany through an *Ausbildungsduldung* ("status of being tolerated" for the duration of an apprenticeship). A migrant who has lived in Germany for four years before turning twenty-one, and who provides evidence of their integration into German society, also qualifies for a residence permit under section 25a of German residence law. An applicant whose asylum request, including the appeal to a rejection, is denied before they are able to obtain an *Ausbildungsduldung*, and who is too old to qualify for section 25a, enters into a highly precarious life with a *Duldung* and is excluded from legal employment, among other things. Besides marrying or having a child with a German partner or hoping for a change in the law, they have little choice but to make do with life at the very margins of German society. This is also true for anyone who cannot prove their identity with a passport, which is a prerequisite for all residence titles, including the *Ausbildungsduldung* and section 25a. Although relatively few rejected asylum seekers are actually deported,[12] the knowledge that in theory one is deportable still casts a heavy pall.

Because of its prevalence and weight in the lives of so many asylum seekers in Germany, it is perhaps useful to provide some more information on the *Duldung*. The word *Duldung* comes from the verb *dulden*, which means to tolerate and also shares the root of the German word for patience, *Geduld*. Legally, a *Duldung* is not a residence title but the "temporary suspension of a deportation." A deportation may be suspended for various reasons, such as pregnancy, illness, or lack of a passport attesting which country the migrant can be deported to. Although the specific conditions vary from one kind of *Duldung* to the next, many include prohibition from work and severely curtailed freedom of movement. One might also argue, however, that rather than only being the product of the impossibility of deporting someone, the *Duldung* is strategically used by the German state because it creates a particular type of labor force, restricted to particular segments of the German labor market. While a regular *Duldung*, for example, might be issued to someone who temporarily cannot be deported because of a medical condition or lack of a passport, an *Ausbildungsduldung* ("status of being tolerated" for the duration of an apprenticeship) suspends deportation for a migrant willing to do an apprenticeship. This often means foregoing high school or university studies, being channeled into the lower tiers of the German labor market, and taking up specific vocations that are in high demand and which too few Germans are interested in, such as nursing care or warehouse logistics. The *Duldung* is thus an example of how policies ostensibly about asylum and refugees can also function as furtive labor policies, even if creating a particular labor force is not their only motivation. In 2020, about 236,000 people were living in Germany with a *Duldung* (Deutscher Bundestag 2022).

In addition to the immediate drawbacks of a *Duldung*, its main danger lies in the fact that it does not lead to a more permanent residence title.[13] The years that one spends in Germany on a *Duldung* do not count toward the residency requirements of permanent residence titles.[14] Besides the particularly precarious *Duldung*, Germany in general has been hesitant to issue permanent residence, let alone citizenship, to migrants. Only in the year 2000, for instance, did Germany make it possible for a child born in Germany to two foreign nationals—at least one of whom must have lived in Germany lawfully (not, for instance, with a *Duldung*) and must now have permanent residence—to become a German citizen. Until then, lack of German citizenship had been essentially passed down from parent to child. Many of the so-called guest workers who came to Germany in the 1960s and '70s from southern Europe and Turkey had thus remained foreign nationals in Germany, despite often having spent the better part of a century in the country. Even when someone receives German citizenship, he or she often continues to be viewed as a foreigner within Germany. This is evidenced, for instance, by the fact that in official statistics, Germany considers anyone to have a "migration background" who has at least one parent born without German citizenship, regardless of that parent's current citizenship status.

Returning to the significance of minority age to residence and asylum, however, it is important to emphasize that the advantages enjoyed by those who were once minors in Germany—better education, networks of caseworkers and legal guardians, well-prepared asylum interviews, and access to alternative residence titles that do not necessitate a successful asylum application—last into adulthood. Such sharp legal distinctions between minors and adults lead many young asylum seekers to believe that being a minor is their only chance at a secure and fulfilling life in Europe. This hope sets off a protracted struggle for minority age status, which is not only tedious but does not always end in the fulfillment of expectations, as the next chapter will show.

2 ⋆ *Complicated Truths and the Promise of Minority*

Age seems like a straightforward category; after all, don't you just count the years since someone was born? It also seems like a particularly democratic one, because everyone presumably passes through the same age brackets over the course of their lifetime. In this chapter I make the case that for many migrants from the Global South—who lack documentation and sometimes knowledge of their birth dates, and for whom youth has often not been an experience of sheltered freedom—neither the first assumption, of the straightforwardness of age, nor the second, of its fairness, holds true. Age becomes remarkably complex when it is not embedded in standardized documentation practices and must consequently be defined and determined anew. It can only be a fair arbiter when everyone is similarly supported and protected in universal life phases of equal duration—and even then, people's individual development will diverge.[1]

The First Months in Germany as an Adult versus as a Minor

The reception of migrants in Germany differs greatly depending on whether they are officially minors or adults. Although in the chaos of 2015–16 new arrivals' actual experiences in Berlin often diverged in ways both small and large from what should have awaited them, I will briefly sketch out what minors' and adults' reception typically looks like in order to contextualize my interlocutors' first months in Germany.

Migrants who say they are unaccompanied minors register with a special clearing office, where either their claims are confirmed or dismissed in a visual age exam, or a forensic age exam is commissioned to settle a dispute. If a migrant's claim of minority age is believed, they are usually transferred to a shelter for unaccompanied minors. Here, social workers help them enroll in a "welcome class" (*Willkommensklasse*) where teenagers learn German until they are ready to join a regular school class, they are assigned a legal guardian, and they eventually move to a youth welfare apartment where caseworkers help them with all kinds of important issues from preparing an asylum application to finding a psychotherapist, a sports club, or tutoring.

By contrast, migrants who register in Germany as adults—or who become adults after unsuccessfully trying to register as minors—live in refugee camps with hundreds of others, often after spending months or even years in even more crowded and provisional arrival centers intended as places to live for only a few weeks. They share small bedrooms, as well as soiled bathrooms and kitchens, with strangers with whom they often share no common language, and thus no means by which to agree on who will shower or cook at what time. Perhaps worst of all, they and many of the other camp residents "have Dublin," meaning that Germany can deport them to their EU country of first arrival. Nights at the camp are riddled with police searches for "Dubliners" and other deportees. Notwithstanding discrepancies between the legal protections officially afforded to minors and their often considerably less secure reality, adult and minor asylum seekers in Germany thus do live very differently from the start, as a comparison of Idris's and Samir's arrivals also shows.

In Italy, Idris had given twenty-one as his age, enabling him to leave the camp and migrate further north. He crossed the Italian-Swiss border by foot and, having heard that train conductors in the more expensive high-speed Intercity Express (ICE) trains were less likely to check the IDs of passengers, he purchased an ICE ticket from Switzerland to Germany. To look even less conspicuous, he sat in the dining car. His friend Kadir, who had come to Germany a year earlier, had advised Idris to say he was sixteen, explaining that minors were exempt from the Dublin III Regulation and had access to regular schools. Idris, who was about twenty-two years old at the time, thought that sixteen was too much of a stretch, but he did want to be a minor; so when he arrived at Berlin's clearing office for unaccompanied minors, he said he was seventeen. A visual age exam confirmed his claim, and he was assigned to a former hostel—Pangea, named after the supercontinent—that had been turned into a shelter for unaccompanied minors. Idris says everyone who lived there knew that most residents were far older than seventeen—some looked thirty—but that everyone just accepted that this was how it was. At Pangea, other Ethiopians urged Idris to say he was from Somalia and that he was orphaned. Giving a wrong nationality seemed too big a lie to Idris, but he did say his father had died. He felt guilty about this soon afterward, and confided in a social worker who, however, advised him to leave things as they were because BAMF and other offices would think "once a liar, always a liar."[2]

Pangea offered German classes, three meals a day, and around-the-clock access to social workers, sports, and other activities for the young men, as well as some pocket money, with which Idris bought phone credit to call his family. Others at Pangea saved their money to buy sex. Once, Aman—who was also living at Pangea—and a few other Ethiopians asked Idris to join them for a walk. They went to one of Berlin's red-light districts, and Idris was aghast when he realized this. He took the subway back to Pangea by himself, and felt alienated from Aman and his friends for weeks after. He was still hurting from the relationship that had ended in his incarceration in Ethiopia almost three years earlier, and was not interested in women—certainly not in sex workers.

At Pangea, Idris met Yakob, who would become his best friend in Berlin, especially after Aman had to move to Dessau following an age exam that determined him to be eighteen. Yakob's hair was usually arranged into long braids, and he seemed to follow the latest fashions among young Africans in Berlin, at one point getting his ear pierced and from then on wearing a large rhinestone stud. Yakob liked to pose as a Casanova, and one could not walk around the city with him without hearing his opinion of every pretty girl who passed by. Yet his talk was mostly a facade, and he stayed with his girlfriend, Masarat, throughout the years of my fieldwork. Yakob and Masarat, an exceptionally beautiful Amhara girl with large traditional tattoos covering her forehead and temples, had fallen in love in a labor camp in Libya. They were separated before the boat crossing, and Masarat went to Frankfurt while Yakob moved to Berlin. Masarat contacted Yakob via Facebook and while he was initially hesitant about having a long-distance relationship, the two soon became a couple and regularly spent weeks in each other's cities. Yakob always returned from Frankfurt with several plastic bags full of *injera*, the Ethiopian flatbread Masarat made to tide him over until their next visit.

Idris and Yakob explored Berlin together, and sat on subway platforms for hours to use the free wi-fi provided by the city's public transportation services. Idris lived at Pangea for his first seven months in Berlin. After the summer, he enrolled in one of the *Willkommensklassen* Berlin had installed for young asylum seekers. With the help of Pangea's social workers, Idris was eventually able to move to an apartment provided by the youth welfare office. Several years later, we would still encounter acquaintances from Pangea when walking through the city, and the young men's faces always lit up as they reminisced about their time there. Idris often showed me pictures from Pangea, marveling at his own full cheeks and carefree smile. Pangea, he said, had been a time without worries, when he was just happy to be in Europe and unaware of the struggles over residence papers that lay ahead. He had been off to a good start.

Samir's memories of arriving in Germany more closely resemble the disarray Franka and other volunteers remember of their nights at LAGeSo. Samir and Idris both arrived in Berlin in summer 2016, but while Idris spent his first months being well taken care of at Pangea, Samir lived in a former gym turned refugee camp with little supervision. He had first arrived in Munich, where his older brother already lived. Since living with family would mean scrutiny of his daily routine, smoking habits, and choice of friends, he decided to leave. He went to Hamburg and stayed with older friends from Sudan. They told him that in order to live with them, he needed to be an adult. He also thought that as an adult he would get more money from the state and be allowed to work. Given his young looks, he even claimed to be married, hoping this would make his majority age more credible. His plan backfired: when he registered as an eighteen-year-old, he was relocated to Berlin and assigned to living in a former school gym with hundreds of others. For the first fifteen—or, since 2019, eighteen—months after their arrival, adults receive less money from the state than do minors, because they are forced to be on a refugee camp's meal plan and to accept other in-kind benefits. This left Samir with nothing to send to his family.

Samir talked frankly to me throughout the years about many sensitive things: the deaths of friends, his job in a brothel in Libya, his drug addiction, his identity. The one topic he was rarely willing to discuss was how he spent his first year in Germany—that is, before I knew him. The regret of having wasted a year, the awareness of how much better his German could be, how much more manageable his drug addiction, how much less obstructed his future, weighed heavily on him. "I was stupid," he finally blurted out one day. "I did nothing for a year and a half."

"But what did you do all day?" I asked. "You must have done something."

"Leave it, leave it," he said.

"It doesn't matter now, Samir, you can't change the past," I offered.

"It was a fun life, but it fucked my head. Time just passed me by. At the gym, I saw all the other people; no one was going to school or doing anything. Everyone just smoked. I looked around and thought: What is this life? I couldn't remember why I had even come to Europe."

"But you could have enrolled in a German class," I suggested.

Samir laughed at my ignorance. "When you're sleeping underneath a basketball hoop, are you in the mood to go to German class?"

So he started dealing instead. As in many of Berlin's refugee shelters, the security staff at the gym were themselves involved in the drug trade, and Samir discovered that they turned a blind eye to his breach of the camp rules when he helped them do business.

How Paul and Samir Reached Minority Age

Idris and Yakob were the only two among my main interlocutors whose age was never questioned by the German state. Most young asylum seekers I knew had held several dates of birth throughout their time in Germany; one was Paul from Guinea, whom I met while he was in the process of becoming a minor again after two age exams with contradictory results.

Paul was a noticeably tall young man with a boyish face, which could go from looking gravely serious to smiling infectiously within a second. Wherever we went, doctors, teachers, and counselors were immediately taken by his childlike charm and moodiness. Paul's dream was to become a professional soccer player. When the chronic pain in his legs and back allowed it, he played for various youth soccer teams in Berlin, spending much of his free time at practice or at the gym. His icon was the French-Guinean soccer star Paul Pogba, and like Pogba, he performed little dances on the field after scoring a goal. But often the pain and the loud clicking noise his knees made since his forced labor in Libya meant that he could hardly walk. He went from doctor to doctor, dutifully attending the physiotherapy sessions and taking the pills and creams he was prescribed. He asked God to restore his health so that he could fulfill his dream of playing professional soccer. In Guinea he had not believed in God, but after his journey to Europe he could find no explanation besides God for his survival.

While jumping off the freight train on which he had hidden to cross the Austrian-German border, Paul had also injured his head and arm, so he spent his first day in Germany at a Munich hospital. When he was released, police who spoke French showed him the way to the Young Refugee Center. Paul thought he was sixteen or seventeen, and unaccompanied minors in Munich stayed at the center throughout their clearing procedure. A visual age exam there determined him to be sixteen, and he subsequently lived in a shelter for unaccompanied minors in Munich. Just as at Pangea in Berlin, life at this shelter was good. Paul's caseworkers played board games with the teenagers, and took them to the cinema or to watch soccer games. Once they even saw a Bayern Munich match, of which Paul posted pictures to his Facebook page, letting his friends in Guinea believe he was another step closer to fulfilling his dreams. If a teenager at the shelter felt unwell, he was taken to a doctor, and everyone was allotted half an hour each week to call his parents. In the evenings, the boys who shared a room talked and laughed quietly until late into the night, interrupted by stern but friendly caseworkers who came in to remind them that it was already hours past bedtime. In the mornings, everyone went to school. It was not always easy to get the sleepy boys out of bed, and sometimes the caseworkers pulled away their blankets amid laughter.

Because of its geographical position at the southern edge of Germany, however, Bavaria had more asylum seekers than other German states, and relocated them across the country for a more manageable distribution. When Paul was redistributed to a small village in the eastern German state of Thuringia, he quickly realized that his life in Germany had taken a turn for the worse. The only public transportation connecting the village to the nearest town was a twice-a-day bus. There was little to do besides take walks or play soccer in the grass. And, as Paul remembers, the caseworkers and other teenagers were unwelcoming, with sometimes brutal conflicts between the Afghan and African boys, and no intervention by caseworkers. Paul lay in bed for hours, pondering what to do. One morning, he quietly packed his few belongings, took the bus to the nearest town, and then another one to Munich.

Back at the Young Refugee Center, his old caseworkers greeted him warmly but insisted he had to go back to the Thuringian village, as it was where he had been assigned to live. No matter how many times he snuck back to Munich, they warned him, he would always be returned. When the bus brought him back to Thuringia, the other boys there laughed at his failed escape. Paul cried silently in his bed that night and again decided to leave—this time to Dortmund, where he knew of a sizable Guinean community. In Dortmund he again underwent a visual age exam—attesting to a lack of information exchange between local communities about previous age exams—and in the process he explained his situation to the translator. The translator advised him simply to say he was eighteen, because then he would not be sent back to Thuringia. Paul agreed. As an adult asylum seeker, he could not stay in Dortmund either; but he was lucky enough to be relocated to Berlin. There, he was assigned to a large and notorious—and since shut down—refugee camp for adults at the city's outskirts. As an adult, Paul now fell under the Dublin III Regulation, meaning that Germany had six months to return him to Italy, the country through which he had entered Europe and which, accordingly, should handle his asylum case. Only if Germany failed to return him within the given time and he had not gone into hiding (which would extend his Dublin period from six to eighteen months) would Germany be responsible for handling his asylum case.

A social worker at Paul's new camp noticed this quiet, withdrawn young man who looked much younger than the other residents. She knew French and began talking to him, eventually learning of his two age exams in Munich and Dortmund, and the minority age on which he still insisted. She called Empower—an organization for unaccompanied minors, at which I volunteered at the beginning of my fieldwork—and reported that someone needed help correcting his official age. To escape the risks of living in a refugee camp—the possibility of a Dublin deportation to Italy, or of being dispirited by the hopelessness of other residents—Paul moved into an apartment funded by private donations that had been established specifically for cases like his: young asylum seekers who were in the process of trying to fix their official ages but who needed a place at which to avoid their Dublin deportation in the meantime.

With the help of Empower volunteers as well as social workers from the sanctuary apartment, Paul wrote to BAMF asking them to give him the benefit of the doubt—given his two conflicting age exam results— and to end his Dublin period, which they agreed to do. Paul then went to family court with the written confirmation that he no longer "had Dublin"—to quote the jargon used by asylum seekers—and that accordingly, even BAMF had doubts about his majority age. The family court accepted this argument and assigned him a legal guardian. With this new legal guardian, Paul returned to BAMF and informed them that the family court was convinced he was a minor, and that otherwise they would not have assigned him a legal guardian. BAMF accepted his minority age, and Paul was now able to submit his asylum application anew as a minor and move to an apartment paid for by the youth welfare office. Different agencies—such as the family court, the youth welfare office, BAMF, and the Foreigner Registration Office—often have various identities on file for asylum seekers, and playing these off against each other—that is, approaching one agency with the identity recognized by another—is one way asylum seekers try to attain certain identities.

Paul took full advantage of his new supportive environment, building close relationships with his social workers, eagerly learning German in his "welcome class," and joining a youth soccer team. As a Guinean, he had a slim chance of getting asylum, but his young age held many opportunities for securing his future in Germany. Living in a youth welfare apartment, he was not deportable. Focusing on learning German and going to school could enable him to get a residence permit through an apprenticeship; and as someone who would have lived in Germany for four years before turning twenty-one, he might eventually qualify for a residence permit under section 25a of German residence law.

That Paul's life had taken a turn for the better was clear from the contrast between his trajectory and those of many of his old acquaintances, who continued to live in the camp as adults. Half a year after Paul left the camp, we visited his friend Le Boss, who had since been moved to another camp. Boss's new camp, a former office building, was located in an industrial part of Berlin. The streets around the camp were empty and unlit. The hallways of the camp smelled musty, and the carpet in his room was blotched and sticky. He shared a small room with two other young men, and the narrow beds were arranged side by side, with only small gaps for getting in and out. The room's windows spanned the whole wall facing the door, and could not be opened—for security reasons, as a camp employee told me. They were mirrored from the inside, so that residents could not look outside and were forced to constantly see themselves. We sat down on the beds and Boss gave us wheat rolls and tiny containers of jam and margarine, leftovers from breakfast. Boss told us he was unable to sleep, but also did not leave his room much, and had chronic pain in his limbs. I offered to make a doctor's appointment for him or look for a French-speaking therapist, but Boss shook his head dejectedly: "My only problem is my problem. Not the sleeplessness or the pain or anything else." I only saw Boss a few more times over the next three years. Paul told me he did not want to be friends with people who "had problems," because they envied his luck and seemed to think he should help them.

Yet becoming a minor is not always as rewarding as in Paul's case, as Samir's odyssey illustrates. Recall that Samir had decided to say he was eighteen when he arrived in Germany. He spent the next two years in three adult mass shelters, including a former gym. He did not go to school, instead dealing drugs at night and sleeping during the day, picking up awry German and a drug habit. Samir soon understood the advantages of being a minor, but his attempts to change his age initially failed.

As in Paul's case, a social worker at the gym had noticed Samir and decided he needed help—maybe because he was slender, with a ready smile and an air of innocence about him despite his constant swearing and provoking. His appearance and conduct made him seem like the minor he officially was not. With the help of a lawyer whom the social worker knew, Samir was able to convince the family court that he was a minor. The legal guardian the court assigned to him, however—a woman who worked for the city and was in charge of many dozens of wards—was not convinced that Samir was a minor; despite signing the agreement and being paid for the guardianship, she refused to do anything on his behalf. We went to the youth welfare office with the court's guardian assignment, but they would only take him in once the date of birth on his ID card had been changed. Samir also switched camps at this time because the gym closed, and so he lost touch with the social worker who had tried to help him.

Samir knew a man back in Sudan who could send him a birth certificate bearing a place and date of birth of Samir's choosing, but it would cost him two hundred euros, which he did not have. The man had sent Samir a screenshot of what his birth certificate would look like, and Samir considered simply printing and submitting it to BAMF as though it were the original. But even if he had cropped out the computer desktop visible in the background, the image would have still had the flickering appearance of a screenshot, and the part that had been highlighted as if it were being copied and pasted would still have been obvious. So he decided not to submit it.

At the official age of twenty—a couple of years below his actual age, as he would later tell me—Samir did not really believe he would be able to become a minor again. But during his asylum interview he told the interviewer he was seventeen, recounting how he had been assigned a legal guardian who had then refused to do her work. To the amazement of both of us, the interviewer changed Samir's date of birth accordingly in the computer system, and instructed him to get a new ID card from the Foreigner Registration Office, which drew its information from the same computer system the interviewer had just updated (the *Ausländerzentral-register*, or Central Register of Foreign Nationals).

The day we went to the Foreigner Registration Office to ask for the date of birth to be changed, Samir had spent the previous night at a park with friends, doing cocaine and listening to Afrobeat music on his phone. He showed up at the office late, so we had to sit in the waiting room for hours with the other hopefuls, who looked up at the display expectantly every time it rang, each hoping to see their own number, as though 30 could ever be followed by anything but 31.

Samir and I eventually went outside to wait by the canal. Samir took his shoes off and wiggled his toes, telling me he had worn his shoes for two days and two nights straight because he had not been home. If only he could be seventeen, he swore, he would turn his life around. If he didn't have to live in a camp, he would stop dealing drugs, enroll in school, and go to bed each night by eleven. He would buy a TV set and spend the evenings indoors, cooking and watching shows to improve his German. Maybe he would even get a gym membership. I asked how I should respond when I saw him dealing or skipping school. "Just ask me why I came to Germany," Samir said. "And if I'm still like that, wait five minutes and then ask me again."

The clerk corrected the date of birth on Samir's ID with a ballpoint pen, and accidentally recorded a different birth month from the one Samir had given BAMF, making him three months "younger" than he had even hoped for. (During the routine renewal of Samir's ID a year later, this mistake of course would not be made a second time. But by then it would no longer matter that he had become a few months "older," because he had already been able to use his minority age. His date of birth was not a safe space; it was the key with which to enter.) Samir barely made it out of the clerk's office before jumping up and down triumphantly. "Seventeen!

Seventeen!" he cried out. He insisted we go to the School Enrollment Office immediately, determined to make good on the promise to change his life if the Foreigner Registration Office changed his age. During the bus ride there, he dreamed of how different his life would be. Then he said, "If I hadn't done all those lines last night, I wouldn't have been late. I wouldn't have gotten that waiting number and that clerk, and I wouldn't be so young now." We laughed, but he was right. Who ended up with which identity and legal status really was sometimes mere coincidence.

Only a few weeks later, however, Samir declared, "Fuck seventeen!" He had indeed enrolled in school, but his patchy German had made him difficult to place. He spoke quite well; but without formal education, he was barely literate, and only knew "street German," as he called it. Being in a beginners' class was frustrating and humiliating. The Landesamt für Flüchtlingsangelegenheiten (State Office for Refugees, or LAF), from which adult asylum seekers receive their money, had stopped paying him because they were no longer financially responsible for him, given his new minority age. His camp had kicked him out, because they were not allowed to house unaccompanied minors. This forced Samir to move into a shelter for youth in crisis, with 24/7 supervision. We went to the Youth Welfare Office repeatedly, reminding them of their obligation to put Samir up in one of their apartments, but the employees there were wary of an asylum seeker suddenly being three years younger. They claimed to be short of suitable apartments, while making no secret of the fact that they did not believe Samir was seventeen. He had lost the only advantage of being a legal adult—his freedom—and had gained little in return.

When Samir got into a fight and had to go to the emergency room, the hospital administrators kept us waiting for hours as they tried to decide whether to admit him to the children's clinic (since his ID said he was seventeen) or the adult clinic (since he was on file from a previous treatment as being twenty). The day before his new official eighteenth birthday, the youth crisis apartment forced Samir to move out because they were not allowed to house adults. We went to a youth homeless shelter, hoping he could spend the night there, but they explained they would have to kick him out at midnight, when he turned eighteen. The adult homeless shelter also refused him because he would only be an adult after midnight and their intakes ended at 10 p.m. Broke, homeless, and humiliated, Samir realized that so far, turning seventeen had solved nothing.

Idris's, Samir's, and Paul's cases thus show that young asylum seekers construct their ages strategically, claiming adulthood to cross European borders and minority to settle more safely and comfortably at their final destinations. They take advice from friends and acquaintances, but also make their own choices and compromises based on their particular goals and concerns, often attempting to offset the disadvantage of their national origin and biography with the benefits promised—albeit not always delivered—to minors. They also repeatedly find their trajectories shaped by chance encounters as well as the arbitrariness inherent in age exams and asylum procedures. Whether they experience their first months in Germany as adults or minors not only determines the legal context of their reception but also circumscribes their likely social contacts: dedicated caseworkers, volunteers, and German as well as other refugee teenagers, in the case of minors, or asylum seekers in legal precariousness struggling alone to endure the hardships of being strangers, in the case of adults. This context of their arrival casts a sweeping light of either optimism and promise or disappointment and doubt on their decision to come to Europe.

Identity Concepts in Countries of Origin versus Germany

Not only does Germany's very different treatment of minors and adults create incentives for migrants to claim minority age; identity concepts there—in terms of both cultural notions and documentation practices—often differ greatly from those in asylum seekers' countries of origin. This includes matters of age, childhood, minority, and practices related to the documentation, application, and commemoration of dates of birth. But it also includes ideas of ethnicity and nationality, as well as other categories of self, such as names and family relations. Categories like nationality, language, and kinship share many of the central theoretical facets of age: social construction and contingency; the potential for fabrication and instrumentalization; and the fact that regardless of certain objective elements, they necessarily involve interpretation and can take on various meanings. In this way, everyone was born on some land, but their national belonging may be complicated; the same letters assembled in the same order do not necessarily acquire universal meaning; and a mother's brother may be called an "uncle" by multiple people for whom the term connotes various familial relations.

Although scholarship on legibility (see, for example, Scott 1998 or Torpey 1999) has suggested that states around the globe have sought to make their citizens "legible"—and thus easier to tax and govern—through the introduction of passports, systematic data collections, and standards such as weights and national languages, migration from the Global South to Germany and other European countries shows that not all of the world's populations have been statistically captured to the same extent. For example, the *tazkira*, an identity card common in Afghanistan, only records how old the person was when the *tazkira* was issued, not a date of birth.

It does not contain security features besides signatures and stamps, and can only be requested in absentia by male relatives (Skiba 2017). In an astute interpretation of truth as the impossibility of deception, Ali, one of my interlocutors from Afghanistan, quipped that a *tazkira* was "always real" when I inquired about the authenticity of his.

In his memoir *Notes from the Hyena's Belly*, the writer Nega Mezlekia (2000) describes his youth in the Somali region of Ethiopia, where Idris was also from: "Mam was like most Ethiopians: she would cite a historical benchmark when asked her age. [. . .] When the Italian fascists invaded the country and when her father took up arms against them, she was five years old. The war itself lasted about five years, so one could figure out her age with a likely margin of error of two or three years" (254). Although Mam is of a different generation, not much has changed; none of my interlocutors knew their birth dates.[3] Birthdays as special occasions are typical of prosperous and individualistic societies. Paul, for instance, had only asked his parents if they knew his date of birth after his coming to Europe made his exact age relevant. In Afghanistan it is common for parents to make a note of their child's birth in a copy of the Quran, and some Afghans try to prove their ages by submitting pictures of such notes. Tellingly, such authentic ways of giving birth dates often meet with more state suspicion than do mere fabrications, which even in their falsehood parallel Germany's exactitude when it comes to age, as the following case illustrates.

In summer 2019, Germany passed a new law—the *Geordnete-Rückkehr-Gesetz*, or Law of Orderly Return—that obliged an asylum seeker to prove their identity by obtaining a passport. In order to apply for a passport from the Ethiopian embassy, Idris asked his brother for a birth certificate. His brother went to the local citizen center in Ethiopia, where he was issued the document without his having provided proof of the information he had asked them to attest. Idris's brother sent the birth certificate to Berlin, but when it arrived, we saw that Idris had made a mistake. He had told his brother his German date of birth, but Ethiopia does not use the Gregorian calendar; and so according to this birth certificate, Idris was now eleven years old. I could not contain a chuckle when I saw the birth certificate, but Idris was very upset—not only because of the additional hassle, as he explained to me, but because the birth certificate that identified him as being eleven years old was an unwelcome reminder of the lie at the root of this mess.

Idris used an online converter to figure out the Ethiopian equivalent of his European date of birth, and his brother obtained and sent a new birth certificate in the same way as he had the first. This time everything worked out: Idris showed the birth certificate to the Ethiopian embassy in Berlin, and was issued a passport that matched his official German date of birth. A few days later, I wondered aloud whether BAMF would be suspicious of the alleged ability of an Ethiopian minor without formal education to arrive in Germany worn out from the journey but convert his date of birth from the Ethiopian to the Gregorian calendar. A social worker agreed with my reasoning but said that BAMF demanded precision even when it was highly improbable, ultimately choosing precision over accuracy, and the tempting simplicity of information over a more complicated truth. An incorrect but precise document has more weight than a note in the Quran that is far more likely to approach the truth.

German state agencies thus continue to treat age as straightforward, applying it to an asylum seeker without a documented date of birth in the same way they would to a German with a birth certificate. Such unrelenting adherence may ultimately contribute to the validation of false information, because it is not the content of the information whose credibility is evaluated, but that of its structure and articulation. Germany is not the only country to pursue this disambiguation strategy, valuing the form of official documents above their content. The US government, similarly, refuses to update naturalization certificates it knows to contain inaccurate information with information it believes accurate, because that would "undermine the credibility of its record keeping" (Stevens 2017, 223).

The story of Idris's birth certificate, which contains patterns repeated in many of the experiences of asylum seekers who obtain documents, also challenges notions of authenticity and fakery. Idris's birth certificate and passport would have passed any authentication test. They were not counterfeit; they had been issued by the institutions authorized to do so. Idris even mused that his new passport was "more real" than the one he had owned in Ethiopia, because it was based on a birth certificate, whereas he had received the old one without any proof of identity. The replicability of "realness" reveals much about the construction of realness and its relation to truth. A "real" document is not one that shows truth. A "real" document cannot be distinguished from a "fake" one except during its creation. What does it mean for a stamp, for instance, to be "real"? According to the forensic measures used by BAMF and other agencies, a "real" stamp is made by the responsible government agency. While you can compare the stamp to known stamps from the same agency—inspecting, for example, the chemical makeup of the ink—a stamp does not show whether the agency was attesting to a fact, rewarding a bribe, or simply signing off unheedingly on whatever was in front of it.

Proving an identity—or rather, attaining category membership—is thus often self-referential. Idris joined his friend Faysal to the Somali embassy one day. Faysal was Ethiopian but had said he was Somali, which was the nationality recorded on his German asylum seeker ID card. Because he wanted to relocate to Sweden to be with his wife, he needed proof of his identity. The two went to the Somali embassy in Berlin and, for 125 euros, Faysal received a Somali citizenship certificate onto which the embassy employee had transferred the information from his German asylum seeker ID card. The information the German state wanted verified then became the verifying information. Whether documents are authentic or fake is thus a complicated question—a point that should not beget more repressive asylum policies but stimulate debate about the standards of truth used to manage migration.

Besides dates of birth being unknown or going unrecorded, notions and realities of childhood and youth also differ greatly around the world. What a seventeen-year-old German expects from life and what is expected of him is not the same as for an Afghan or Somali teenager. While many of my interlocutors had led quite responsible lives in their home countries, caring for younger siblings and working to provide for the family, Idris insisted that a twenty-five-year-old African was not comparable to a German of the same chronological age. A German in his mid-twenties was formally educated and had learned how to plan and organize his own life, something Idris said Africans never learned. Sure, maybe they worked or got married at a younger age, but the family still decided everything for them. In Europe they felt young because they had not yet learned to make decisions for themselves. When comparing himself to Germans, he said that he felt eighteen or nineteen—and so he thought his official age actually appropriately reflected his circumstances.[4]

Nationality also does not work as neatly as the asylum procedure assumes. For asylum seekers from countries that border on Eritrea and Somalia but have much lower protection rates—as in the case of Ethiopia, whose people often speak languages also spoken in Eritrea and Somalia—the incentive to claim to be from one of the countries with higher protection rates is high. Mother tongues do not map neatly onto the postcolonial political geography of Africa and other sending regions, where "geographic mobility is ancestral history" (Belloni 2019, 11). People who have grown up along former or novel borders in geopolitically unstable regions like the Horn of Africa often have native knowledge of multiple languages. People from eastern Ethiopia speak Amharic as well as Somali, people from northern Ethiopia speak Amharic as well as Tigrinya, and people from eastern Sudan might speak Amharic or Tigrinya in addition to Arabic. Many asylum seekers speak an African language in addition to the language of their former colonizer. Paul, whose native tongues are Susu and French, insisted on being interviewed in Susu, so as to prove that he was from Guinea. Had he given his interview in French, the interviewer might have thought he was from a Francophone African country with even lower protection rates than Guinea.

Languages, then, are an asset for asylum seekers, with which they can prove or feign national and ethnic membership. Extensive migration within Africa also means that people have citizenships of countries in which they have never set foot. In an oversimplification of national identity, BAMF often conflates native language and country of origin, conducting language tests to determine applicants' nationalities. Ethiopians who speak Tigrinya may successfully claim to be Eritrean, whereas Samir, who is *actually* an Eritrean citizen but does not speak Tigrinya because he grew up in Sudan, was not believed because of the perceived language-nationality mismatch, as I will show later. In recent years, citizenship has also arguably experienced an instrumental turn (Harpaz 2019; Joppke 2019), meaning that personal strategizing has actually become socially acceptable in this formerly sacred domain.

Different conceptions of family relations also lead to misunderstandings and unfair accusations that asylum seekers are giving false information. In Arabic, for example, terms differ between maternal and paternal aunts and uncles. When Samir was asked to list all his relatives during the asylum interview, it was impossible for him to translate his family tree accurately because German does not discriminate between maternal and paternal relatives. When he was again asked to explain his family composition in a subsequent interview, the interviewer accused him of having lied the first time. Similarly, in some cultures only brothers are listed as siblings, which again has led to accusations of inconsistencies.

Names, too, are less strictly regulated in many common countries of origin. The first name on the birth certificate Paul eventually submitted differed from the one he had given in Germany, but he insisted that this was his genuine birth certificate and that certain first names were considered the same in Guinea, and that therefore it did not matter which of them was written on the birth certificate. (The similarity between his two names was comparable to that of James and its diminutive Jim in English.) Interestingly, the authenticity of Paul's certificate was doubted by several agencies, whereas that of his friend, whose birth certificate listed an Italian nickname he had given himself upon arrival in Europe, was accepted. This again shows that Germany values precision over accuracy.

Finally, last names do not work the same way in Germany as they do in asylum seekers' countries of origin. I met people who did not know their last names and who simply made up names that in their mind fulfilled the function of surnames, such as using a father's name. In many Muslim societies, a first name is chosen for both girls and boys and their second and third names (equivalent to a Western last name) are the names of their father and paternal grandfather, respectively. This often leads to names being recorded as first name, middle name, and last name, when really there is only one first name and two last names, not to mention spelling mistakes resulting from problems in transliterating from other alphabets. I encountered families in which nearly every member had a slightly different last name due to transliteration mistakes various administrators had made. Such mistakes were sometimes used by officials to accuse asylum seekers of identity fraud.

When conceptions of identity differ greatly between migrants' countries of origin and their destinations, honesty and deception are not always easy to distinguish. Belloni (2019, 119), for example, describes how Eritrean migrants often harbor notions of marriage that are at odds with what Italian officials deemed a "real" marriage (that is, one based on love and intimate knowledge of the other). Therefore, marriages that are "real" in the Eritrean spouses' eyes may get sorted out as fake. This is similar to different notions of nationality, age, or family names being considered false by the German state.

When I told other Germans about my research, they would often think of corresponding anecdotes from their own family histories, such as a great-grandfather whose date of birth varied considerably across documents, and who appeared to have made himself older when seeking employment and younger to evade military service. Childhood as a life phase of special protection is neither globally nor historically universal. It is a relatively recent idea even in Europe, and my interlocutors described their own notions and time frames of childhood as being quite different from those they encountered in Germany. Philippe Ariès (1973) argues that the main change toward "modern" notions of childhood, youth, and adolescence in Europe took place only in the seventeenth century. It was then that youth became associated with vulnerability (thus deserving of support) and innocence (deserving of forgiveness). Asylum laws that provide minor asylum seekers with legal guardians and do not punish their clandestine border crossings rest on such assumptions of vulnerability and innocence.

The role of children in Western countries—first among middle-class families and eventually across larger swaths of society—changed from one measurable in economic terms to "priceless" only at the turn of the twentieth century (Zelizer 1994). "Adolescence," similarly, was only coined as a term in the early twentieth century to acknowledge trends that "extended dependency beyond childhood and delayed entry into adult roles" (Crosnoe and Kirkpatrick 2011, 440). Age-related norms, both informal and legal, vary considerably across time and space. Even within otherwise similar societies, there are considerable differences when it comes to the legal age thresholds for various rights and responsibilities from voting to criminal liability (Buchmann and Kriesi 2011; Juárez and Gayet 2014). Conceptual shifts over time and space between defining age relationally, socially, functionally, subjectively, and chronologically (Treas 2009), as well as the instrumental turn of citizenship (Harpaz 2019), further evidence the contingency of categories like age or nationality.

To register in Berlin, Idris had to give a date of birth, but he did not know his date of birth and was even unsure about the year. So, he reasoned, giving any date of birth would have been a lie. To me, this was not simply a self-serving splitting of hairs but a justification that actually revealed the bigger issue: the incompatibility of identity concepts and practices from the Global North and the Global South. Vastly different cultural understandings and ways of documenting (or not documenting) personal identifying information thus not only create a "margin of liberty" through which asylum seekers can "play with the rules," as Didier Fassin has put it (2018, 42), but also provide ample fodder for genuine misunderstandings and unwarranted accusations of deceit. The long-winded conflict over Samir's nationality shows this perfectly.

The Back-and-Forth over Samir's Nationality

One of the most important goals of the asylum interview is to establish the nationality of the applicant, which indicates whether he has made false declarations or can generally be considered trustworthy and whether his return would be safe, irrespective of his individual experience of persecution. The long back-and-forth over Samir's nationality is revealing both in terms of the social construction of nationality in the asylum process, and the emotional attrition such a drawn-out process causes in the applicant.

After his Dublin period was over and before he was accepted as a minor, Samir and I went to an asylum counseling service specializing in migrants from the Horn of Africa. The walls of the counseling room were covered with maps of Somalia, Ethiopia, Eritrea, and Sudan, which visualized not only their geography and the names of cities and landmarks, but also the dispersion of the many resident ethnic and linguistic groups. Samir had reluctantly told Julia, the counselor, that he had been born in Sudan to Eritrean parents with few rights and opportunities. When he came to Europe, he had said he had been born and raised in Eritrea, because other asylum seekers had told him that would make it easier for him to claim Eritrean citizenship. Julia warned him that he would not be able to answer the interviewer's questions about Eritrea, and that the fact that he didn't speak Tigrinya would raise a red flag. She advised him to start the interview by apologizing and asking for the chance to correct his story. He should say he was young and scared, and had been listening to the advice of older asylum seekers. We left the counseling appointment with a cheat sheet of things Samir could say in the interview.

The weekend before his interview, Samir worked. It was Saturday night and well below freezing, so instead of lingering in a park or near a subway station, he set up shop in a crowded bar, sitting at an unplayed piano, right next to where people lined up to go to the bathroom. Squeezed side by side, we sat on the piano bench, and Samir used the closed fallboard to lay out his rolling papers and the other equipment he always carried with him in his small black pouch. He sipped all night on a glass of Coke, which he placed on the fallboard, leaving a new wet rim mark on the wood every time he picked up his drink. As a special service to impatient or clumsy smokers, Samir rolled joints or cigarettes laced with meth or cocaine that he pulverized with his health insurance card, the only surcharge being that he got to take a couple of drags first.

While working, he talked about his mother and how much he loved and missed her. I knew his mother only from the picture of her Eritrean ID: a handsome woman with the same round eyes and disobedient smile as her son's. Samir had sent me pictures of his mother's and grandmother's old IDs so that I could print them for the interview, and so that he could convince BAMF that he was Eritrean. As during many other such nights, he said that if only his interview went well, if only he "got papers," he would turn his life around. He would stop dealing, go to school, get a regular job, and live the life he was already telling his parents he was living. Throughout the night, Samir kept checking the cheat sheet Julia had made for him. He had propped it up against the piano's music rack and occasionally glanced at it and read it slowly: *I want to apologize. I lied. I was young and stupid and didn't know better than to listen to the advice of other asylum seekers. So when I arrived in Germany, I said that I was born in Eritrea. But now I want to come clean. I was born in Sudan. But my parents are Eritrean. So, although I was born in Sudan, I am Eritrean, too.*

We decided to call it a night. The subway was crowded with tourists and clubbers on their way home that Sunday morning. We stood in the back of the subway car, and Samir leaned against the wall, with one foot up against it. He stared at the dirty floor. Just before I had to get off, he said, without taking his eyes off the subway floor: "I hope I get three years. Because three years would be a home." Three years may not seem like long-term security to a person with a comfortable citizenship whose once-a-decade passport renewal is merely a formality, but to someone like Samir, who had never owned an ID that allowed him to travel anywhere—and who until recently, while he had Dublin, had had to renew his temporary residence permit every few weeks with the Foreigner

Registration Office—three years indeed appeared like a luxuriously long time—a *home*, as it were.

Samir spent the night before his interview on my guest mattress. He wanted to be well-rested, and his snoring roommate, altercations between security and residents in the hallways or common rooms, and middle-of-the-night door banging made rest unlikely in his camp. Hearing neighbors get deported, he decided, was not the best backdrop for relaxing before a decisive asylum interview. And he wanted the interview to go well. "It has to," he said.

Samir's interview was scheduled on an icy February morning. We walked to the subway slowly, so as not to slip, and then, after the ride, we again walked slowly from the subway to the BAMF office. We each did slip on the sidewalk a few times, landing on our bottoms and giggling in pain. When we passed a flower store, Samir suggested getting the interviewer a bouquet to get them onto Samir's side. Samir theatrically handed a hypothetical bouquet of flowers to an imaginary interviewer. Then he took on the part of the interviewer, and bowed while stretching out his right hand in respect and declaring: "Here you go, three years for you!" We both laughed.

After searching our bodies and backpacks in a makeshift security area, the staff told us to sit down and wait to be called. Samir was visibly nervous, telling me in a surge of words how he had learned to walk when he was only nine months old, and how his uncle had called him "little runaway," because even as a child he was always running away. Then, as a young teenager, he had stayed out all night with friends, drinking Sudanese coffee and smoking. He had always had a glass of water right after getting up in the morning, and had continued this habit in Europe. His mom had asked him on the phone whether he still drank his morning glass of water, and praised him when he said that he did. Samir held the transparent envelope with the copy of his mom's Eritrean ID card that he wanted to give to the interviewer. "Do you know *jannah*?" he asked me.

"Yes. *Jannah* is paradise," I replied.

"*Jannah* is my mom," he said, and kissed the clear plastic over the picture of his mother's face.

Bored, Samir started playing a game. He looked around at the other tense faces in the waiting area and pointed at them arbitrarily. "You out! You three years! You one year! *Y'Allah*, you out! Get lost!" he hissed, and flung his foot as if kicking a soccer ball off a playing field. Then, after two years in Germany and four hours in this waiting room, a guard finally approached. "No interview today. You'll be sent a new appointment."

The next appointment came two months later. By now, Samir had forgotten most of Julia's advice and had misplaced the cheat sheet. With the passing of time, he had lost momentum. Instead of resting the night before the new appointment, he worked. We had agreed to meet two hours before the interview in order to go over what he wanted to say, but he was late. Wearing too many jackets for the spring weather, a backpack hanging deep on his back, with cracked lips and reddened eyes, he looked like he had been out all night. But when I asked him if he would rather reschedule, he said no. After more than two years in Germany, he just wanted to get it over with.

The interviewer's office was plastered with aphorisms: "The world holds enough for everyone's needs but not for everyone's greed." And a Bertolt Brecht quote: "A man who doesn't know the truth is just an idiot, but a man who knows the truth and calls it a lie is a crook." The woman asked Samir when he had gone to bed and gotten up, and whether he felt fit enough for the interview. "Nine p.m., 8 a.m., yes," he lied.

Irritated by a self-proclaimed Eritrean conducting the interview with an Arabic translator, she asked, frazzled: "So who or what are you? Eritrean? Sudanese? Or maybe Libyan?" Samir nervously dreaded his hair between thumb and index finger, and tiny locks snowed onto the table underneath his elbows. The interviewer asked which country code Samir dialed to call his family in Sudan; but because he only called via WhatsApp or Facebook Messenger, he did not know the Sudanese country code. The interview continued in a testy tone, as Samir explained that he was Eritrean but had grown up in Sudan.

If an asylum seeker claims to be from a country with a high protection rate, especially if his native language is also spoken elsewhere, BAMF might do a language and phone evaluation.[5] So, three months after his interview, BAMF invited Samir for a mobile phone readout and language analysis. More than worrying about the language evaluation, he worried about the phone readout. A caseworker had told us that BAMF was only going to look at Samir's phone's metadata—its waypoints, the dialect used in messages, country codes, and websites visited. Still, Samir feared they would see his texts and photos, and realize that he dealt drugs.

The night before the appointment, we looked through his phone together for incriminating photos and texts. "I have so much shit on my phone," Samir said, "I'm afraid. I swear, Ulrike, I'm terrified they'll send me back." He contemplated whether he should delete pictures as well as his social media accounts, but he did not want to lose the memories of nights spent with friends. He deleted sixty-three pictures and several chats, then decided he would not be able to finish by the morning. Either he would have to delete everything or not give his phone to BAMF. The next morning, as we entered the BAMF building, Samir slipped his phone into my jacket pocket and said "I lost it at the park. I have no other choice."

While BAMF used to use human dialect assessors, they were eventually considered to be biased, and were replaced by software. The language test therefore took place in a computer lab. The clerk instructed Samir to pick up a telephone receiver and speak for two minutes about "anything at all." Samir said he might not be able to think of anything, and asked if he could read something instead. The clerk said no, that they were as interested in his choice of words as his pronunciation, but handed Samir a stack of pictures—the Golden Gate Bridge, a Tuscan hillside, a plate of falafel—and instructed him to describe what he saw. Making light of the situation, Samir raised his fists to the ceiling, like an athlete about to compete, then picked up the receiver and spoke.

Samir received his rejection letter two months later. In it, the BAMF adjudicator wrote that "the truthful description of an actual event should be marked by concreteness, clarity, and richness of detail," and that Samir had failed to meet this standard in his descriptions of the discrimination he had supposedly experienced in Sudan. Furthermore, when Samir first registered in Germany he had given wrong information regarding his nationality, date and place of birth, marital status, and country of usual residence, and this now decreased his overall credibility. While Eritreans almost always receive protection because of Eritrea's mandatory lifetime military service and the repercussions for deserters, the adjudicator wrote that he had no way of knowing if the woman on the Eritrean ID card Samir had submitted was indeed his mother. Franka, who worked at the youth welfare apartment where Samir was by now living, suggested that Samir could submit a picture of himself with his mother to prove the relation. Since he had no such picture, he took a screenshot the next time he video-called his mom. In it, the woman pictured on the passport—older but recognizable—beamed into the camera, and Samir's own smiling face, somewhat covered by a baseball cap he always wore during video calls with his family to hide his un-Islamic hairstyle, was suspended in the upper left corner. But BAMF did not accept this screenshot as evidence, arguing that talking to the woman from the ID card did not make him her son.

Franka and I read Samir's BAMF file carefully, and kept shaking our heads in disbelief. "Why should the applicant have Eritrean citizenship if he was not born in Eritrea?" it read.

"Because there are citizenship laws, you moron," Franka retorted, talking at the paper.

"The name and physical appearance of the mother indicate Ethiopian origins," the paper read.

"Jesus!" Franka exclaimed. "Which idiot wrote this?"

BAMF lamented that Samir's maternal half-brother, who lived in Munich as a recognized Eritrean refugee, had a different last name; but Samir had explained during the interview that last names were passed down through the father, not the mother. The translator, on the other hand, was quoted as suspecting that Samir was indeed an Eritrean who had grown up in Sudan. Franka: "The translator is not even allowed to say anything. But still, good for Samir."

The places and countries of birth were mixed up in the file. Sometimes it read "Al Showak [Samir's Sudanese city of birth], Eritrea." Franka laughed: "Showak, Eritrea. It's in Sudan, but who gives a fuck?" The language analysis showed Samir to be from various Arabic-speaking countries with low double-digit probabilities—Iraq, the Levantine region, Egypt, the Gulf states—but not Libya and Sudan, the two countries in which he had actually spent time.

In consultation with Samir, Franka and I wrote a long appeal to BAMF's rejection. We met at Samir's new youth welfare apartment to discuss it. When Franka plopped Samir's four-hundred-page BAMF file onto the table, she said: "You know what it says in there, right?"

Samir pretended to read, and said, moving his eyes from left to right: "*Y'Allah*, fuck off!"

"Yeah, something like that," Franka laughed.

When Franka and I told Samir about the ridiculous arguments we had found in his file, we thought he would laugh with us and be encouraged because nonsense was easy to rebut. But he was discouraged, and he wondered whether he should go to a different country. "They're all crazy," he said resignedly. "First they tell you to back up your claims with documents, but when I give them my mom's Eritrean ID, they say her face looks Ethiopian. All the fake Eritreans get papers just because they speak Tigrinya, and I am really Eritrean and get nothing."

He eventually had the idea that his mother could record a video message in which she would explain in Belen, a language spoken only in Eritrea, that she was Eritrean and that Samir was her son. In the video Samir's mother later sent, she wore a shimmering turquoise dress and headscarf and gold jewelry around her forehead, clearly dressed up for the occasion. In a firm voice, sometimes stopping mid-sentence and looking out of frame as if to remember her words, she said: "My name is Mariam Jamal. I am the mother of Samir. I am Eritrean, as is my whole family. But we live in Sudan where we have no papers. I speak Belen and Tigrinya, but my son only speaks Arabic because he grew up in Sudan." We submitted the video along with the appeal, in which we explained the 1992 Eritrean Nationality Proclamation, according to which anyone is an Eritrean citizen who has at least one Eritrean parent. We also explained that from an ethnic perspective, Ethiopians and Eritreans were both *habesha* people, and that it was insolent to claim that Samir might be Ethiopian based on the facial features of his mother—about as reasonable as claiming that someone looked East or West German based on the shape of their nose. As of this writing, more than four years after his first interview, Samir has still not heard back about his appeal.

National origin, then—like age and other categories central to the classification of asylum seekers—is not as straightforward as it may seem. Parents have different nationalities; people are born in one country and reared in another; ethnicities and languages do not fit neatly within official state borders, especially when those borders have been traced at the drawing table by colonial powers. Asylum applicants in Germany may have been refugees in other countries, even for their whole lives. Borders shift, people move, and the offices that produce bureaucratic evidence of people's citizenship differ greatly around the world. Significantly, Samir's citizenship claims were accurate and based on citizenship laws, yet they were the ones most contested by BAMF, presumably because they did not conform to assumptions about the relationship between native language, residence, biography, and citizenship. Such cases, in which "modern" notions of the relationship between language and the national order are applied to "postmodern" realities—such as a person who only speaks the language of the country in which he grew up, but is claiming a different citizenship in another country—are not unique (Blommaert 2009). Western immigration authorities and courts often do not adequately engage with the complicated political realities regarding citizenship and documentation in regions like the Horn of Africa, or with the international laws that would relieve people like Samir of the bureaucratic failings of their home states (Campbell 2011). The rigidity and blind spots of the German asylum system thus often inhibit truth, as do its inherent notions of believability and standards of verification.

The Asylum Interview: Three Ways

The asylum interview centers around the question of the applicant's national origin—as the above examination of Samir's experience shows—but also their experience of persecution. In the wake of the 2015 "long summer of migration," free interview prep workshops and individual counseling appeared throughout Berlin, with lawyers and professional asylum experts as well as self-taught volunteers instructing asylum seekers how to master the interview. I attended dozens of such workshops and consultations; they usually advised asylum seekers to tell the truth,[6] but in a way that aligned with definitions of asylum-worthy persecution, as well as with a German narrative culture. The counselors advised:

Germans think chronologically and find stories more credible that explain why something happened. Give as much detail as possible, but if you do not know a name or date, do not make it up. Bring physical evidence, such as school certificates, doctor's reports, photos, or newspaper articles. Treat the interviewer like a child to whom the world needs to be explained; for example, that a policeman in your country is not a friendly helper with a badge number, and that there is no due process of law. Most importantly, do not contradict yourself. The interviewer might ask how long the bus ride was between your home and your school, when you have told him two hours earlier that your city had no public transportation; this is a test. Finally, always talk about yourself. It is not enough to say: "The Taliban persecute the Hazara people." Say: "The Taliban persecuted me because I am Hazara."

In the interview, an asylum applicant must explain why he left his country of origin and why he cannot return there. Nothing that happened during the flight—such as the traumatic boat journey—is relevant to the asylum application, except to substantiate claims to a psychological trauma that could justify a deportation impediment. I will now turn to the asylum applications and interviews of first Idris, then Paul, and finally Guled—each of which epitomizes a different characteristic feature of the asylum procedure.

IDRIS: MAKING THE TRUTH MORE CREDIBLE

Friends urged Idris to increase his chances for asylum by saying he was from Somalia. Having grown up in the Ethiopian-Somali border region, he spoke native Somali. Nevertheless, he decided against giving a wrong nationality, for fear of being found out by, for example, tripping over questions on the complex Somali clan system, and also, he insisted, because he loved his country and felt that denying it would be a betrayal of that love. What if he became famous one day, and had to hold the Somali flag instead of his own? He sometimes joked that Ethiopia would become extinct if every Ethiopian claimed to be from somewhere else.

Despite giving his real nationality, Idris gave a wrong ethnic group. He had been imprisoned following his secret relationship with a Somali girl whose politically powerful parents viewed his Ethiopian origin as below them, and who successfully brought him before a sharia court for supposedly having kidnapped and raped their daughter. After his release from prison, her parents continued to threaten Idris and his family for having dishonored their daughter (though Idris could not mention their having beat up his father, because he had said earlier that his father was dead). Idris did what many asylum seekers do: he invented something to make the truth more credible. While his girlfriend was actually from the Somali ethnic group Ogaden, and he from the Ethiopian ethnic group Gurage, he told BAMF that he was from the Somali ethnic group Goboya, because people from that group are known to be seen as lower by other Somalis, and are prevented from "marrying up." He hoped this would make his already true story more believable. While in reality he had been imprisoned once for his relationship, and bailed out by his mother, he now invented a second prison term, from which he had supposedly escaped by jumping over the prison wall. Because he was unsure whether the problems with his girlfriend would suffice for asylum, he also said that his girlfriend's parents had accused him of fighting for a separatist rebel group, the Ogaden National Liberation Front (ONLF). BAMF, however, did not believe he could have jumped over a prison wall, and thought it did not make sense that his girlfriend's family, who were themselves Ogaden, would accuse him of fighting for the *Ogaden* NLF. Accordingly, they doubted his relationship, imprisonment, and endangerment altogether, and rejected his asylum application.

PAUL: INVENTING THIN STORIES

When I first met Paul, he told me and his caseworkers that he had left Guinea after the death of his parents. On July 16, 2013, he had come home from school and found his parents dead. There had been terrible interethnic violence that day in his hometown of N'Zerekore, so he assumed that his parents had been killed by another ethnic group. He left and spent three years in a Libyan labor camp before coming to Europe. I looked up the incident and found news reports and a Wikipedia entry about the clashes that indeed took place in N'Zerekore around July 16, 2013. I was surprised that Paul knew the exact date of his parents' death, since I had grown accustomed to asylum seekers using only approximate time specifications. But I did not think it was my role to play detective, so I said nothing.

Eventually, however, a social worker saw pictures on Paul's Facebook page that showed him in Guinea in summer 2016. When confronted with the pictures, Paul admitted that his parents were living in the Guinean capital, Conakry, where he had grown up, and that he had left in 2016 to escape the poverty and because he dreamed of a soccer career in Europe. He had spent only half a year in Libya. When he told me for the first time that he missed his parents, I was more moved than during the times when he had stoically talked about finding their dead bodies. During the asylum interview, Paul then described a childhood of poverty, parental neglect, and frequent fights with teenagers from other ethnic groups, which he said were politically motivated, but which BAMF interpreted as normal conflict between adolescents. He received a rejection shortly after the interview; the adjudicator believed his story but did not consider his experiences asylum-worthy.

GULED: DEALING WITH A EUROPEAN ASYLUM SYSTEM

Guled had filed for asylum in Sweden when he was fourteen and received his rejection when he was fifteen. He had stayed in Sweden another three years, and left when turning eighteen made him deportable. After his Dublin period in Germany had passed, he had filed for asylum again and had his interview shortly thereafter. According to European asylum law, however, Germany had to respect Sweden's decision, unless Guled had new reasons for claiming asylum or new evidence for the old reasons. During his interview, Guled thus spent hours describing how he had been kidnapped by Al-Shabaab when he was eleven and kept at their labor camp for a year before being found by government troops and imprisoned, as the troops feared Al-Shabaab might have brainwashed him into "blowing something up." Either Al-Shabaab or the government would retaliate against him if he returned to Somalia now, he feared. In its rejection letter, BAMF did not comment on the credibility or protection-worthiness of his story, but simply stated that it had to uphold Sweden's previous decision. So, while Idris's story may have been deemed protection-worthy but was not believed, and Paul's was believed but not deemed protection-worthy, Guled's story did not need to be assessed by these criteria at all, because another EU country had already made a decision.

Strategic Identities

Wherever we see extreme stratification—whether it be by age, by nationality, or by some other characteristic—we can expect to see strategic memberships. People, unsurprisingly, seek the best place within a system that seldom rewards honesty. Yossi Harpaz (2019) has shown that people, in order to advance their position in a radically unequal world, try to obtain "compensatory" or "strategic citizenships"—that is, purely instrumental citizenships of countries to which they have no emotional attachment but whose citizenship they qualify for, on the basis of ancestry, for example.

It should not come as a surprise, then, that asylum seekers also approach laws in ways that are "pragmatic and entrepreneurial" (Kim 2015,

47, in Menjívar and Lakhani 2016) and adopt strategic, piecemeal identities, often compensating for a disadvantageous aspect of their identity with an advantageous one. Idris decided to say he was seventeen but thought sixteen would be too young; he did not want to say he was a Somali national, but he did say he was an ethnic Somali from Ethiopia. And asylum seekers' statements are not always easy to distinguish into truths and lies, either. Is someone who does not know if he is seventeen, eighteen, or nineteen lying when he says he is seventeen? Is Samir lying when he says he is Eritrean, given that he had never thought of Eritrea as home before his request for asylum made emphasizing this part of his family history useful? Citizenship, in fact, can mean very different things depending on a country's specific citizenship laws, including having been born in the country (*ius soli*), having parents who were born in the country (*ius sanguinis*), living there (*ius residencia*), or having married a citizen (*ius matrimonii*).

Because existing scholarship has largely focused on state efforts to verify migrants' identities and—to a lesser extent—the role of intermediaries acting on migrants' behalf, we do not know much about how the demand for official vulnerability, such as being a minor or being from a country considered unsafe, is experienced by migrants. We might expect the role of migrants to be minimal or at most symbolic because of their disempowered position vis-à-vis the German state, but migrants' imaginations and strategies actually do have an impact. Their official identities are always compromises between what the state agents and what the migrants can "prove." They contain elements of fiction and truth, are often self-contradictory and changeable over time, and cause friction with a bureaucracy that does not tolerate ambiguity. Such strategic identities dovetail with the literature on strategic citizenship (Harpaz 2019), which highlights an instrumental attitude toward nationality that is analogous to the at least initially instrumental—but eventually more conflicted—attitude toward age among asylum seekers in Germany.

It is important to note two things. First, initially purely instrumental identities may over time have lasting and profound effects on the people who adopt them, as I will examine in later chapters. And second, acknowledging migrants' agency in their own classification should not obscure asymmetric power relations between them and the states they are up against. Saba Mahmood's (2005) reminder not to focus on people's resistance at the expense of trying to understand the workings of power is an important one here. Resistance can instead be used as a diagnostic of power. Young asylum seekers and those who advocate for them face the same dilemma as do all those engaged with identity politics: "Fixed identity categories are both the basis for oppression and the basis for political power" (Gamson 1995). In other words, can one claim minority and its attendant benefits and at the same time challenge the minority/adulthood binary? Asylum seekers do not necessarily believe they can have real impact on politics, but they understand how the existing system works, and they navigate its lines not necessarily with the goal of exposing their arbitrariness but with the hope of traversing them to their advantage. As Michel de Certeau describes, people cannot always reject or alter rules, but they may subvert them "by using them with respect to ends and references foreign to the system they had no choice to accept" (1984, xiii). By actively seeking out a particular position within the stratification systems I have described, asylum seekers conform to the rules without resigning themselves to their predeterminations. The rules provide them with opportunities for being outwitted.

Judith Butler suggests that norms themselves are not only powerful but also enable resistance to such norms, making agency "a reiterative or rearticulatory practice, immanent to power" (1993, xxiii). Drag queens, in this way, use the imitable structure of gender to debunk claims about its naturalness. White converts to Islam challenge ideas of Muslims as a racial group (Galonnier 2017). The successful performance of age or national origin similarly exposes their falsely assumed naturalness. When people cross category boundaries, the performability of the category becomes evident—whether this has been intended by the crosser or not. Helpers do play an important role, of course. For language reasons alone, Samir could not have written his appeal without Franka's and my help. Paul and others were lucky to be noticed by social workers who believed in their minority age. In this chapter, however, I wanted to shift the focus to asylum seekers' own important and often unacknowledged part in negotiations over their identities.

To avoid writing on this issue for fear of breaking with images of refugees as consistently virtuous victims would not only be condescending to their complexity as humans but also ultimately harmful, as it would leave those discussions to ill-intentioned and not empirically minded commentators. How to write about the role of lies in asylum seekers' lives without contributing to the defamation of a population already under sweeping suspicion nonetheless remains an important question, and I will take it up again in chapter 7 and the epilogue.

No one enjoys lying about their identity. Everyone who openly talked to me about false identity claims insisted that they felt they had no other choice if they wanted to be given a chance in Germany. "You shouldn't lie, but you have to," one young man told me. Comparing his own living situation, health, German language skills, and career prospects to Samir's, Idris said he thought their official age largely accounted for the difference.

And yet, he said, if he had known when he first arrived in Germany what he knew now—that is, how much shame and fear he would feel about his false age—he would not have lied. On other days, reflecting on the truthful declaration of his nationality, he said: "If only I had said I was from Somalia, I would have papers now. The liars all got papers." But one must live with a lie, in practice and conscience. Later chapters in this book will examine both sides of the dilemma: the emotional and practical costs of living with a false identity, and the reality of living without the resources afforded to people with more advantageous official identities.

Before examining how young asylum seekers live from day to day with the identities whose negotiation and attainment I have tried to show in this chapter, however, I will first turn to the state's side of things. Using the case of age determination exams, the following chapter will show how the German state responds to the possibility that asylum seekers may be lying about their ages. Together with this chapter, it thus also makes the case that age is anything but obvious or straightforward when the documents that normally would show it do not exist.

3 * The Impossibility of Determining Age

A bus with twenty asylum seekers arrives in Germany, and they all claim the same date of birth; the probability of randomly drawing twenty people with identical dates of birth is 2×10^{-49}. An asylum seeker in Greece claims to be seventeen; three years later in Germany, he again claims to be seventeen—"forever seventeen." These two anecdotes are presented at the twentieth annual meeting of Arbeitsgemeinschaft für forensische Altersdiagnostik (the International Working Group for Forensic Age Diagnostics, or AGFAD), held in a posh conference hotel by the River Spree. Most attendees smile at the punch lines, and some laugh out loud or shake their heads.

I know some of the attendant scientists from my fieldwork, and recognize the name tags of others whose articles I have read. Forensic age examiners from all over Europe—Sweden, England, Greece—have come to Berlin for this day. In their presentations they all tell similar stories of young migrants claiming to be under eighteen, of local governments being overwhelmed, of an increased demand for age exams, and of a growing controversy over whether the work of forensic examiners is unethical, unscientific, or both. Most had estimated ages their whole careers, without receiving any flak, in order to combat child prostitution or identify trafficking victims, to validate international adoptions or athletic competitions, to decide whether criminal offenders should be tried as juveniles or adults, and, of course, to assess dead bodies.[1] No one seemed to take issue with their labor—until the 2015 refugee crisis. Suddenly, age examiners' motivations, methods, and results were under attack.

My fieldwork on age exams began at my desk. For a while I thought it would stay there. I had made several discouraging calls to age examiners whose numbers I had found on their institutes' websites. Some admitted that they feared I was a journalist hunting for defamatory details of age examiners "pulling pants down" or "measuring pubic hair." Others lied that I must have misunderstood the listing and that their institute did not conduct age exams. I briefly considered making do with the fact that participant observation was out of reach, as did Hugh Gusterson (1996) in his study of the secretive world of nuclear scientists. Then I decided to try to show that I was uninterested in lurid headlines and willing to put in the work. I collected hundreds of articles on age determination from forensic, pediatric, and generalist medical journals as well as newspapers, and I began to read. Becoming an expert on the technical nitty-gritty of these exams, it turned out, was a better key to entering the world of age exams than a threatening bouquet of sociological questions. This chapter, in which I explain how age determination works and show just how controversial and ambiguous it is, should be read as a foil to the matter-of-factness with which a date of birth thus determined is subsequently treated.

Age Assessment in Germany: History, Legal Framework, Controversy

German forensic scientists have been examining young migrants with disputed ages since the late 1980s. They compare X-rays of the left hand and wisdom teeth, as well as CT scans of the clavicle, to atlases of skeletal development which show typical images of hands, jaws, and clavicles at various chronological ages as well as distributions among the reference population in order to determine the probability that someone has crossed a legally relevant threshold: fourteen, sixteen, eighteen, or twenty-one years. While age exams are subject to other laws, such as the German X-Ray Ordinance, Germany does not have specific regulations on how to conduct age exams. To unify age exams across the country, forensic scientists in Berlin founded AGFAD, which regularly publishes updated best-practice reports, holds an annual meeting, and conducts tests to screen the quality of the exams that its members perform.

In the 1990s and 2000s, age exams on living subjects were rare and could easily be integrated into work weeks filled with autopsies and other common tasks of forensic science. At the University Medical Center in Hamburg, which conducts age exams for all of northern Germany including Berlin and is where I shadowed examiners, 699 age exams were done between 1990 and 2000, 946 between 2001 and 2008, and 2,578 between 2009 and 2015 (Mansour et al. 2017). Dr. Peters, an age examiner at the University Medical Center, told me that he did about 700 exams just between the summers of 2015 and 2016, the height of the refugee crisis. As age exams increased in prevalence, they also became more controversial among politicians and refugee rights activists as well as within the medical community itself, though the public-political controversy cannot easily be separated from the medical-scientific one. People even began using different terms for age assessments to show where they stood: while practitioners referred to their work as "age determination," "age diagnostics," or "age distinction," critics preferred the terms "age fixing" or "age estimation."

Pediatricians, social workers, and activists hold that the variance of the chronological ages associated with specific developmental stages is too large to ever exclude minority, that radiological exams expose young refugees to medically unwarranted doses of radiation, and that the studies medical examiners reference are not suitable for assessing today's asylum seeker population. Greulich and Pyle's *Radiographic Atlas of Skeletal Development of the Hand and Wrist*, for example—the atlas medical examiners use to interpret hand X-rays—is based on the Brush Foundation Growth Study from 1931–42, but pediatricians argue that ossification has accelerated over the past eighty years. They also invoke biological conceptions of race, arguing that the physical development of white study subjects may not be comparable to that of other races. Several people explained to me that they did not doubt that certain developmental stages roughly correlate with chronological ages, but that forensic age examiners were inferring the wrong way around: atlases of skeletal maturity could be used to see whether a teenager with a known date of birth was developing normally—that is, if their physical development approximated what would be expected given their age—but that it was a logical fallacy to think that such tables could be used the other way around to infer age.

Besides criticizing such scientific aspects of forensic age exams, opponents argue that need, not chronological age, should determine the resources a refugee gets. They told me countless stories of severely traumatized asylum seekers who, because they were classified as adults, were denied the resources they deserved. They also told me how their own family histories—involving flight from Nazi Germany, or from the German Democratic Republic (East Germany) during the Cold War—had informed their stance on refugees and age exams. (Some even brought up physicians' role in the Holocaust, implying a comparison to forensic scientists working for the state today.) By contrast, forensic medical examiners rarely told me anything personal about themselves—especially not in connection to their work—because they strove for neutrality and expertise rather than positionality.

The German Medical Association has repeatedly voted against physicians' involvement in age exams. While these decrees are not legally binding, they are important professional resolutions that critics of age exams use to argue that medical examiners are shirking their profession's guidelines. As one opponent of age exams said, "Doctors' job is to heal, not to separate the good guys from the bad." All of the medical examiners

I met firmly denied that age exams were unethical, and were irked by the allegations that they were flouting medico-professional norms. They explained that other physicians sweepingly defined the physician's task as that of healing in accordance with the doctor-patient contract, but that medical examiners occupy the role of expert as part of a contract with the commissioning government agency or court. They asserted that radiation exposure during age exams was no higher than at an airport. They also pointed to the German X-Ray Ordinance, which states that in addition to being ordered due to medical indication, X-rays can be ordered due to legal indication, and are warranted not only when there is a benefit to the individual but also when there is an expected benefit to society (RöV 1987). Nonetheless, several forensic scientists are working on developing radiation-free or low-radiation methods of age assessment, such as ultrasound and magnetic resonance imaging (MRI). The debate over whether individuals should be exposed to radiation in the interest of society or solely for their own medical benefit echoes a larger juxtaposition of individual and society inherent in age exams. As one presenter at the twentieth annual meeting of AGFAD noted, from the standpoint of the individual, false negatives of minority should be low, while from the standpoint of society, false positives should be low. Forensic medical examiners also refute the importance of race to age exams, claiming that, if anything, ossification depended on socioeconomic conditions, meaning that refugees' ages were most likely being *under*estimated.

Many pediatricians advocated improving visual age exams, now conducted by social workers, and putting them in the hands of pediatricians—what they called the psychosocial method of age assessment. This is intended as a holistic examination because, as one critic of forensic age exams put it, "a human being is not just skin and bones." Several pediatricians regularly use their own psychosocial methods to reexamine asylum seekers who have already been forensically assessed, and then send their reports to the respective judge, who usually ignores this addendum. Many age exam critics told me about doing things similarly on their own initiative. Social worker Julian, who had been working in refugee camps in Bavaria years before the refugee crisis, told me how he, two colleagues, and a translator set up shop in the waiting room of the government office that was then conducting age exams. They approached any asylum seeker who entered the waiting room, asked him what he thought his age was, and then asked him what age the government had determined for him after his assessment. They put these numbers into two columns and made a third column for the average of their own guesses. Julian showed me these tables, which included hundreds of rows of asylum seekers. The government almost always estimated an age above both the asylum seeker's declaration and the social workers' guess. Julian handed these tables to the government and youth welfare office of Bavaria. After half a year, the government reassigned the task of assessing age to the youth welfare office, and Julian believes this was partially thanks to his experiment. While he is also critical of visual age exams conducted by the youth welfare office, he sees them as a definite step up from the "age raffle" the government had been holding, in which a government employee briefly looked at the asylum seeker, often through a glass panel, and came up with a number.

Youth welfare offices across Germany began conducting visual age exams, in which social workers assessed an asylum seeker's physical appearance and demeanor, when the country's federal government mandated in 2005 that youth welfare offices had to take in asylum seekers who were below the age of eighteen, rather than only those below sixteen. Youth welfare offices started implementing this new law about five years later. Until then, asylum seekers under eighteen had been deemed minors, but were considered of age when it came to their asylum procedure. When the legal age to submit an asylum application was raised from sixteen to eighteen, unaccompanied minors were housed no longer in refugee shelters but by youth welfare offices, thus causing those offices to take the scope of this population into their own hands, as several of my interlocutors noted.

Forensic scientists deride both visual age exams and the psychosocial method as silly. First, they say, no scientific studies exist on the correlation of psychosocial development and chronological age. And second, psychosocial age assessment confuses need with chronological age. They concede that were the task to determine need, the psychosocial method would indeed be appropriate. But that would call for a new legal framework in Germany. Chronological age—not need—matters legally, and so chronological age and need are two entirely different questions. Stefan Timmermans (2007) has shown how various groups in society develop their own notions of suicide (biographical, statistical, and medicolegal). Various groups in Germany similarly advance different notions of age: while social workers and refugee rights activists define age socially or biographically, medical examiners do so biologically, and public institutions, including family courts, youth welfare offices, and migration offices, work with chronological or calendric definitions of age.

Forensic age examiners see justice as the central value of their work. They argue that age exams ensure that no adult will accidentally be allowed into a youth shelter, which is, after all, supposed to be a safe space for children. They stress that material support is necessarily limited and should go to those who most deserve it—children. Forensic age exams, they told me, uphold the state of law—the absence of which in other countries is a common cause of flight. Forensic scientists were especially upset about claims that they _loved_ to do age assessments because it earned them a lot of money, made them feel important, or allowed them to act on their right-wing political beliefs or pedophilic tendencies. They emphasized that age assessments were a totally unpopular job that they had agreed to do only when no one else would. It was such a hot topic that one could only lose by being involved with it. Andrew Abbott has argued that the relative status within professions depends on the work's perceived purity; the work of medical examiners is, in Abbott's terminology, "tainted by nonprofessional issues" (1981, 825) as well as by their collaboration with law enforcement. Forensic science is already not a prestigious field within medical science, and age exams are a forensic subfield of particularly low prestige.

The controversy around age exams is so difficult to resolve due not only to obdurate political camps but also because it is impossible to know which side is factually right. Age examiners—unlike many other scientists, such as weather forecasters—can never know whether their reading of the evidence was correct. There are no provably false or correct outcomes to appeal to. The University of Münster, where AGFAD is now based, evaluated 594 age exam reports it had written between 2007 and 2018, and found that 40 percent of those migrants who had claimed to be minors were determined to be eighteen or older. But even such striking findings remain self-referential, as they only assess the work of age determination and not the true share of minors in the asylum seeker population.

When I began my research in 2016, very little public attention was directed to age exams; but the few existing media reports, were, to my knowledge, univocally critical, insinuating that age exams were harmful and even unlawful. By winter 2017, constant media reports of asylum seekers using false identities to claim resources, and several high-profile crimes committed by young male asylum seekers who had lived in Germany under false or multiple identities, discomfited the German public. A survey among readers of the center-right newspaper _Die Welt_ immediately following one such crime showed that 78 percent of respondents were in support of mandatory age exams for young asylum seekers (_Die Welt_ 2018). Even the Green Party, which is generally lenient on immigration, and which just a year earlier had tried and failed to forbid forensic-medical age exams, now called for reexamining the identities of every asylum seeker who had entered Germany in the past two years, lest they had been misclassified.

There are also no reliable official statistics on age exams and the ages of refugees, and this has caused each side of the controversy to produce its own numbers. Germany's largest organization for unaccompanied minor asylum seekers, Bundesfachverband unbegleitete minderjährige Flüchtlinge (Association for Unaccompanied Refugee Minors, or BumF), surveyed thirty-five youth welfare offices across Germany, asking them how many asylum seekers they had classified and with what results. BumF never published these numbers, but a staff member showed them to me. After youth welfare offices began conducting age exams, the share of minors in the total asylum seeker population in Germany plummeted, which this staff member saw as a sign that youth welfare offices have used age exams as a method of gatekeeping. They have a limited number of spots in youth welfare apartments, and so they classify accordingly. Several of my interlocutors pointed out that it was absurd that the youth welfare office could manage access to its own system, saying it would be as if I could evaluate my own research grant applications. More startling to me was the age pyramid of young migrants in Germany as revealed by the BumF survey. Unsurprisingly, there were very few migrants below fourteen years of age and the numbers per group rose steadily until the age of twenty-five. However, there was a remarkable plunge at age seventeen. That is, there were many sixteen- and eighteen-year-old asylum seekers, but far fewer seventeen-year-olds. The BumF staff member speculated as to why: "It could be that asylum seekers say especially often that they are sixteen. But that does not make sense to me. If I am twenty-one and want to pass for a minor, I'll say that I'm seventeen. So, if anything, the number of seventeen-year-olds should be disproportionately high. So this gap, the one thousand seventeen-year-olds who are missing in 2014 alone, those are the ones the youth welfare office sorted out."

For the sake of ethnographic depth, I will mainly present the experiences and reflections of two age examiners—David, a social worker, and Dr. Peters, a forensic medical examiner—whom I found to be in many ways typical of their respective professional groups. Unless I indicate otherwise, the quotations are from them. Both men have the ultimately impossible task of determining ages, but they meet this challenge differently.

"That Then Simply Becomes My Professional Opinion": Social Work and Visual Age Exams

"I had nightmares for the first week," David recalled of his early days conducting age exams. "I think it's awful to judge people, and I couldn't care less how old someone is." David is tall, with curly hair and glasses. (In his own words: "Receding hairline, many white hairs, forehead wrinkles. Obviously not under eighteen.") After completing his masters degree in social work, David worked with Roma and Sinti families for twelve years before applying to work for his local city government. He wanted to be a caseworker for asylum seekers and help them get settled. Three days before his first day of work, he received a phone call: "Herr Mayer, we have assigned you to our age exam unit." David was stunned, but thought he could not afford to refuse the job.

In the month of August 2015 alone, 135,000 asylum seekers arrived in Bavaria, the state where David works. The German federal police began patrolling train stations and other public transit areas, sorting newly arrived asylum seekers into the appropriate shelters. When an asylum seeker enters Germany and claims to be both unaccompanied and under eighteen, he is sent to a local youth shelter for refugees—like the Young Refugee Center in Munich, where Paul spent his first weeks in Germany, or Pangea Hostel in Berlin, where Idris met Aman and Yakob—and undergoes a so-called clearing procedure, which includes appearing before three social workers who try to verify his age claim. "That's German bureaucracy," David explained. "[Without an age,] a person can't exist." During the zenith of this refugee crisis—between the summers of 2015 and 2016—David classified about twenty asylum seekers a week, completely filling his part-time work schedule.

David and his colleagues had one hour to estimate the age of each asylum seeker. David called it "work on the assembly line." With the help of a translator, these social workers—who were not specially qualified to conduct age exams—would interview and inspect the asylum seeker. They first asked the asylum seeker to recount his biography, including information about his family, home country, education, and flight. They would listen for possible contradictions, as well as for chronologies and durations that made minority age unlikely. They also took notes on the asylum seeker's skin, build, hair growth, voice pitch, and demeanor.[2]

The manual that social workers used to assess age tried to minimize subjectivity. It instructed social workers to write down, "if at all possible, objective and actually observed details rather than interpretations." It also cautioned that certain behaviors, such as avoidance of eye contact, might be related to the asylum seeker's cultural background, and that certain physical attributes, such as individual white hairs, might be related to shock or stress. The instructions also appealed to social workers to "review your inner attitude. [. . .] Don't think 'they're all lying,' 'they're all criminals,' 'they're all older than they say.'"

After forty-five minutes, the asylum seeker and translator would leave the room. The social workers would share their impressions and decide on a new birth date, often December 31 (to give the asylum seeker the bonus of being as young as possible within the estimated year of birth) or the birth date originally given by the asylum seeker, even if the year changed. This was because the social workers believed that piece of self would be especially important in times of flight. Unlike forensic age exams, which conclude with determination of a minimum and probable age, visual exams culminate in assignment of an exact date of birth. "This is really just horse-trading," said David. "Usually we've agreed on an approximate age, but then we have to decide whether he turned sixteen yesterday or is turning seventeen tomorrow. And that always seems absurd." The social workers would then inform the asylum seeker and translator of the results. Everyone reacted differently to being given a new age. "Some don't react at all," said David. "Occasionally someone says, 'Yeah, I know. I just wanted to give it a try. I'm actually older.' Some become angry. And some just start crying." Those asylum seekers who were classified as adults had to leave the youth shelter that same afternoon, and were relocated to a camp for adults. If the team of social workers could not decide on an age, or if the asylum seeker appealed the decision, he would undergo a forensic medical age exam to settle the dispute.

Despite the detailed instructions laid out in the manual, David found it impossible to tell someone's age, especially from their demeanor: "Some argue, 'He was so stand-offish. He must be older.' But I've heard the opposite argument, too: 'He was so quiet, he must be older.' You can interpret it this way or that." Other social workers told me that they found it difficult to judge voice pitch in languages they did not speak, because every language has its own tonality. One social worker said that people from certain countries were more difficult to classify than others.[3] Another said girls were more difficult than boys. Most recognized the predicament of never knowing whether they were right. They could feel more or less certain, but their final decision could never be validated. "Sometimes there's this moment when you tell someone which date of birth you've determined for them, even though you weren't there during their birth," said David. "Sometimes their reaction gives you the impression that you were probably right or probably wrong. But this is just an impression. Ultimately, we're always working in vagueness." Sometimes, social workers changed their opinion too late, *after* having made someone eighteen. This happened to David on one of the days we met. He was visibly upset when he explained what had happened. That morning, he had estimated someone to be over eighteen, but afterward talked to the translator who explained why the teenager had appeared older, thus convincing David that he had made a mistake. Translators occupy a peculiar role in age exams: they often know the asylum seeker a little better, since they can talk to him and have sometimes accompanied him to other appointments, yet they are strictly forbidden from saying anything during the age exam or influencing its result in any way.

Michael Lipsky (1980) defines street-level bureaucrats as public workers with discretion over the dispensation of benefits—that is, the ability to use their professional judgment when making decisions. As is typical for street-level bureaucrats, David's work was highly scripted, yet he also had to improvise. "Just today," he told me, "we had a guy whose whole family died, he said. He seemed really burdened, so of course we left out any questions related to family. And this happens often." Like other street-level bureaucrats, David faced a dilemma: bureaucratic fairness means treating everyone the same, but that seems unfair in some individual cases. For example, minors have access to better medical care than do adults. David would sometimes let this influence his decision. "When you have someone who is half-tattered by bombs, and this could potentially play a role in the decision, some colleagues, maybe even I, might let this enter the decision.[4] [. . .] In such extreme cases I look at the case more closely, and I simply conclude that it is possible that he is still seventeen. That then simply becomes my professional opinion." I asked David what he thought about the bureaucratic ideal that it is fair to treat everyone within one population group the same—that every minor, for instance, should have one set of rights and every adult another. He responded: "One could also say it's fair when a person who's been shot to pieces, whose extremities—ah, I won't go there—when this person has the chance to receive full medical support [regardless of their age]."

Another social worker described as some of the toughest situations those in which asylum seekers who were obviously children insisted that they were eighteen: "Time and again we get ten-, eleven-year-old Eritreans, or twelve or nine; they don't know their exact age. But they say they're eighteen, because they think then they'll be able to work [and send money to their families]. And those are the onerous cases with the most tears, because we have to decide against their will. [. . .] But of course in the end I have to tell them, 'You're just a little squirt. You belong in second grade.' But they insist that they're eighteen, absolutely insist. And they never budge from that. And then we have to give them a new age—against their will but, I would say, in their interest."

David had never imagined he would do age exams for a living. He was critical of the fact that age mattered so much in the first place, and also doubted the validity of the criteria used to assess it. He oscillated between seeing his job as only a small part in the process of assigning age (perhaps to soften his responsibility) and being extremely self-critical of his own involvement. On the one hand, he would explain to the asylum seekers, "from the beginning, that our conversation has nothing to do with asylum,[5] that it's just about their age, simply to see which agency will be in charge—the youth welfare office or the government of Upper Bavaria." Yet at other times he told me, "Most [social workers] would never be willing to work here [in the age exam unit]. Initially, I wasn't either. You could have offered me ten thousand euros and I would have refused. Now I ended up here and, yeah, I do it. I have to take responsibility for that."

David used his discretion whenever it helped him maintain his conception of the social work profession as "the dismantling of exclusionary mechanisms." Classifying severely injured asylum seekers as minors is one example, but he exercised discretion in many other situations as well. When confronted with children who had been separated from their relatives somewhere in Europe, and who would only be allowed to leave Germany to be reunited with them if they were over eighteen, he would find "special solutions. I could imagine that in such a case, I wouldn't know, [. . .] but I could imagine that during the exam you would have to conclude that the kids aren't feeling well and the exam has to be terminated, and as chance would have it, at just that time there's a translator around who can call the relatives and discuss a few things. And it might just be that the next day, those children are gone." In situations like these, David used his discretion to subvert the equation of fairness with equal treatment.

David did not choose to work in the age exam unit, and only did so because he was ordered to do so and could not find another job. He knew immediately that this work aligned neither with his personal values nor with his professional self-understanding as a social worker. He began his job with nightmares and still felt guilty, calling it a "scandal" that age mattered so much for the life chances of individual asylum seekers. His social worker friends were appalled that he would do such a job, and they either teased or berated him. David was part of the Working Group of Critical Social Workers, a loose association of social workers with branches across Germany.[6] They met once every month or two to discuss recent developments in social work. For David, these meetings were both an outlet to be openly critical of age exams and a place where he faced criticism for his complicity. In mid-July 2016, an asylum seeker who had been classified as a seventeen-year-old Afghan attacked passengers on a Bavarian train with an ax. Two days later, it came out that he was neither seventeen nor from Afghanistan. I spent the day following this news with David and members of the Working Group of Critical Social Workers, who mocked the public outrage over the attacker's age and nationality. When one of the social workers told the rest of us about the newest state of investigations—that the seventeen-year-old Afghan was now in all likelihood an eighteen-year-old Pakistani—everyone burst into laughter, and one sneered, "That, of course, changes everything!" David partook in this mockery, but it was also directed at him. After all, through his work he validated daily the notion that identity markers like age lie discoverable in individual bodies and should be consequential for individual lives.

The European belief that a person's age was unequivocal and simply needed to be determined came up again and again in my interviews with social workers and others working with asylum seekers. When I first brought up the subject of age with Monika, who had been working with unaccompanied minors since the 1980s, she laughed and said: "It's just a fictional entity. Just a number. It's all a giant circus." Monika was not as vehemently against age exams as were other social workers; she found them comical. Just a few months earlier, she had received a call from one of her former wards who confessed she was actually twelve years older than she had claimed. Monika found this amusing: "She was twenty-seven when we all thought she was fifteen! They didn't even order an age exam for her, because there was no doubt. But she completely slipped into this role of a girl: she wore little skirts and white bobby socks, and just generally acted like a fifteen-year-old."

Nearly all social workers I talked to admitted that asylum seekers lie about their ages; most found this justified, and some actively supported false claims—such as Viktoria, who told asylum seekers, "It can't hurt to try." If age did not matter so much, they said, no one would be forced to "bullshit." Sophie, another social worker, also supported false age claims. "There's no recognition of what a shitty situation someone has to be in to lie about their age, which is also a part of their identity," she said. "If someone is willingly denying a part of their identity, their situation demands our support, no matter their age." The social workers insisted that by denying traumatized young people the support they needed to integrate into German society simply because we "latch on to our age myth," as Julian put it, we were producing social problems.

Viktoria provided legal and bureaucratic advice to refugees. She told me that many of the refugees she sees every week simply do not know their birth dates, because those dates play no role in their home countries. They can often say approximately when they were born—during which season, or around the time of what event—but that is meaningless to German courts. She remembered two Guinean boys who had grown up in the same village, were best friends, and had experienced their milestones together. Then they came to Germany, and one was assessed to be seventeen, the other twenty. She called this absurd: "How would we feel if someone told us: 'You weren't born on October 6 but on December 31, and not in this year but in that year?'"

Social workers also insisted that fleeing ages a person, and that age exams should not be conducted immediately upon an asylum seeker's arrival in Germany, if at all. They said that sleep deprivation and malnourishment make people appear older, and that stress messes with a person's hormones, which can affect men's facial hair growth. They told me about newly arrived asylum seekers who had looked like old men: haggard and bent over, shuffling their feet, with hands hanging limply, dark circles around their dull eyes, and thinning hair. After a few months in Germany with food, sleep, and medical care, they had transformed into young men.

"We Simply Find Certain Things and Describe Them": Forensic Science and Forensic Age Exams

Besides visual age exams, most German cities also use medical-forensic age exams to estimate the age of asylum seekers. In some cities, such exams are a method of last resort, employed only when the social workers cannot agree on an age. In others, every asylum seeker who is not clearly recognizable as a child or adult is sent to a forensic age exam. Most forensic age examiners follow—more or less closely—the suggestions of AGFAD, which recommends taking three radiological images: an X-ray of the left hand, a panoramic X-ray of the jaw area (orthopantomogram), and a thin-layer CT of the medial clavicular epiphysis. These images are compared to atlases of skeletal development that show typical images of hands, jaws, and clavicles at various chronological ages, as well as distributions among the reference population.[7] Medical examiners then write a report comparing the asylum seeker's radiological images to these reference populations, and suggest a minimum age (the age of the youngest study participant with the same skeletal development) and a probable age (the average age of study participants with the same skeletal development). Age exams are based on the idea that humans all follow the same developmental path through distinct stages at roughly the same speed. If images suggest different minimum ages, the medical examiner indicates the highest minimum age. A judge then uses this report to assign a new date of birth.

Dr. Peters did not choose to work in age exams. Trained as a dentist, he spent most of his professional life in radiodontia, and identifies as a radiologist. He began working in forensic pathology early on in his career, helping to identify dead bodies by examining their teeth. Starting in 1995, he was asked to do age exams, mostly to determine whether criminal offenders were twenty-one (and thus subject to adult criminal law).

After several interviews, Peters invited me to be present during forensic age exams. The exams I observed all followed the same routine. I would arrive at the forensic lab early in the morning and watch Peters prepare the paperwork for that day's exams. Although age exams took place in different rooms than did autopsies, it was impossible to forget that this was the institute of forensic *pathology*, not age determination. Peters's office was often littered with pictures and other artifacts from autopsies. He and his colleagues were working on autopsy reports while I was writing my field notes at a big table in the middle of the large office, and sometimes they would make a remark about something that had happened during an autopsy before they shifted their attention to the age exams at hand.

In the mornings, Peters would piece together identifying documents for the asylum seekers he was expecting that day, so that the X-ray technicians would later know whom they had before them. He was usually disgruntled that age exams were not afforded much importance within the hospital; he did not have his own secretary, and the hospital radiologists were often annoyed at having to slot healthy people into their schedules when they had patients with massive brain hemorrhages in urgent need of care. At around 9 a.m., the asylum seekers scheduled to have their age assessed would arrive together with translators and social workers. Peters and his assistant quickly slipped on their white scrubs, and we greeted everyone in the forensic lab foyer. A roll call usually revealed that names had been misspelled, that first and last names were mixed up, and that some asylum seekers scheduled to have age exams had not shown up. After some back-and-forth about who was there, we would walk over to the adjacent hospital as a large, quiet group to get everyone's dental panorama images taken.

I would join Peters and his assistant in the X-ray lab to observe the taking and initial interpretation of the X-rays. One by one, the asylum seekers came in, held on to the panoramic dental X-ray machine, and left the room after their images had been taken. Peters and his assistant intently watched the screen on which each image unfolded, and voiced initial impressions as teeth began to appear. As the panoramic dental X-ray machine rotated around one young man's head, the image of his teeth appeared on the computer screen behind him, disclosing itself from right to left, centimeter by centimeter. Peters looked at the screen and said, "The wisdom teeth are there."

"Sixteen, seventeen," his younger colleague said.

"Seventeen, sixteen," Peters replied. He moved one step closer to the screen and put on his glasses, watching the now complete image intently for another ten seconds. "A not entirely clear seventeen," he concluded.

Based on these initial impressions from the orthopantograms, Peters decided whether to also X-ray the hand. He would usually forego a hand X-ray, arguing that the teeth were the most diagnostically conclusive part of the exam anyway, and that a hand X-ray would only expose the asylum seeker to unnecessary radiation. The tradeoff between wanting more images to analyze and wanting to avoid excessive radiation is actually a source of conflict among forensic medical examiners. Many sweepingly order radiological images of everyone's teeth, hand, and clavicle, and only then look at them. The AGFAD guidelines, in fact, recommend taking all three images so as to infer chronological age from a range of developmental characteristics, not just the teeth or hand. Peters, who identified as a radiologist, said that medical examiners often did not fully understand radiology, and therefore did not think twice before ordering clavicle CTs, which exposed the patient to much higher doses of radiation than either hand or teeth X-rays (0.4 mSv, instead of 0.026 and 0.0001 respectively). He recalled a conversation with a colleague who had casually mentioned the many CT scans he ordered every week. When Peters asked the colleague why he did not instead do orthopantograms, which come with just a fraction of the radiation, the colleague looked surprised and said he did not really know. "He was just flinging radiation all over the place," huffed Peters, who only ordered a hand X-ray when in doubt, and only asked for a clavicle CT when he had to determine whether a criminal offender was at least twenty-one, because at that age the hand and wisdom teeth are often too far developed to be of any use in assessing a person's age. Peters always stressed the reliability of his exams. "Our system works," he would say. "Odontogenesis is so consistent. You can drop a bomb outside, but teeth keep on growing." He laughed. "That's the beauty of teeth. They're reliable evidence."

During one age exam I observed, the asylum seeker had no wisdom teeth, but Peters still decided against hand X-rays. "I can't make him over eighteen, right? He does have some atrophy, and so I can say in all likelihood he's seventeen. But I'm not going to do an extra hand X-ray. Nonsense! The hand is also going to show a minimum age below eighteen. Just based on the orthopantomogram and my experience. You always have to weigh between the radiation and all the rest. And in this case, I just have a feeling, I just know, it wouldn't bring anything new to the table. Let's say the hand looks developed; that means it's the image of a nineteen-year-old. And then I have plus and minus fifteen months [standard deviation], and I'm again below eighteen, right? [. . .] Empirical value, you know?"[8]

Back at the forensic lab, the asylum seekers are asked to enter a treatment room, one after the other, for their physical exams. They are weighed, measured, and asked about their health, their family health history, and any medications they are taking. Their pulse, blood pressure, heart, thyroid, and lungs are checked. The primary point of these exams is not to estimate their age—though a "general impression" is included in the final report—but to rule out developmental disorders that could distort the results of forensic age exams. Dr. Schmidt, a medical examiner in Münster, told me that he almost never finds signs of such disorders. He attributed this to the selection process that asylum seekers go through:

the poorest cannot afford to flee, families tend to send their fittest members with the highest chance of success, and the flight itself is strenuous, withstood by only the most robust.

While age examiners were consistently polite to the asylum seekers, I often witnessed police—who were present only when criminal offenders were being examined—taunt them. They would make mocking jokes about the radiation: "You will be glowing when we're done here." In the waiting room, one police officer showed an asylum seeker a magazine article about Afghanistan with pictures of bombed-out buildings, to gauge from his reaction "if you're really from there." The police voiced their opinions about the refugee crisis: "We can't save the whole world. It's like that boat you came in on: when it's full, it's full." This was something the medical examiners never did. Police also did not hide their suspicion of self-proclaimed minors, and teased one migrant who had quietly endured the physical and radiographic exams: "Didn't cry at all. . . . You *are* a big boy after all!" They also sometimes speculated about the age of an asylum seeker on the basis of biographical information gleaned in small talk during waiting periods: "So you were in Afghanistan until you were ten, then four years in Iran, two in Syria, then again Iran, and a year ago you came to Germany. And you say you're nineteen. But you also say you worked as a painter for twelve years. So you started when you were four?"

A medical examiner does not make the final decision about an asylum seeker's age. The examiner gives a minimum and a probable age, and explains the conclusion in light of the asylum seeker's exam result and the atlases of skeletal development in reference populations. The examiner's report is presented to a judge, who bases a decision on it. But something always gets lost in the attempt to translate information from one field of professional expertise (medical) to another (legal). Medical examiners told me that judges often do not understand the difference between minimum and probable age. The judges are tasked with drawing conclusions from medical evidence they cannot fully comprehend. They sometimes simply opt for the average of the minimum and probable ages, a practice not in keeping with the meaning of either concept. Dr. Peters did not like giving the probable age, because judges tended to latch onto it and completely ignore the minimum age. Judges, youth welfare offices, and other agencies, he said, do not understand that age examiners cannot determine an exact date of birth, only the probability of having crossed a legally relevant age threshold.

The reports medical examiners write are invariably factual and sure-sounding, despite the ambiguity I observed during the exams. They vary greatly in length and detail. In the case files I reviewed, some reports were only a page in length, others twenty-five pages, and most around ten. The reports did not contain personal information about the asylum seekers, only observations made during the exams and about how they compared to the reference populations. In fact, I witnessed multiple times that Peters and other forensic age examiners stopped translators and social workers when they were about to disclose something personal about a person to be classified. When Peters's colleague Anna was tasked with classifying a criminal offender who was to be tried under either juvenile or adult criminal law, she instructed the accompanying police not to tell her what he had done. "I don't want to be tempted to make him older," she said. "If he raped someone, yeah, he is an asshole, but it's not my job to judge that." Medical examiners prefer to remain scientists, and become politicians only reluctantly, "expecting others to determine the implications of their findings" (Timmermans 2007, 272). The times when forensic age examiners did learn something personal about an asylum seeker were noticeably also the times they began to struggle with their classification task, as the following incident illustrates.

One of the few girls I saw at the lab had a German ID that said she had been born on May 5, 2002, which would have made her fourteen. Peters and I met the girl and her caseworker in the hallway to tell them the results of the exam. "I can't be sure just yet," Peters explained. "But the minimum age is, I'm guessing, around fifteen. I have to look at the X-rays some more, and also when [my colleague] is here. But the teeth are already so developed that I really don't need to take an X-ray of the hand. We can definitely say the age here on her residence permit is too young."

The girl looked disappointed. Her caseworker said, "Sixteen would be ideal for her," and laughed uncomfortably.

Peters deliberated and then said, "We'll see. Probably not sixteen, but not fourteen either. Again, my guess is a minimum age of fifteen."

Back in his office, Peters told me that the girl had just given birth to a baby who was taken away, because she herself was an unaccompanied child and was thus seen as unfit to raise one. If she was sixteen, she could have her child back. I asked whether there was a chance that he would give her minimum age as sixteen.

"Oh well," he said, "I cannot exclude sixteen, right? But I'll have to look more closely. You know, when I say minimum age, meaning 'not younger than this,' of course she could be older. Based on this radiograph, she could be sixteen."

"So it's possible?"

"That's the statistical leeway. But I really have to look at the reference books some more, to see the numbers. All I can say is she's stage E or maybe even F, because if I just take the upper jaw, the roots there were pretty long. If I compare this with the dental crowns, I can say it's stage

E or F. And F is sixteen–nineteen, on average. And E is fifteen–nineteen on average. That's why I told her fifteen. She told me sixteen would be better, though. They took her baby away, you know? But it's because she's so young, you know? All we're doing here—we can't give a date of birth. It's possible she could be sixteen; we can't rule it out."

Peters later wondered whether he should have X-rayed the girl's hand, to see if she might be sixteen after all. "But would I have been any the wiser?" he said.

"So you'll have to take another close look at the orthopantomogram?"

"Yes, definitely. Because if the teeth had been less well developed— let's say only the crown had been sitting there, and then just the beginnings of a root—then I'd definitely have said we have to do the hand, you know? But the roots seemed so developed, so I didn't think it was necessary. I can always protect myself by saying I won't agree to a dose [of radiation] that isn't necessary."

Dr. Peters seemed to struggle sincerely with his decision about whether to give the girl a minimum age of either fifteen (his professional judgment) or sixteen (her wish).[9] He was sympathetic to her desire to raise her baby, but did not want to compromise his scientific standards of evidence-based judgment. Medical examiners are not used to their work having these kinds of consequences.[10] For the most part, they deny the politics of their work, pointing to the objectivity of forensic science, and particularly of radiological images. "Age exams belong with forensic science," as opposed to social work or pediatrics, Peters insisted. "Because this is a neutral space. I think it is, right? We're not pursuing any interests; there's no ideology here. We simply find certain things and describe them." Medical examiners did acknowledge some degree of uncertainty, but only to the extent that was normal and acceptable in science.

I asked Peters what happened when he and a colleague disagreed on what age someone's teeth indicated.

"Well, then you have to discuss it," he said. "We don't want to harm anyone, so in the end one of us budges and says, 'Fine, then he's not eighteen; he's seventeen.' It's not the end of the world, you know? He got lucky." Peters laughed. "It's not like we ever have huge differences in opinion. If there are five developmental stages, and I say stage 2, and he says stage 5, that's impossible. One of us is wrong. The disagreement could only be between 3a and 3b, or something like that. Nuances, you know? X-rays are hard to read. That's just what it is."

Age examiners are aware of the consequences of classifying someone a certain age, and while they must avoid letting this influence their decisions, so as to retain their professional and scientific credibility, they insist that the concept of minimum age and its primacy over the concept of probable age shows that they do not take lightly the consequences of their work to the lives of young asylum seekers. Similarly, in Timmermans's study of the determination of causes of death (2007), death examiners are well aware of the stigma of suicide. While all avoidance of classifying deaths as suicides would undermine their professional credibility, they are nonetheless careful to opt for this classification only when its correctness is very probable, and are aware of the emotional and sometimes even financial and legal repercussions it could have for relatives. Because of this fear of losing credibility, "compromise cases," such as that of the young mother who wanted to be sixteen, "rarely appear in professional journals but are instead the stuff of hallway conversations" (2007, 239), and also are occasionally picked up by the media.

Most forensic medical examiners reject visual age exams as subjective and unscientific. Peters imagined visual age exams as "a group of, I don't know, psychologists or something. And then they start talking about the hairline. 'Since it is all the way up here . . . it usually isn't this far up.' Completely wishy-washy!" Medical examiners contrast visual exams with their own methods, which, they insist, are substantiated by hundreds of scientific studies. One medical examiner even speculated that if more asylum seekers got forensic rather than visual age exams, more would be under eighteen. One medical examiner said it took a "virtuoso" to correctly determine age; another described age assessment as an extraordinarily complicated task for which there existed almost no experts in Germany. I accompanied Dr. Peters several times to court, where his assessment would help determine whether a criminal offender should be tried under juvenile or adult criminal law. While waiting for a hearing to commence, he would whisper to me that neither the defense nor the judge understood his medical report. The defense, he quipped, had found "some article from South Vietnam from 1980," and thought it had disproven him. Another time, the defense commented on the result of Peters's age exam: "So if he is 21.4 today, then he was under 21 six months ago [at the time of the criminal offense]."

"That's not how it works," Peters protested. "We could only say how old he was at the time of the exam, not how old he was six months earlier."

Once a year, AGFAD organizes a test to screen the quality of the age exams that its members perform. Members are sent a panoramic radiograph of teeth, an X-ray of a left hand, and a CT scan of a clavicle. They must then write a report arguing for the subject's minimum and probable ages. Interestingly, the images do not come from patients whose date of birth is known. Rather, they come from the actual case files of an unaccompanied and allegedly minor asylum seeker whose age was at one time assessed by forensic medical examiners. Passing the test, then, is not about approximating the patient's *actual* age, but about the minimum and probable age previously *assigned* to him by a preeminent medical examiner. Peters explained this method of quality control, which seemed circular to me: "It doesn't really matter whether I estimate someone half a year too old or too young. What's crucial is the *how*. It's like math class back in the day, you know? When you got the wrong result, but the method was correct, maybe you got points off for a calculation error or something. It's kind of like that. You don't have to get the age 100 percent right." These quality checks, then, like other areas of migrants' identity verification, aim for internal coherence, not external validity.

Age as Infrastructure: The Social Construction of Age in Age Determination

When I submitted my research proposal to my university's Institutional Review Board (IRB), the response was puzzlement. Did my research involve minors or not? I explained that some of my interlocutors did not have official ages, others had multiple ages, and still others might move in and out of minority throughout my research. I reaped more puzzlement. The IRB insisted that they needed to know whether minors were involved in my study. Thankfully, my research was eventually approved; but the IRB's bewilderment was telling.

When an official date of birth decides the future of a young asylum seeker, age is treated as straightforward, even natural. Yet a close look at the practice of age determination shows the complexity and social constructedness of age—involving margins of error, examiners' uncertainties, and altogether divergent approaches to the task and to dealing with the ambiguities that inevitably emerge in its course. One might almost come away finding age determination rather arbitrary. Indeed, social workers and forensic scientists seem to have wholly different things in mind when they determine an "age." While forensic scientists view the vulnerabilities and needs of an asylum seeker as distractions from their *true* age—the maturity of their bones—social workers view these same vulnerabilities and needs as indicative of the asylum seeker's *true* age—their social and personal maturity, about which a narrow focus on bones can hardly reveal anything. There is disagreement about what a "valid" age exam—that is, one informative about age—is, because age itself is a contested category. What initially appears to be merely a question of determination is equally one of definition.

Sociologists have shown that many of the categories that structure our political systems and daily interactions are socially constructed (Berger and Luckmann 1967; Bowker and Star 2000; Espeland and Stevens 2008; Lamont and Molnár 2002; Lampland and Star 2008; Timmermans and Epstein 2010). But while scholars have written extensively on the social construction of race and gender, for example, and are increasingly recognizing the sociality of categories such as sexuality (Brubaker 2016) and physical appearance (Monk 2015), age as a socially constructed, culturally contingent, and politically charged category has not received quite as much attention. Perhaps the chronological facticity of age, the undeniable truth that everyone was indeed born on a certain day, still confers an air of naturalness to age that other categories have shed.

Standards and classifications are all around us, but the conflict over their creation and the tension with a world they do not perfectly fit are usually hidden (Bowker and Star 2000). Categories reveal themselves as contingent and, thus, social under exceptional circumstances, such as the migration of young people without documents to a country that relies on chronological age for the allocation of rights and resources. In 2017, 75.2 percent of asylum seekers in Germany were under thirty years of age, and 45 percent under eighteen (BAMF 2018). These, at least, are the official numbers. Such statistics, however, obscure the ambiguity behind categories, the often merely provisional belonging to categories, and the negotiations about who will be admitted to which. Categories emerge through political struggle but are made to look natural, so that once a classification system is established, it is nearly impossible to reconstruct its inception. Star and Bowker write: "If one examines any category, or any classification scheme, and looks at its genesis, it is clear that a category is something like a treaty or a cover of some sort that hides the messier version of what is inside" (2007, 274). Only a study of the concrete practice of constructing a category, such as age, can begin to recover this "messier version."

Age can be conceptualized in various ways, including psychosocial age (need), biological/somatic age (body), and chronological/calendric age (date of birth). Age exams are both premised on ideas about how these three relate to one another, and contested because of such ideas. That a seventeen-year-old asylum seeker has fundamentally different rights than an eighteen-year-old one is based on the notion of psychosocial age—the assumption that cognitive and emotional maturity determine a person's needs and, thus, their rights. Psychosocial age is usually not attempted to be measured directly; rather, chronological age serves as its proxy. That is, a seventeen-year-old's rights change automatically when they turn eighteen, because we assume their vulnerability to have decreased, and their wisdom to have increased. Chronological age, then, is legally privileged. When an asylum seeker's chronological age is unknown, yet another proxy is needed to estimate their chronological and, by extension, psychosocial age: their biological or somatic age, that is, their physical appearance and skeletal development. Age exams are controversial because some criticize the legal privileging of chronological age, or question whether the various kinds of age indeed approximate each other in the way they must in order for age exams to work.

Before the eighteenth century, most Europeans did not know their ages; this changed only due to the hope of improving administrative practices (Treas 2009). Likewise, Americans only developed an age consciousness around the middle of the nineteenth century (Chudacoff 1992). Yet in contemporary Germany, chronological age is central to a person's rights and responsibilities, and is considered a proxy for vulnerability. This is as true for young refugees as it is for native-born Germans, but without the arrival of large numbers of people without documented ages, the importance of age would largely remain hidden. Age exams—and the surrounding debates about what age is, how it should be measured, and the indignation when an asylum seeker does not give his true age—reveal just how much age matters. The controversy surrounding age exams also reflects the equivocality of the figure of the unaccompanied minor in the European refugee crisis: at once the human face of the crisis, an emblem of innocence and vulnerability, *and* the embodiment of public anxieties over false identities and the violent potential of young masculinity (Lems et al. 2020).

Age seems natural or self-evident only until we delve into its varying conceptions (relative, psychosocial, biological, somatic, calendric, chronological) and ask why we privilege one of them (calendric/chronological) in our laws and culture. Age loses its banality when someone's minimum or probable age is considered to determine the rest of their life. Age is not self-evident to the various groups laying claim to its interpretation and application. Of course, age is not sweepingly ambiguous. Most of us know our birth dates, and our age will only upset us occasionally due to vanity or nostalgia. But that, too, is a characteristic of social categories and markers: they tend to be contested most in the lives of those individuals for whom they are most consequential. They seem most certain to those for whom they matter least.

Asking the Impossible

The stakes of age determination are enormous. As street-level bureaucrats are generally incapable of living up to the demands of their role, they bring their understanding of these demands in line with their capabilities. When I interviewed age examiners—forensic scientists and social workers—about the purpose of age determination, their answers were bold: "protecting the rights of the child" or "upholding the state of law." When, however, I asked similar questions *during* age exams, or just after talking about the actual practice of age determination, their answers were far more modest. "We simply find certain things and describe them," said a forensic scientist. "We're trying to do a good job, knowing of course, that we could always be wrong," said a social worker.

Moral dispositions, which are shaped by professional norms (Zacka 2017), can provide psychological relief from this mismatch between role demands and capabilities. Consider how David and Dr. Peters—and the other age examiners from their respective professions whom I interviewed and observed—reacted to asylum seekers' preferences to be certain ages. First of all, Peters and other forensic scientists actively avoided learning personal information about the asylum seekers. They did not ask them personal questions, and they stopped social workers, police, and translators who were about to slip any in. David, on the other hand, asks asylum seekers personal information as part of the age determination interview, and sticks around after the interview to chat with the translator, often obtaining more personal information in that way. When David learns that an asylum seeker would especially benefit from being a certain age due to a particularly high need for medical care, or a desire to be reunited with relatives, he determines an age accordingly: "That then simply becomes my professional opinion," he says. Peters, on the other hand, is visibly moved by the girl who will not be able to raise her child as long as she is under sixteen, yet in the end decides to stick with his initial professional opinion and makes her fifteen. While David embraces his personal responsibility in the asylum seeker's future, Peters "protects himself" from the implications of his decisions by relying on radiology's maxim to "avoid unnecessary doses of radiation," even when a dose might help establish the age an asylum seeker desires.

Both age examiners have the same two-part task: to classify, and to enable resource allocation. Yet while David routinely talks about the second part—that is, the consequences of his classification—Peters stresses the first, the classification itself, and does not talk about its repercussions. In fact, whenever I asked Peters what would happen to an asylum seeker whose age he had just determined, he waved my question aside, saying it was no longer his responsibility and would be handled by a court or the youth welfare office. Importantly, David personally informs the asylum seeker of his decision and has to face their reaction, while Peters writes the report after the asylum seeker has left the forensic lab, and sends it to the court or youth welfare office that has commissioned the exam.

There is ardent debate over the standard deviations, the radiation exposures, and the appropriate reference populations of age determination.

But no method exists to determine a person's exact age. There is no controversy about that. And yet, as long as laws distinguish so resolutely between minors and adults, down to the day of birth, someone has to do the determination. Thus, age examiners face an impossible task. And they hardly receive accolades for it. Instead, they are castigated by activists, politicians, the media, their own colleagues, and other professionals, for underestimating, for overestimating, and even for estimating at all. Street-level bureaucrats often deal with the problems that the rest of society has the luxury to ignore, and this includes contested categories. They are not equipped to handle these problems, but are held responsible for their remaining unsolved. The street-level bureaucrats charged with classifying migrants are not the tyrants of the state they are often portrayed to be, but are instead conflicted by the political and emotional facets of their work.

Being confronted with an impossible task is actually something age examiners share with the asylum seekers they examine. While age examiners are expected to discover something that is by definition hidden, asylum seekers are expected to speak the truth in a system that rarely rewards their doing so. In the previous two chapters I have shown the dilemma in which asylum seekers find themselves, and in this chapter I have shown the one encountered by age examiners. In the next three chapters I will examine the consequences for asylum seekers of living with a contested age.

4 * "Fuck Seventeen!"— Why Being a Minor Is Hard

Samir and I were skipping down the stairway of the youth welfare apartment he had finally been able to move into the previous week, four months after an administrator at the Foreigner Registration Office had changed his date of birth from January 1, 1998, to November 24, 2000. We were on our way to the euro store to buy little white rubber bands for his black dreads. At the bottom of the stairs we ran into his new caseworker, Nelly.

"You know what I found out?" Nelly called cheerfully to Samir. "You're a Sagittarius. Remember, I told you about star signs?"

Samir looked at her, confused. The three of us came to a stop, and Nelly continued reading from an astrology site on her phone.

"I just looked up what Sagittarius is like, because you were born on November 24 now," she said. "And it fits you perfectly. Spirited, a strong sense of justice, a lot of energy. Sagittarius loves his freedom, loves adventures. And he is cosmopolitan."

"What is that?" Samir asked me.

"You're tolerant," I said. "How people live in Africa or in Germany or in America, you're OK with it all."

"And where do I live?" Samir asked Nelly.

"It just says cosmopolitan," she said.

"No country?"

"No country. But Sagittarius is funny and playful. You like to play."

"Love to play," Samir smiled.

"And he likes company, likes to be surrounded by people."

"It's a must," Samir agreed.

Nelly continued. "Sagittarius is always looking for the meaning of life. Why am I alive? What am I doing with my life?"

"And what does it say?" Samir asked.

"That's what you're trying to find out. You're still searching. And Sagittarius loves honesty."

"See, there you have it," Samir said, winking at me.

Situations like these—in which a completely arbitrary date of birth, once printed on paper, was treated as if it were natural and real—seemed particularly remarkable in light of the immense ambiguities and uncertainties of age determination. From the tension between dates of birth produced through negotiation and their subsequent treatment as non-negotiable arise a host of delicate and bizarre circumstances and practices, which stand in stark contrast both to the great hopes that asylum seekers place in minority age and the arbitrariness through which their age is determined.

As cumbersome as the pursuit of minority age is, living as a minor is perhaps the greater challenge. Once you adopt such a date of birth, you must live with both the constraints of minority and the burden of deception—if, indeed, you believe you have been deceitful. In this chapter I will describe how asylum seekers try to fulfill the social roles that come with their official minority and how they struggle with its implications, such as infantilization and emasculation for young men who are now boys and, more generally, feelings of guilt and fear of being found out. This unease permeates asylum seekers' relationships with other asylum seekers and with volunteers and caseworkers. I show how asylum seekers' relations with each other are at once characterized by both camaraderie and secrecy, and how many German "helpers" cultivate an attitude to asylum seekers' identities that is reminiscent of the collective willful ignorance parodied in Hans Christian Andersen's folktale "The Emperor's New Clothes." A date of birth thus affects both the self and social relationships. I also show how asylum seekers are sometimes able to use their ambiguous identities to their advantage, drawing playfully on the uncertainties that an official determination seeks to erase.

Effects on the Self: Infantilization, Emasculation, and the Internalization of Minority Age

When Samir ranted, "Fuck seventeen!" just weeks after finally becoming a minor, I was reminded of the age examiner conference I had attended two years earlier, where one of the speakers had quipped that asylum seekers wanted to be "forever seventeen." Yes, Samir had desperately wanted to be seventeen, thinking of minority as a panacea. But after years of self-determination, and in light of the perennial hope for Europe to be the place where he could finally be a man,[1] being a minor was hard. Like other young men from the Global South, Samir had hoped to achieve "a new sense of self" (Aguilar 1999, 87) through migrating.[2] Instead of a rite of passage to adulthood, however, he experienced what Chiara Galli (2018) has called a "rite of reverse passage," a deliberate regression into boyhood upon realizing that minority would put him on a much kinder track in Europe.

A rite of passage to adulthood, after all, is intended to bring about a number of concrete transitions: toward employment and financial independence, detachment from parents' decision-making power, and the beginning of a family of one's own. None of these are possible for minors in Europe. The realities of being a minor in youth welfare therefore feel even more infantilizing. It is, in fact, a catch-22: to become the success story that would justify the risk and sacrifice of coming to Europe, asylum seekers believe they must be minors. But being a minor means waiving the dignity and self-determination which to a large extent has motivated the migration.

After turning seventeen, Samir had to spend the three months leading up to his new eighteenth birthday in a shelter for youth in crisis, because the youth welfare office, skeptical of his purported minority age, shirked its obligation to properly house him. I interpreted its reluctance as an attempt to stall until the passage of time would once more allow it to refuse Samir on the grounds of his age. When he turned eighteen—now for the second time—he had to leave the youth shelter, and the youth welfare office ended his welfare, arguing that the previous two years he had spent in a camp had made him too self-sufficient to receive youth welfare past the age of eighteen. When Samir and I went to the shelter to pick up his belongings—some clothes, toiletries, the prayer rug he had yet to use, his school supplies, and the crutches he had received after being injured in a fight—Tom, the shelter's manager, called us into his office to say goodbye. Tom had always treated Samir warmly; but now that Samir was eighteen, Tom was legally obliged to put him out on the street.

"Why does nothing ever work out for me?" Samir asked no one in particular, as he pulled a scab off his left ring finger and flicked it away.

"Because life just is what it is," Tom said.

Samir reeled off the names of other teenagers from the shelter who he knew had gotten a residence permit, or for whom a different, more lenient youth welfare office happened to be responsible.[3]

"That's unfair," Tom said. "*Chéri*, you have every right to feel that injustice. But it's in your hands to make sure this setback does not lead you to give up on a regular livelihood in Germany. I wish you the best of luck!"

Samir did not want to move back to a refugee camp, which would have seemed akin to conceding that becoming a minor had been for nothing. Instead, he moved to the sanctuary apartment where Paul and Guled had lived while they had Dublin, and he eventually was able to renew his youth welfare with the help of the Berliner Rechtshilfefonds Jugendhilfe

(Berlin Legal Aid for Youth Welfare, or BRJ), an organization that mediates impartially between the state and claimants of youth welfare but, according to its mission statement, seeks to balance out the unequal distribution of power between those two parties.

Now that Samir's youth welfare had resumed and he in theory was able to leave the sanctuary apartment, we viewed several youth welfare apartments. Two rejected his application because they thought it a bad sign that he had lived in Germany for two years and was still learning German at the beginner's level. I wondered in those moments whether someone who had turned seventeen after being twenty regained those years, or whether that time was still lost and wasted, as the social workers and Samir himself often seemed to think. The social workers at the apartment viewings asked Samir what he wanted to be. Most scoffed that he needed a "reality check" and was light years away from his "child's dream" of becoming a car mechanic—a popular profession in Germany for which one needed to complete three years of vocational training. One of them even said he could consider himself lucky if he got to sweep the street one day. During these weeks of apartment searches, I often picked Samir up from his literacy course and tried to encourage him to see this time as a temporary rough patch. We sat by the river near his school, and between yelling at the tourists passing by on boats, Samir wondered aloud whether he should go to BAMF and say there had been a mistake and that he had actually been twenty all along. School was difficult for him, the rules at the sanctuary apartment were infantilizing, and his dream of a room of his own was still unfulfilled. The social workers, moreover, who should have welcomed him in youth welfare and helped him formulate goals toward which he could work, merely derided his dreams.

When Samir was finally able to move into a flat share provided by the youth welfare office, it did not take long before the problems began. The facility that took him in ran ten one-bedrooms and shared apartments spread out over two street blocks. Samir lived in a shared apartment with two others. The social workers were present on weekday afternoons, but also checked in unannounced at other times. Samir was expected to participate in a weekly group dinner, attend biweekly meetings with his caseworker, and go on a weeklong field trip in the summer. Living in the apartment was contingent on following the rules laid out by the social workers: no smoking, alcohol, or drugs inside the apartment; no parties; daily school attendance; a 10 p.m. curfew on school nights; sleepovers only on non-school days with the permission of his caseworker; friends allowed to visit only after first introducing themselves to the social workers; and a requirement to inform the social workers if he was sick. His caseworker was in close contact with his teachers and doctors. Samir was paid his youth welfare in small weekly installments, was expected to save fifty euros a month, and had to contribute to a group account from which household items, group dinners, field trips, and other communal expenses were paid.

I expected Samir to resent these rules, but initially he was highly motivated and saw them as his chance for a new life. On his move-in day, his main caseworker, Nelly, articulated what was going through my own head: "I really think he wants to use this chance, but he might eventually find that he is simply not able to." And indeed, Samir's motivation soon yielded to old habits. Only a week after moving in, he used the Christmas holidays, during which he rightly assumed no social workers would check in, to invite about two dozen friends to his new room, where they smoked cannabis and listened to loud music. I asked Samir why he would risk his youth welfare, which he had longed to have for so long, for a party, but he brushed me off. Only a few days later, a social worker came to the apartment unannounced and found cannabis on Samir's table. Within the first month, Samir also broke a window and his desk, missed group dinners and meetings with caseworkers, was sent home by his teacher for talking back, smoked in his room, and was having people over daily.

While Nelly was well disposed toward Samir and wanted to help him make it against the odds, the project's other social workers were skeptical from the day he moved in. To them Samir looked like a drug dealer, skinny and quick, with dreaded top hair and shaven sides, and always carrying a small black pouch. One social worker even claimed to have seen him dealing at a concert hosted by the youth facility. Samir had been lingering in a corner all evening with another Black teenager, and had left the concert multiple times to stand outside. But he later insisted, even to me in private, that he had not been dealing. Despite lack of proof, he was suspended from the youth welfare apartment for a week. A few days into his expulsion, however, the social worker admitted she had not actually seen anything except two Black teenagers loitering outside the concert, and Samir was allowed to move back in. This incident, however, confirmed to Samir that regardless of how hard he tried, regardless even of whether he succeeded, he would always be viewed with suspicion or deemed as failing.

Samir ended up staying much longer in youth welfare than I had dared to hope. I often talked to Nelly after her shifts. She had taken a genuine liking to Samir despite his transgressions, and was the only one at the facility advocating for him. She seemed happy to talk to me, since I also liked Samir and listened patiently to the excuses she made for his behavior. She believed Samir was severely traumatized, and that behind his caustic facade hid an unlivable sadness. His German was not getting better, which she interpreted as a protective mechanism: "When you cannot speak, you don't have to justify yourself." For all these reasons—along with his drug abuse, which he was unable to hide from the social workers—she believed that he needed a sheltered therapeutic accommodation specifically for traumatized and addicted youth; but these had long waiting lists, so she feared that he would eventually have to return to a camp.

Ten months after moving into the youth welfare apartment, Samir left. He was tired of the supervision, the scolding, and the small installments of pocket money. He returned to the camp, where he would again share a bedroom with other adult asylum seekers but there would be no curfews or check-ins, and he would receive his monthly state allowance all at once. Despite initially welcoming the rules and placing all his hope in them, Samir was ultimately unable to overcome behaviors he had adopted throughout his years of being an adult.

Samir's problems in youth welfare were, undoubtedly, extreme because of his personality and addiction, and because he had spent such a long time on his own. But most young asylum seekers who live in youth welfare take issue with its rules at some point, framing their grievances in terms of emasculation and infantilization. "I'm not a child!" they complained to me. Even entering youth welfare involves making oneself small. In the application and during the interview, one must argue that one is delayed in personal development and unable to care for oneself. One must repeat this self-debasement every six months in order to be allowed to stay in youth welfare.

The behaviors and personality traits that are advantageous to making it *to* Germany are, in fact, a liability to making it *in* Germany. To endure the journey, many young asylum seekers had to be extremely self-sufficient and adopt a kind of "street kid mentality," as several social workers put it. But once in Germany, they had to downplay their self-sufficiency and shed manners formerly essential to their survival. In fact, their autonomy was held against them by employees of the youth welfare office, who argued that surely they did not need help since they had made it to Europe all on their own.[4] Such arguments once again show the difficulty of defining youth and vulnerability. A young man like Samir, for example, who has been away from his family for years and helped raise younger siblings before he left, may not have trouble cooking for himself—one of the skills the youth welfare office inquires about—but may need help planning his education or acknowledging and addressing his emotional trauma. The youth welfare office even often used asylum seekers' success as an argument for not admitting young adults. When Guled applied for youth welfare at eighteen so that he could finally leave the camp, the youth welfare office rejected his application with the argument that since he had done well in school despite living in a camp, he clearly did not need help.

I had met Guled through his classmate Paul. The two were not exactly friends—friendships between asylum seekers from such countries as distant from each other as Guinea and Somalia were rare—but Paul felt sorry that Guled "had Dublin," meaning that he was supposed to be returned to Sweden, and thought that perhaps I could help. Guled usually wore jeans and a short-sleeved button-up shirt. He had two very large identical scars on the inside of each wrist, remnants from a bloodletting treatment he had received for a childhood disease. One of these scars was hidden behind a beaded light blue bracelet with a white diamond shape resembling the Somali flag. Guled said few words and made little eye contact, a shyness people often mistook for unfriendliness. He had left Somalia as a young teenager and had spent long periods of time in Libya, Malta, and Sweden before coming to Germany. The years spent on his own had left their mark. He was so self-sufficient and modest that it truly was sometimes easy to forget that this was still a very young person living with a highly precarious legal status in a foreign country. Guled had a few Somali friends and acquaintances at his camp, but mostly kept to himself, never missing a day at school unless he had a conflicting appointment, and spending his free time at the gym or the mosque.

For young men, then, being a minor comes at the cost of masculinity. In a phase of life when other young men accentuate every physical sign of impending manhood and try to behave in ways that make them seem older—and, by extension, more masculine—young asylum seekers regress into boyhood in search of protection. While other young men play up their financial independence, sexual prowess, and rebelliousness, young asylum seekers go to school with people much younger than them, are given small allowances by female social workers and guardians, conceal past sexual and work experiences because these would challenge their fabricated timeline, and refrain from the legal transgressions that young people with secure legal status simply take a chance on. One of the costs of portraying yourself as younger is that of being emasculated at a time of life when masculinity is often a primary source of identity and self-esteem.

This clash between the practical need for acceptance as a minor and the emotional need for recognition as a man can be especially difficult for young men who are also poor, without secure residence permits, and with diminished control over their lives, given that asylum-seeking itself can be patronizing (Barnett 2017). Behaviors that might help them assert their masculinity,[5] moreover, would be at odds with their performance as minors. Minority and youth welfare, then, are not only emasculating in themselves, but also impede asylum seekers' ability to compensate for the infantilization in one area of their lives with emphatic masculinity in another. Instead of playing up their manhood and independence, as other young men with few socioeconomic and educational means may do, these young men have to act like helpless boys to get a shot at a future in Germany. This is exacerbated because they have to take orders from mostly female social workers and legal guardians. At the guardians' meetings I regularly attended, in fact, women told me they felt a special responsibility to show their wards what an emancipated German woman looked like, which in practice often meant an even more infantilizing treatment of the young men.

In youth welfare, social workers are involved in nearly every aspect of the youths' lives. Idris thought about leaving youth welfare many times, usually after something happened that he viewed as an infringement on his privacy and autonomy. Once, for instance, his caseworker told him that neighbors had filed a noise complaint at night, and when Idris told her he had not even been home on the night in question, she reminded him that he was required to let her know if he slept elsewhere. Another night, Idris had to stay at a hospital, but did not tell his caseworker. When he told her after the fact, she was angry and held that it would have been her job to accompany him. She insisted on joining him for the next appointment. She also called his doctor and had him explain Idris's diagnosis and prescribed therapy. Idris was upset about this and complained to the doctor that he had broken his physician's confidentiality. The doctor agreed, and apologized.

overbearing

Similarly, when Paul was eighteen, doctors had given him large quantities of antidepressants, and he often took more than the recommended dose. When he became seventeen, however, his caseworkers held onto the pills and only handed them out in small portions, despite Paul's protests. Social workers sometimes withheld information from the asylum seekers in their care, even about important medical diagnoses or the rejection of their asylum application, as they waited for a "better moment" to tell them. When I remarked that I thought the asylum seeker in question had a right to know, caseworkers shrugged, and said it was just part of being a minor.

Idris, Paul, and Ali often told me about their friends back home who had gotten married, built homes, and become fathers. While showing me baby pictures, they speculated as to how many children they would have had by now had they stayed at home. I thought about how their regression into boyhood was even more stark relative to the situation of their former peers, who were launching adult lives. Moreover, as Julian, the Bavarian social worker, observed, young asylum seekers have truly existential worries, and then "some social worker comes along and says, 'You can't use the wi-fi anymore!' or 'Turn off the TV!' Of course you are going to think, 'Fuck her!'" For teenagers who have had traumatic experiences of powerlessness, it may be especially difficult not to simply see rules as instruments of repeated malevolent exercise of power.

In addition to struggling with the desire for adulthood and the need for minority, there is another possible response to officially being designated a minor: trying to internalize the official age. It is impossible to experience one's own life as a permanent state of exception. Perhaps this is why an initially instrumental and foreign identity is often eventually internalized so that it can be sustained in the long term. The internal experience of falsehood may simply be too taxing otherwise. A few months after Samir's age change, I noticed that he started referring to himself as seventeen, and later as eighteen, even when it was just the two of us. When he calculated how old he might be at one of life's milestones, he took seventeen as his starting number. He also told me about a woman who was interested in him, but said that at twenty-three she was too old for him since he was seventeen. I assumed he was joking, and laughed; but he added matter-of-factly that he was seventeen now, and was no longer dating women over twenty.[6]

Roberto Beneduce has called for asking what the long-term consequences of invented memories are—or, put differently, at what point "the narratives of (false) personal experiences become memoirs, gradually embodied by these subjects" (2015, 563). Cecilia Menjívar and Sarah M. Lakhani (2016) have shown that the personal transformations migrants undertake to improve their legal status—such as volunteering, joining the army, or getting married—can have genuine, profound, and lasting effects on their behaviors, outlooks, and selves that far outlast the need for residence papers and eventually become meaningful in their own right. A person and their representation are truly mutually constitutive: "People get put into categories and learn from those categories how to behave" (Bowker and Star 2000, 311). Ian Hacking has called such looping between classification and self-identity "dynamic nominalism" (1986, 161). Classification and ontology are indeed entangled: the procedures aimed at identifying minors also make them minors. Someone categorized as a minor may start acting like one to convince people, to make the cognitive dissonance easier to handle, because he is put in situations that facilitate young behavior, because he reflects back how others see and treat him, because he now has the resources to act like a minor, and because he is surrounded by people also acting like minors. Social category and social role affect one another: minors are expected to behave like children and are treated as such, thus reinforcing the perceived need and legitimacy of the category.

Effects on Relationships

THE FEAR OF BEING FOUND OUT

Besides affecting the self through feelings of infantilization, emasculation, and the possibility of internalizing minority age, a negotiated date of birth also affects asylum seekers' relationships to others, which tend to be marked by suspicion and secrecy. Gaim Kibreab (2004) has argued that refugees lie because they feel morally accountable to their families and communities, not to the bureaucrats in the host country. While this may be true, the guilt they feel nonetheless indicates that they do eventually want to align themselves with the moral framework of the host society, and that a lifelong lie may keep them from ever being a full member of it.

Idris especially struggled to maintain his self-image of a good, honest person in the face of his false age claims. He would shudder when recounting that one of his social workers called him and his friend Yakob "my children." "Shame!" he exclaimed to me, and shook his head bashfully. Idris also suspected that certain people assumed he was not a teenager. His German teacher, he insisted, who herself was only in her mid-twenties, treated him and another student more strictly than the other young refugees in the class, and he was sure this was because she had correctly guessed their age. Idris also advised me not to congratulate other asylum seekers on their birthdays, because most, he insisted, would only be ashamed or wonder whether I was mocking them.[7] Idris himself avoided seeing people on the day of his official birthday who might congratulate him or give him presents. For Idris's twentieth birthday, his apprenticeship supervisor gave him a card that read: "I have exactly the right age; just need to figure out what for." Idris showed me this card nervously, and asked whether I thought his boss suspected something.

Idris had a complicated relationship with his religion, Islam: believing in it firmly, but finding it difficult to follow its rules in Berlin. During one of the phases in which he was especially critical of how moving to Europe had changed his religious practice, he wondered whether his false age claim had violated the Islamic dictate to tell the truth, or whether this fell under the exemption that breaking rules was permissible when the believer's life was at stake. He contacted his brother in Ethiopia, a mufti (Islamic jurist), and asked for advice. The brother thought this an especially knotty case and referred Idris to a more experienced mufti, whose verdict Idris eagerly awaited. When this man eventually informed him that he had committed a great sin and needed to repay the state welfare he had "stolen" or face Allah's punishment on Judgment Day, Idris was very upset and even contemplated correcting his age. But then he considered the implications. Would he have to tell people that he was now five years older? Would he have to repay thousands of euros in youth welfare? He deliberated back and forth, imagining in horror that he would be stuck with this lie for the rest of his life, but ultimately decided that the consequences of admitting to lying were too severe.

Idris developed two strategies for assuaging his feelings of guilt and reestablishing his identity as essentially good: suspecting everyone else had lied, which lessened his unique culpability, and establishing a hierarchy of more and less acceptable lies. He insisted that most others had lied even more than he, since he had at least given his true nationality and had actually been to prison, even if only once and not twice, as he had told the interviewer. He seemed to relish in speculations about others' lies, and came up with ever more hyperbolic descriptions of the deceit around him. When I showed him official statistics about where asylum seekers in Germany were from, he laughed and said, "The Iraqis are from Iran, the Afghans from Pakistan, the Eritreans from Ethiopia, and the Syrians from Lebanon. Take my word for it."[8] Idris even came up with his own tongue-in-cheek methods for verifying the nationality of those around him. For example, to determine whether an "Eritrean" was an Eritrean national or an Ethiopian with Tigrinya language skills, he joked, one simply had to play for them a recording of Tigrinya music from Ethiopia. If the person in question said "I know something better," and played a recording of Eritrean music, he was really Eritrean.

It seemed to me that Idris wanted to convince me that his lies did not result from flawed character, but were an almost inevitable result of the situation. He also explained to me that lying about one's age was less bad than lying about one's nationality, because he too had been a minor once, whereas he had never been Somali or Eritrean. He proudly wore an Ethiopian soccer jersey and a bracelet bearing the design of the Ethiopian flag. At his first youth welfare apartment, he had lived with two other Ethiopians who had both successfully claimed to be from Eritrea. They sometimes told Idris that they admired his honesty—at least that is what Idris told me—and wished they could openly show their love for their country. Both had received residence permits as Eritreans; but even when one of the two took over Idris's spot in school because Idris, as an Ethiopian with a rejected asylum application, was forced to drop out and start an apprenticeship to secure his residence, Idris insisted that he did not regret his honesty. At the same time, after we encountered a young asylum seeker with poor German language skills, Idris would sometimes tell me, "See, the people who didn't go to youth welfare don't speak German," as if to assure himself that being a minor had been for the better.

The fear of being found out permeated even the most intimate relationships. I would sometimes hear the young men speculate as to whether a friend or girlfriend they had argued with would go so low as to rat them out to other people, or even to the public authorities in revenge. This fear was a basic component of everyday life for asylum seekers, and also shaped relations to helpers. Yakob was invited to spend Christmas with Marie, a volunteer from Empower, the organization for minors. Marie suspected Yakob's real age, but did not explicitly tell him so. She also recounted that her sister, who was older than Yacob's official age but younger than his real age, said over Christmas dinner: "Yakob, you don't look your age at all. You look much older."

Yakob seemed uncomfortable and responded, "Yeah, the flight really ages you."

Marie and I smiled at this double entendre.

Sometimes people would accidentally reveal something about themselves that did not fit with their purported identity, and would later tell me they hoped no one but me had noticed. Guled, for example, told a social worker that he had worked as a gardener in Somalia, but this did not fit with his story of being recruited by al-Shabaab at eleven and leaving Somalia immediately after his escape. Yakob often accidentally referred to Ethiopia as "our country" when other Ethiopians were around, even though he was officially from Eritrea. He also told a social worker that Ethiopia and Eritrea were really one nation and should be reunited—a viewpoint very uncommon among real Eritreans, who tend to think of Ethiopia as their intra-African colonizer.

When the new Law of Orderly Return, passed in summer 2019, required every asylum seeker to prove their identity by obtaining a passport from their respective embassy, many panicked because they feared this would reveal their false identity claims. For the most part, these fears eased when they realized that embassies often either issued documents without verifying the applicant's identity or issued no documents at all. The new law also included the option to state one's identity under oath if one was unable to obtain documents. While several social workers mocked this arrangement—"So you just say, 'W'Allah, my name is Mohammed,' and that's that"—most asylum seekers I talked to insisted that they would never cross the line of lying under oath because of its religious connotations.

Inventing aspects of identity also means practically losing access to other aspects. Since Paul had told us he was orphaned, he was not initially able to have his family send a birth certificate, though this would have helped prove his minority age. In his appeal, Idris was unable to cite lootings by Somalis against Ethiopians in his home city, even though they directly affected his family, because he had claimed to be from a Somali ethnic group. The war in northern Ethiopia, Yakob's home region, which started in late 2020, did not aid his chances of receiving protection, because he had claimed to be from Eritrea. When Samir's father passed away, he could not tell social workers or teachers why he was so sad, because he had already told them his father had died when he was a child.

ACCEPTING HELP WHILE NOT TRUSTING EVERYONE

Many young asylum seekers told me they avoided getting too personally close with Germans, so as to retain a flexible identity. The more they revealed about themselves, they worried, the more their biographical parameters would become testable. Just as other people in exceptional and potentially risky situations, such as young men on the run from the police (Goffman 2014), learn to see the harbingers of danger even in seemingly ordinary encounters, young asylum seekers learn to suspect fake identities in their personal environment and to recognize situations that might expose them.

The most common way through which I met asylum seekers was when my main interlocutors introduced me to friends who needed help with their residence papers, which I became better at giving over time. I would usually receive a text message saying, "Ulrike, I have a friend, he has a problem," or "I know someone, he has Dublin. Can we meet with him?" We would then meet the person at my apartment, their camp or, in warmer months, outdoors. The tragic absurdity of the situation was never lost on me. The three of us would sit on a park bench and the young man with "the problem" would bring a plastic bag stuffed with documents and official letters he only half understood. I would start reading through these very private documents despite being a complete stranger, and if I did not speak the young man's mother tongue, our mutual friend would translate for us, despite himself being a beginner in German. I usually suggested requesting access to the BAMF files, and the young men readily gave me written permission to get their personal files after only an hour of knowing me. These encounters made clear how precious is the ability to decide whom to distrust and to whom to entrust oneself.

I met Ali, a stocky young man from Afghanistan with a Swiss accent—a relic from the years he had spent near Bern before turning eighteen made him deportable—when to pass his Dublin period he tried to get church asylum, a particularly precarious form of temporary protection I will describe later. Ali introduced me to Tasneem, a girlfriend of his. She was living in a German village and was desperate to get permission to relocate to Berlin so that she could enroll in German classes and find work. Ali, Tasneem, and I met whenever Tasneem was in Berlin for a few days. During the first few meetings, as soon as Tasneem saw me, she began wailing and pleading with me to help her get permission to move there: "Please, I can work. I can clean toilets, I can do any job. I don't care. Honestly. I have worked all my life. Please, I just need to move to Berlin." She eventually understood that I was only a friend of Ali's and happy to help her as much as I could, but that I did not work for the government, and that she did not need to convince me of her misery to activate my alleged superpower to end it.

My interlocutors' friends often asked me why I was helping them with their residence papers, and smiled amusedly when I responded that it seemed like the right thing to do and that I—in a kind of golden-rule, karmic world view—hoped that I would be helped if I ever sought asylum in a foreign country. Understanding that volunteers in Germany help without recompense and that social workers are part of an extensive state infrastructure aimed at helping, but that helpers are not always as knowledgeable or well-intentioned as they purport to be, is an important skill for young asylum seekers, as the following examples will show.

Deportations from youth welfare apartments are prohibited in Berlin. Yet one afternoon, Idris called me in tears because the night before, a group of police officers had entered the apartment of his best friend Yakob, who was in the last week of his six-month Dublin period. The police had opened the door to Yakob's room and told him he had five minutes to pack his things. Yakob called us two days later from a camp in Rome, where he would stay for two months in a drab room with barely enough space for the seven cots on which he and six other Dublin deportees from all over Europe slept.

Because his deportation from inside a youth welfare apartment, which is supposed to be a kind of sanctuary space, had been wrongful, his anonymized case received some media attention, and several local politicians promised that they would do everything in their power to right this wrong and bring him back to Berlin. Yakob's caseworkers had the idea of presenting his case to Berlin's hardship case commission (Härtefallkommission), a board that can award a residence title to a foreigner with no other legal options on moral or humanitarian grounds. For this, however, the commission needed to know more about Yakob and his reasons for fleeing Eritrea. Not being from Eritrea, Yakob evaded their attempts to learn more about his story, and eventually just returned to Berlin on his own, turning down the papers that were offered to him as compensation for his erroneous deportation, because he did not want to be questioned about his national origins. He was able to return because he knew about routes and tricks that the Germans who assumed he depended on their help were ignorant of. "Helpers" often think they know more than they actually do.

Guled also had Dublin, and desperately needed a place to escape the possibility of deportation from his camp—which, unlike in Yakob's case, was likely and would have been lawful. I suggested we go to Berlin's central church asylum counseling office, where Dublin cases as well as people in danger of deportation to their own countries could present their situations to church asylum volunteers in the hope that they would be found noteworthy enough to be connected to churches willing to take them in. But when Guled realized he would have to recount his kidnapping by al-Shabaab—which, regardless of whether it had really occurred, could at least cast some doubt on his age and biographical timeline—he decided against applying for church asylum.

Michael, an officially eighteen-year-old Nigerian who had Dublin and was supposed to be returned to Italy, lived in a camp from which he had seen many other young men deported. Terrified of experiencing the same, he tried to sleep at his camp during the day, and spent the nights sitting at Alexanderplatz, eastern Berlin's main plaza, or riding the subway. When he did spend the night at the camp, he hid in the communal bathroom stalls. A volunteer from the camp brought him to Empower, where our only idea was to try to get church asylum for the duration of his Dublin period, to which he agreed.

Later at night, however, he called me in agitation—presumably because I was associated with Empower but was enough of an outsider to vent to—and said that he had reconsidered, and did not want the organization to help him. He did not want church asylum because he could not be sure that the church was not actually cooperating with the state and setting him up to be deported. I assured him that it was not the case, but he insisted that it was a trap. In the wee hours of the morning he called again and said he had decided to give church asylum counseling a try after all. A few hours before the counseling appointment, he canceled. A few weeks later, Michael sent me a picture of his temporary ID card (GÜB) that apparently was now being renewed for only three days at a time, and said he did want help after all. He apologized for being suspicious of the church and our organization, and said that he was new and did not understand the system. Michael cycled in and out of seeking help several more times, and eventually left Germany for another European country. He made me promise not to tell his whereabouts or give his new number to anyone at Empower.

Most asylum seekers do not make the decision about whom to trust by themselves, but discuss it with their friends, usually from the same country. Paul, for example, who had only had positive experiences trusting Germans, retaining their support even when he admitted to having invented stories, always advised his friends to accept all the help that was offered them. When an older couple wanted to become legal guardians to his friend Amadou, Amadou asked Paul whether he should accept, and Paul's advice was firm: "Look, you're here without your family, you have nobody. If there are people in Europe who want to help you, just do what they say." Noelle Brigden and Cetta Mainwaring have pointed to "the purposeful surrender of agency as a survival tactic" (2016, 417) among migrants. Temporarily and deliberately giving up agency to helpers was ultimately Paul's best shot at the eventual achievement of his long-term goals.

The realization that social workers and guardians help professionally, however, can also be deeply hurtful. Ali had spent two years in Switzerland before coming to Germany. He had lived in youth welfare there, and had developed an especially close bond with one of his caseworkers. Ali was a quiet, reserved young man who opened up only slowly. This was the case in his interaction with Laura, his Swiss caseworker. He would often come to her office and they would chat about his day, his childhood, his plans for the future. During one of their conversations a group of teenagers began a fight elsewhere in the building, and an alarm called all social workers to the scene. Laura left the office hastily and did not close her laptop or put away any paperwork. Ali walked around to her side of the desk and saw, on her laptop screen, a document with his name on it. He began reading, and realized that day after day, when he had thought they were having private, heartfelt conversations, she had been writing reports on him, often concluding, "Ali was irritable again today," or "Ali is not following the facility's rules." When Laura returned, he yelled at her about how she could have betrayed his trust and turned their private conversations into reports. Laura, bewildered, responded, "Ali, what did you think? This is my job." Ali told me that on that day he had learned not to trust social workers.

Social worker Franka and I often talked about the spectrum of blindly trusting and unwaveringly distrustful asylum seekers. Franka admitted to never knowing where she stood. Sometimes she thought that someone really trusted that she was trying to help, and was ready to follow her lead through the thicket of asylum and youth welfare—only to disappear the next day, having changed their phone number, so that Franka never heard from them again. Franka worked at the sanctuary apartment for young asylum seekers with contested identities. At every new intake I observed, she would tell the young man moving in: "All you have to do now is sleep, eat, and go to school. All the rest, your papers, your asylum, your age, we're taking care of that for you." As lucky and comfortable as this position was in comparison to the aloneness of most asylum seekers, entrusting one's future and identity to near strangers was still extremely difficult.

Idris, Franka, and I took a walk together about a year and a half after Idris, during his interview prep counseling session, had told Franka the story about jumping over the prison wall, and she had angrily shouted at him not to take her for a fool. He now apologized and explained that he had told the same story to the caseworker who was responsible for him when he first arrived in Berlin. At that time he had thought all social workers worked for BAMF. So he had feared the first one might have already told his story to BAMF, and that he would have to stick with it. Ending up with lies that have to be maintained often starts with wanting help from a particular person and being unsure whom exactly that person answers to, and whether the person will keep information confidential. Many asylum seekers told me they had initially not understood that social workers would be unable to influence the outcome of their asylum case in any way. Idris and Aman recounted how the boys living at Pangea hostel would text their caseworkers at night, telling them they were unable to sleep because of their terrible past, or that they felt sick. They explained to me that the boys did this only because they wanted to increase their chances of getting asylum, and stopped once they realized that the social work services they received as minors and the scrutiny they were to receive as asylum seekers were unconnected, even if the same state had commissioned them. Another young man who had told his caseworker that his parents had disappeared could not refuse her offer to file a missing person report with the Red Cross search service, even though he was in regular contact with his parents.

Julian, the Bavarian social worker, told me that many young asylum seekers in Germany actually plan to move on to England or Scandinavia, but do not say this so as not to jeopardize Germans' willingness to help them. This secrecy, Julian said, made it difficult to establish genuine, close relationships with the young men in his care, who, moreover, often avoided emotional attachments because, given their precarious legal statuses, their social ties might be merely temporary.

Asylum seekers can benefit from accepting the help of people who speak German natively and can navigate Germany's intricate bureaucracy more easily; but they are also proud grownups and do not want to be made to feel like helpless children, especially since they have often already led very independent lives. Gifts, which is how many volunteers think of the help they provide, are, in Pierre Bourdieu's words, "an attack on the freedom" (1998, 94) of the receiver, who is put "in an obliged and dominated state" (100); helpers often expect gratitude in the form of truth, and are offended when they find out they have been lied to, as I will now discuss.

THE EMPEROR'S NEW CLOTHES: HELPERS' TAKE ON THE TRUTH

Marie and I, the only two volunteers at Empower under the age of thirty, talked to each other openly about the fact that most of the unaccompanied minors whom the organization served were not actually minors. We assumed that everyone at the organization knew this, and that they helped regardless, out of moral conviction. One day, however, Marie irritatedly told me of a conversation she had had earlier with another volunteer, Daniela. Marie and I had noticed that the birth certificate of a young man from Guinea, supposedly issued at birth, stated his nickname, which he had told us he had adopted only a few years earlier. To Daniela, Marie had said something along the lines of "He should have at least been smart enough to not put his nickname on the certificate." Marie told me that Daniela's face had frozen, and that she had snapped at Marie that if this was what was on her mind, she should either keep it to herself or leave the organization.

I had a much calmer conversation with Daniela a few months later in which I confessed to having assumed it was an open secret that many asylum seekers were older than they said. Daniela avoided responding to my claim directly, but said the organization would be dead if any of this came out, and that it would make good copy for xenophobes who would gladly present helpers as gullible or, worse, criminal. Even if we each believed it should not matter whether we were helping seventeen- or twenty-two-year-olds, she said, saying so would jeopardize donations and delegitimize the organization's campaigns against age exams. Daniela's reluctance to acknowledge the intricacy of her clients' ages mirrors that of "people who care about vulnerable border crossers" but, as Hamlin points out, "are afraid that exposing the dilemmas of classification will erode public support for protecting refugees" (2021, 152).

Most social workers and volunteers whom I encountered seemed to take this emperor's-new-clothes approach to asylum seekers' identity, acting absolutely convinced of asylum seekers' claims and dismissing allegations to the contrary as political bigotry.[9] Georg Simmel has already argued that secrecy is an elemental part of social life and can enable the simultaneous existence of several social worlds (Simmel 1950). As in the tale of the emperor's new clothes, "open secrets" (Zerubavel 2006) are a collective effort, which may even be needed to prop up certain societal conditions.[10] Moreover, social facts are collaborative products, and age is co-constructed. For example, the way two people see and behave toward each other will be affected by whether they have met with the possibility of becoming a romantic couple or with the intention of becoming guardian and ward.

By feigning ignorance, asylum seekers and those who consider themselves their allies collectively maintain a cycle of pretense and play—until the open secret can no longer be maintained. When it came out that one young man was actually older than he claimed, his caseworker took it as a personal affront, and complained that she had expected her help to be at least rewarded with honesty. Some guardians and volunteers broke off contact with young men whom they had helped when it turned out that they had been lied to. When something happens that makes it impossible to maintain that the emperor is dressed—or that an asylum seeker is a minor—the construction of pretense unravels and exposes the instrumentalization of helpers. Helpers seemed not to take issue with the fact that asylum seekers lied to migration officials, but they did take issue if they themselves were lied to, since they prided themselves on close relationships with the refugees in their care. After recovering from the consternation of having been deceived, one volunteer said the young migrant in question would always be a child to her, even though she now knew she and he were the same age; and she celebrated his next official birthday as if nothing had changed.

So, while in theory many social workers and guardians were sympathetic to asylum seekers not saying the truth, they usually treated the identity an asylum seeker claimed for himself *as if* it were truthful. They were offended when they realized that they, too, were being deceived, because this meant that the asylum seekers with whom they believed themselves to have genuine relationships considered them not as members of their intimate social world, but as part of an antagonistic state infrastructure.

A few helpers, however, did take a more realistic, relaxed approach to honesty. Several guardians told me they were fully aware that not everything their ward said was true, but that this did not matter to them. Some even assumed that lying was the default. They seemed sympathetic, explaining their wards had no way of knowing they could trust them. Franka sometimes speculated as to how old someone actually was. After working with hundreds of young men, she said, she had developed an eye for this. For example, if someone's face and body changed over the course of a year or two, she assumed they must be younger. When someone complained to her that he did not want to be eighteen, she just said, "I don't want to be forty either, but it is what it is." She told me about a guy who looked at least thirty, but whose application somehow was still accepted by the youth welfare office. Franka had expected him to take issue with the rules and supervision, but he flourished, and gratefully used the resources now offered to him. "It was like he was making up for the childhood he probably didn't have," she said.

Franka had a no-nonsense approach to asylum seekers' identities and stories. She asked for honesty not because she thought she was entitled to it, but because in her experience it was difficult to help otherwise, and because she was unwilling to lie when writing appeals. When someone said, as Idris did, that they had had to leave their country because their girlfriend's parents disapproved of the relationship, she just replied sarcastically: "OK, so like everyone." When Michael said he had come to Europe to find his mother, she replied: "Ah yes, the most popular story for Nigerians these days."

FRIENDSHIP, CONFLICT, SECRECY

I noticed early on that asylum seekers often did not know the official identities of even their closest friends, and avoided giving personal information that the friend might accidentally reveal to others or deliberately use against them if the friendship turned sour. Samir had sleepovers with his friend "Whizz" several times a week, during which they would pool their money to buy weed and then hang out at the park before going home to doze off to Netflix. I had hung out with them about a dozen times when Samir left Whizz and me alone one evening to go to a *Späti*, Berlin's version of a convenience store. While he was away, I said something to Whizz about Samir; and when Whizz quizzically replied, "Who?" it took me a few seconds to realize that he did not know Samir's name. The next day, I asked Samir about Whizz—his real name, where he was from, his age—but Samir said he had no idea, and that it was none of his business. Samir saved all his friends' numbers, including mine, on his phone under invented names or even emojis. (My number was saved under the words "Get Up," because, he explained, I was always telling him to keep moving after setbacks. And besides, "get up" sounded similar to *kitab*, the Arabic word for "book"—which, after all, had been the impetus for our friendship.) When Samir saw that I had saved his number on my phone under his real name, he grabbed the phone indignantly to change it to a nickname. When he lost touch with a friend and pondered how he could find him, I suggested that we call around to camps in the city to ask where he was living, or even that we go to the citizen center to see if they would give us information. Samir grinned at my naïveté: "You think I know his European name or birthday or anything?"

I once asked Idris why asylum seekers did not lie about their names. He seemed amused, and asked, "What makes you think they don't?"

Genuinely taken aback, despite having grown accustomed to the abundance of fabrications in the lives of the asylum seekers I knew, I asked, "Like you don't think Yakob or Guled or Samir are their real names?"

"*W'Allah*, I don't know," Idris shrugged.

Unlike Samir, who insisted that his friends' identities were none of his business, Idris frequently speculated about others' identities. He sometimes worried that I did not appreciate how much his openness with me could socially ostracize him and make him look suspicious to other asylum seekers. Before he agreed to take me to social gatherings, he always made me promise not to ask anyone about their nationalities or ages, or make remarks that might reveal that I knew their identities were probably complicated. This was something I would not have done even without Idris's instruction.

Social workers sometimes expected boys with almost identical stories or legal situations to bond and develop friendships or at least solidarity; but this was rarely the case, because they tended to keep stories that could have formed the basis of solidarity private.[11] Although they did not discuss their official identities and asylum claims with each other, asylum seekers, especially among others from the same country as themselves, did help each other with things they did not consider potentially sensitive. Idris frequently lent his youth welfare apartment to near strangers who were visiting Berlin and needed a place to stay, or to young men who wanted to spend time with their girlfriends but could not find privacy at their camps. He did not seem offended to hear from people only when they needed to use his apartment, saying it was a matter of course to help other Ethiopians. But he also let Guled, a Somali, stay at his apartment whenever he was away for a few days, so that Guled could use Idris's wi-fi and have the privacy his camp did not offer.

Whenever we were out and about, Idris knew immediately whether a person was *habesha* (Ethiopian/Eritrean) or Somali, and would greet them and start a conversation. This is how many asylum seekers seemed to make their friends: by identifying co-nationals on the streets and talking to them. Once, Idris and I were walking across Alexanderplatz and saw two Ethiopians drinking beer. As we approached them, they tried to hide their bottles. "Brothers," said Idris in German, "why are you doing this to yourself? You did not come to Europe for this." I expected the two to be angered by this intrusion and judgment, but they agreed with Idris and said they were having too much stress with their residence papers. They invited him that same evening to dinner at the place of a friend, who turned out to be the founder of an Ethiopian-Muslim association, in which Idris became very involved in the following years, and whose meetings I also attended on several occasions.

Solidarity, however, was fragile, and easily corroded by suspicion. Paul called me on the phone one evening in tears, shouting that his friend Amadou had told him that he knew Paul had initially given a false story about his parents being murdered. Paul yelled at me to tell him who had told Amadou about this. I tried to calm him down, and said I had no idea but that it definitely had not been me. And besides, I added, what did it matter if Amadou knew about the story? Paul sobbed that his story was *his* story, and his problem *his* problem, and that he did not want anyone else to know. I saw friendships end altogether because of this kind of mistrust.

Asylum seekers' paths are nearly all the same—some version of arrival, age determination, Dublin, welcome class, asylum interview, rejection, appeal, apprenticeship—and this results in comparisons but little actual help, as the asylum seekers keep their legal status a secret even from friends. The day before his asylum interview at BAMF, Paul and I took a walk through the big, forestlike park near his apartment—something that had become a Sunday tradition for us. He admitted how nervous he was about the interview, and that he did not know what to expect. I asked if he had spoken to other Guineans who had already had their interviews. Paul said that no one talked about their interviews, and that if he asked a friend how his had gone, the friend would be suspicious and say, "Why are you asking me this? It's none of your business."

When Yakob asked Idris—his closest friend, after all—how his asylum case was going, Idris only joked: "The BAMF sent a letter and said I can find my residence permit in the toilet, but I've been too grossed out to look."

On Ali's Facebook page I saw that he had posted his arrival in Germany. A friend from Switzerland asked why he had moved to Germany, and Ali responded, "Just because, brother." In reality, he had had to leave Switzerland for fear of deportation.

On Samir's birthday, when his youth shelter had kicked him out and we had not yet found a new place for him to stay, a friend of his called and asked where he was living. Samir paused, then said in a cheerful tone, "I might move to Kreuzberg [a popular area of Berlin] tomorrow!"

"*Stabil* [Awesome]!" came the immediate response.

Samir did not tell his friend that Kreuzberg just happened to be where the homeless shelter I had found as a last resort was located.

When Guled's appeal was rejected and he received a *Duldung*—the most precarious status—he did not carry it with him in his wallet, as was required, but hid it at home in his binder of documents. He said he did not want other Somalis to see it, and that due to shame, Somalis never admitted to getting a rejection. If a friend were to ask him, he said, he would just tell them he had the "normal ID." Such secrecy also led to the spread of false information. Sometimes the young men would tell me about a residence title a friend had supposedly received, but which actually did not exist; thus making it clear that the friend must have lied.

Taking Advantage of Ambiguity

Maintaining an identity means reading situations and deciding which identity to perform. Which nationality? Which native language? Which age? Orphaned or not? Drug dealer or law-abiding? Asylum seekers with negotiated identities must constantly weigh the advantages and disadvantages of presenting themselves in a specific way. From my observations, their default was usually to give their official identity. At doctor's offices, in school, and in other public or official settings, they would give the age, nationality, and other information they had submitted with their asylum application. If personal relationships had ties to official ones—as, for example, in friendships with other teenagers living in youth welfare— they would also maintain this official identity even if they felt close to a person, because they thought it too risky to do otherwise. The only times I saw asylum seekers live out their actual identities were either in settings where people were anonymous and information was extremely unlikely to get back to officials (such as in contacts with strangers at nightclubs) or in interactions with people they had already known in their countries of origin.

Erving Goffman (1959, 1967) showed that audience segregation is a basic premise of social life, and that people can switch between multiple roles without much dissonance. But audiences sometimes overlap, meaning that one must meet the expectations of multiple audiences, a scenario that has been theorized in media studies as "contextual collapse" (Marwick and boyd 2010). When the consequences of misjudging audience segregation and collapse are as potentially severe as in the case of asylum seekers, it is prudent to default to one identity for all situations, and to adopt a different role only in select relationships and after careful deliberation.

Goffman also drew a sharp distinction between the "front" and "backstage" of people's behavior and identity. Essentially, he argued that, much as in a theater, social actors will behave differently before and behind the figurative curtain. "Backstage," people are supposedly free of the norms that guide their "front" behavior, and can be their true selves. However, the internalization of official identities by asylum seekers shows that

Identify

decisions about the front have backstage repercussions. When a person spends much of his time in front of the curtain, and can often be unsure whether what appears to be the backstage will not turn out to be part of the front after all, it is much easier to treat life itself as a front, just in case. Leading a minor's life surrounded by other minors also makes it increasingly hard to act older when the curtain does close for a few hours; and it challenges the idea that there is a true self, easily distinguishable from a false one, at all. This is more in line with a view of performativity that doubts that a sharp line ever exists between acting and reality, or that an authentic person predates a performance, and instead holds that a person is continuously made through performing—if that is then even an appropriate term.

I generally occupied a middle position between these two poles, of maintaining the official identity and revealing the actual one. Several of my interlocutors—above all, Samir, Idris, and Paul—told me explicitly about their identities. Others told me explicitly about some parts of their identities but not all. Yet others never explicitly told me they had made false identity claims, but also made no effort to maintain their official identities—saying, for example, "When I have papers, I am going to visit my family in Addis Ababa," even though they were officially not from Ethiopia, or saying about a twenty-five-year-old that he was "my age" despite officially being eighteen, or freely telling me about their teenage years in their home country even though they had officially left it at age thirteen.

Just as Aurora Chang (2016) has developed the concept "undocumented intelligence" in opposition to a wholly deficit view of undocumentedness, asylum seekers with uncertain identities also develop a certain savvy and agility, akin to "learning to be illegal" (Gonzales 2011). Sometimes they are actually able to use their identity and uncertain legal status to their advantage by transforming ambiguity into flexibility. They can evoke situationally advantageous category membership, and a lack of identity can even be legally advantageous. Paul, for example, continued to visit night clubs where bouncers had so often admitted him as an adult that they eventually refrained from checking his ID, which would now have revealed him to be a minor. Samir referred to himself as a minor or as an adult depending on whether the situation called for innocence (as when the police found cannabis on him) or masculinity (as when introducing himself to women at a night club), and he owned multiple IDs from variously aged phases of his life in Germany to back this up. Depending on whether they wanted to bond with Eritreans, Ethiopians, Somalis, or Sudanese, multilingual and multiethnic men like Yakob and Idris identified themselves as having come from those countries.

Michael told me he could not go to school, given that his only form of ID during his Dublin period was a GÜB (*Grenzübertrittsbescheinigung*, or certificate of having crossed a border). But he also did not go when I assured him that anyone, regardless of legal status, was allowed to attend school in Germany. Yakob told me he did not care about dodging the fare on public transit, or other minor legal transgressions, because if you do not know whether you can stay in a country, "the rules don't really apply to you." Samir used his change of age, nationality, and spelling of his name to open a new bank account at the same bank where his old one had been frozen until he balanced out his debt. And after recovering from the initial shock of having his Eritrean citizenship crossed out on his ID card by an unconvinced asylum interviewer, he took to declaring that he was glad to be from nowhere, because "without a country, they have no country to deport me to."

In German, the word *Maskenfreiheit* refers to the freedom you feel when you are wearing a mask or acting. Samir was playful with his identity in situations where it was of no real consequence. As a drug dealer, he would often tell customers he was from Colombia and was just making some money during his holidays in Germany. Once, a tourist asked us for directions and also inquired where we were from. While I dutifully said I was from Berlin, Samir said he was from the Gambia, and, asked about his native language, said it was "Ulika" (his pronunciation of my first name), a rare language only spoken by a few Gambians. He taught the tourist how to say "How are you?" and "My name is . . ." in "Ulika," and the man carefully repeated Samir's gibberish. Samir would also regularly bum free food from the Arab grocer on his street corner who correctly thought Samir was Eritrean, and therefore assumed he did not speak native Arabic. Samir and I would enter the store, and Samir would yell "*Ammo* [uncle]!" *Ammo* would come to the front of the store with a big smile on his face, wipe his hands on his apron, and ask us what we had learned in Arabic class that week. Samir had told *Ammo* that we were both studying Arabic, and while I could earnestly try out some new phrase I had picked up, Samir would invariably impress *Ammo* with a sentence that was far too advanced for a beginner-level Arabic student but which still somehow did not sound native. *Ammo* would then praise us for our studiousness and give us free canned beans or tomatoes, and we would go home and cook *ful*, a Sudanese breakfast dish.

High-Maintenance Identities

Because several of my interlocutors had been diagnosed with tuberculosis, I had to go to the public health department and get tested. Besides taking a blood sample and X-raying my lungs, the clinician also wanted to know the names, countries of origin, and dates of birth of those patients I had spent at least forty hours with, because, she explained, they were trying to get better epidemiological data on which age groups and origin countries were most affected. As I made the list—naming the "minors" and "Eritreans" I had spent time with—I realized that I, too, was participating in the fabrication and maintenance of identities. Identity is not established by one person at one time; it can never be a fait accompli. As Idris realized with dismay, a false identity follows you around, and you have to keep it up every day whether you want to or not. Belloni uses the term "entrapment," from gambling studies, to capture how refugees feel "caught in a condition that obliges them to keep moving onward, no matter the risks" (2019, 131). To have obtained a particular identity is a similar trap: even if someone regrets his false claims, correcting them poses an incalculable risk, so the safest bet is to uphold them. Antoine Burgard's historical study of the resettlement in Canada of young European Holocaust survivors, who manipulated their ages in an attempt to fit the eligibility criteria of resettlement programs, shows that they often ended up living "their entire life with a false age" (2021, 184). Imagine not only the psychological burden of never again being able to be yourself, but also the practical consequences of forever being younger than you actually are: from having to work years past the normal retirement age to not qualifying for preventive medical checkups that health insurance companies only cover for policyholders above a certain age.

In contrast to the previous chapters on negotiating identities, this chapter has examined the maintenance of asylum seekers' identities, by themselves and others, in everyday life—an effort that is particularly fraught because it takes place at the tense junction of the complex experience of the self, protracted negotiation, and consequently assumed factualness. Scholarship on refugees' identities has focused on their difficult attempts to attain these, their "narrative tactics" (Beneduce 2015). Yet perhaps the more difficult—because indefinite—task is living with such an identity. A false identity affects the self, as it produces a sense of guilt and fear; and for an official minor, whether they are actually older or have simply lived an independent, grown-up life, it can feel infantilizing and emasculating. Such feelings affect relationships with helpers, who must also be distrusted to some extent, and whose help can exacerbate feelings of infantilization and emasculation. Helpers themselves contribute to maintaining asylum seekers' identities by acting, for the most part, as if the asylum seeker's official identity were real. Such collective silence and secrecy marks even friendships among asylum seekers, who, despite otherwise constituting important social networks for each other, rarely talk about their identities and legal status, thus cultivating suspicion even in the intimate realms of life. Asylum seekers can only use their ambiguous identities to their advantage in relatively anonymous, low-stakes situations. Negotiated identities and minority age, in particular, thus profoundly affect asylum seekers' selves and relationships. The coveted legal protections and social support for minors come with a heavy emotional and interpersonal burden.

Classification, then, does not simply harm asylum seekers through its outcomes. Many are actually able to use their young looks, their compelling storytelling, their multilinguistic abilities, or the incompetence of overwhelmed administrations to their advantage. Rather, the asylum seekers suffer from the practical and emotional consequences of being "entrapped" (Belloni 2019) in a system that, they believe, requires them to lie continuously. In the next two chapters I will focus on these consequences. I will examine what it is like to live with uncertain legal statuses and identities and be forced to maintain two very different possible futures—staying in Germany, or having to leave—not knowing which one will eventuate.

5 * The Liminal Lives of Young Adults

One day, Ali and I talked about interfaith relationships, and I asked if he cared what religion his children would practice. He said it did not matter to him, as long as they embraced one religion fully. To be half this and half that, or outwardly this and inwardly something else, like the Afghans and Iranians he knew who were passing their Dublin period as provisional Christians in church asylum, drove a person "crazy," he said. The liminality Ali describes—being half this and half that—is emblematic of the lives of asylum seekers, particularly young adults. In the previous chapter I showed that minority age, despite its legal and social perks, is often overshadowed by feelings of guilt, infantilization, emasculation, fear of being found out, and cognitive dissonance between the practical need for minority and the emotional need for manhood. In this chapter I focus on those who are classified not as minors but as young adults, and show that they live in what Cecilia Menjívar has called "liminal legality." Menjívar defines liminal legality as a legal status that has qualities of documentedness and undocumentedness, that is temporary but often of indefinite duration, and which is not part of a linear process toward full documentedness (2006, 1008). She borrows the term "liminality" from the anthropologist Victor Turner, who describes people who "are at once no longer classified and not yet classified" (Turner 1967, 95–96) as liminal. "No longer classified" and "not yet classified" characterize asylum seekers' legal status *and* official identities—first and foremost, age—which turn migrants into multiply "transitional beings" (Turner 1967).

Although such liminality is largely created through state policy, the German state actually punishes asylum seekers' liminal identities. In summer 2019, Germany passed the so-called Law of Orderly Return (*Geordnete-Rückkehr-Gesetz*), a set of laws with, among other things, the goal of facilitating deportations by intensifying efforts to verify identities. Having an unverified identity—defined as giving contradictory identities to different agencies, or not having a passport—is a deportation impediment. For every asylum seeker who does not obtain a passport, the new law offers a new kind of *Duldung* for "those persistently refusing to have an identity" (*hart-näckige Identitätsverweigerer*), colloquially referred to as *Duldung light*. With a *Duldung light* one is not allowed to work, receives less money from the state, does not qualify for a *Duldung* for the purpose of an apprenticeship, and can be imprisoned for missing appointments with the Foreigner Registration Office, among other sanctions.

Obtaining a passport is not as easy as the new law implies, however, because many common countries of origin do not have civil registry systems comparable to that of Germany. The Guinean embassy in Berlin, for example, plainly states on its website that it does not issue passports and that applicants will have to travel to Conakry, the Guinean capital, if they want to obtain documents, or wait for the Guinean delegation that comes to Germany to issue passports every four years. The Afghan embassy's waiting period for appointments increased to nearly two years during my research; and it also often refused to issue passports, claiming that it could not find the applicant in its computer system. Moreover, many asylum seekers fear that instead of securing their legal status, a passport will aid their own deportation. For this reason, Guled avoided getting a passport, even though it meant having to live with the retrenchments listed above. Many young asylum seekers are thus scared into continuing to live with a liminal legal status, as attempts to secure their legal status would temporarily demote them from legal limbo to illegality and deportability. Thus, because many asylum seekers cannot obtain passports or avoid doing so out of fear, the new law may not increase verified identities and deportations as much as it increases the number of people living in Germany in liminality as punishment for their unverified identities.

In this chapter I will examine four particularly stark examples of liminality—or "inbetweenness"—in young adults' lives. First, many young adults "have Dublin," as they call the period during which Germany may deport them to their first EU country. This is a time of serial temporary documentation, when asylum seekers live between the jurisdictions of two countries, one of which is no longer fully responsible and the other not responsible yet. Asylum seekers who have Dublin sometimes try to pass this time in church asylum, another site of liminality in which the state vows not to deport a person but that person is also ineligible for any kind of state support—again, in limbo between expulsion and inclusion. Second, I recount Yakob's ambivalent deportation, which I mentioned in the previous chapter, in more detail: as a young adult he was deportable, but he should not have been deported from his youth welfare apartment. This incident shows the merely liminal protection youth welfare can offer to young adults as well as the fact that it is deportability—a state between being in and out—rather than only actual deportation that contributes to asylum seekers' sense of precariousness. Third, I discuss the circumstance of having different ages recognized by various agencies. Multiple, contradictory dates of birth again create liminality, as one is recognized neither as a child nor as an adult, and falls between the jurisdictions of the agencies responsible for minors and those responsible for adults. Fourth, I show how the liminal legality of young adults makes it more difficult for them than for their younger peers to access medical care, and how their precarious legal situation makes them more vulnerable to being exploited by employers, helpers, and lawyers. The legal precariousness in which all asylum seekers live is thus even greater for adults, because certain laws that produce precariousness, such as the Dublin III agreement, apply only to adults, and others that cushion the effects of precariousness or even provide stability apply only to minors.

"Having Dublin" and Living in Church Asylum

Ali had been telling me about a church in the affluent western Berlin district of Steglitz, whose German pastor gave his sermons in Farsi as well as German. He had apparently specialized in church asylums, giving out dozens but requiring the respective asylum seekers to convert to Christianity and live on the church premises for the duration of their asylum. This seemed curious to me, so I asked Ali to take me with him to the Reformation Day service. The benches of the large church were nearly completely filled, and I estimated that about a quarter of the audience was German and the rest of the people were from Afghanistan or Iran—mostly weary-faced young men, and a few women with small children.

After the service, the German pastor and his Afghan assistants waited at the door and personally greeted all the attendees as they exited. Some left the building, but most descended the stairs into the church basement, where they poured themselves tea from large thermos flasks and stood around waiting to talk to the pastor, who entered his office and received them one by one or in small groups. With a wave of his hand toward the crowd, Ali said to me, "All Dublin." I recalled a pithy remark by Basit, another young Afghan I knew who was also in church asylum: "Sweden or Switzerland, it's all Dublin." Ali explained that most of the church attendees had only recently arrived in Germany and now lived in the church, waiting out the months during which Germany—in accordance with the Dublin III agreement—could return them to the EU country in which they had first arrived. Indeed, many were wearing thin tracksuit bottoms, their bare feet in shower shoes despite the freezing temperatures outside. Their clothing suggested that they did, in fact, live here. We talked to a young man with an ashen complexion and deep bags under his eyes;

Ali translated for me that the man had been inside the church for a year already, with another six months to go. I found it hard to fathom that a young man could be confined to the inside of a small church for one and a half years of his life. Ali translated the young man's response to my incredulous facial expression with a shrug: "I have the yard."

When it was Ali's and my turn to speak with the pastor, I asked a bit about the church, and the pastor told me that 1,500 of his 1,600 parishioners were asylum seekers from Iran or Afghanistan. Those living inside the church passed the time by studying German and the Bible. During the process of appealing a rejected asylum application, judges examine whether an applicant's conversion to Christianity—which could be grounds for persecution in Iran and Afghanistan—is merely opportunistic. A court ruling from Bavaria, for example, specifies that a conversion must have occurred "not for tactical reasons but due to an earnest, permanent religious change of opinion shaping the religious identity of the person." This ruling found the convert in question to be sincere, because he had been able to describe "peace and love as the central tenets of the Bible" and to show credibly how those things had been missing from his previous religion, Islam. His answers about Christianity and his faith had been "spontaneous but without hesitation" (Bayerische Staatskanzlei 2016). Judges might ask what the applicant considers contentious within Christianity. But how is an uneducated, perhaps even illiterate man supposed to answer? In fact, too much theological knowledge also raises suspicions, as it turns religiosity into a mere feat of the mind, not the heart. "In the end," the pastor said, "it is often those who know how to act well who are believed. The simple people with honest hearts are the ones who are given a hard time."

After we said goodbye to the pastor, Ali and I went to an Iranian restaurant nearby for a late dinner. On the way, Ali threw away the church schedule flier that the pastor had given him. Other Afghans who had been at the service saw him, and Ali laughed. "Don't tell him," he said. The pastor regularly sent Ali text messages, and Ali had the feeling that he wanted him to convert. But Ali, as he saw it, was not in a bad enough situation to need to do so. A friend of Ali, by contrast, had a wife and children in Afghanistan whom he desperately wanted to be able to join him in Germany through family reunification. This friend was considering the possibility of conversion and church asylum, and, given the circumstances, Ali was sympathetic. Ali told me that the pastor always complained about being used, and that the asylum seekers stopped coming to church as soon as they had passed their church asylum period and received their residence papers. But I wondered: Who was to say who was preying more on whom, or who was the greater opportunist? The people who pretended to be

Christian for residence papers, or the pastor who filled his church's empty pews with desperate asylum seekers? As Ali saw it, the stakes were much higher for his compatriots, who, as he put it, had the choice between "the police outside, or the pastor inside." As in the age exam labs and asylum interview offices, so it was here inside the church halls: the predicaments of rigid protection categories left little room for good guys or bad guys, right choices or wrong.

Ali himself had come out of church asylum only two years before we attended the Reformation Day service together. My first introduction to him had been Daniela's rhetorical question: "Have you ever seen someone's eyes turn black with fear?" Ali had been referred to Empower by one of his camp's social workers because he needed church asylum to bridge his Dublin period. The woman running Berlin's church asylum counseling service, a retired lawyer notorious for her unfriendliness, had taken an inexplicable liking to me when I had accompanied asylum seekers to her office before, so Daniela suggested I join Ali. Although I had never met Ali in person, Daniela's description helped me recognize him immediately. While I had earlier thought of Daniela's characterization of "eyes black with fear" as hyperbole, I now understood exactly what she meant. Ali looked nervous and jumpy, his eyes somehow turned inward even while constantly scanning his surroundings.

The church asylum counseling took place twice a week on the ground floor of a church. Asylum seekers wrote their names on a list, and then waited in the foyer to be called into a small room where two elderly women listened to their stories, usually with the help of a translator, and decided whether their situations merited contacting one of the parishes they worked with. These women were the gatekeepers. The waiting room was always packed with men whose faces looked as if they had been summoned to their Last Judgment. No one spoke, and the silence made the lofty church room feel eerie.

Ali and I were finally called in, and with a Swiss accent, Ali told his story. He had left Afghanistan on the insistence of his mother, who had lost her husband to the Taliban and feared the same for her only son. He had settled in a small town in the German-speaking part of Switzerland, where he lived in a large home for unaccompanied minors. He had learned German, gone to school, and spent his free time with the other teenagers. Life was good, he remembered, until his asylum application was rejected and he had to decide whether to stay in Switzerland—on the barely livable allowance afforded to rejected asylum seekers, prohibited from work and study while under the looming threat of deportation—or to leave the country. He left Switzerland long enough before his eighteenth birthday to file for asylum in Germany again as a minor, which would, among other benefits, exclude him from Dublin—meaning that Germany would not be able to return him to Switzerland, and would be responsible for processing his second asylum application in Europe. In Hamburg, however, the youth shelter where he lived ordered an age exam, which found him to be eighteen.[1] Ali was relocated to Berlin, where he now lived in a camp for adults, in fear of a Dublin deportation to Switzerland.

When Ali had finished telling his story, the two counselors looked skeptical and remarked that they had seen Ali smoke outside, which in their view did not speak for his minority age. In an attempt to distract from the smoking, I argued that Berlin does not deport to Afghanistan, whereas Switzerland does, so that risking Ali's deportation to Switzerland would ultimately risk his deportation to a country that Berlin did not deem safe—what is sometimes called a "chain deportation" (*Kettenabschiebung*; Bohm 2021). The women hesitated, and scolded Ali, maintaining that if he claimed to be young, he should not smoke like an adult. But then they gave us the address of a pastor in the former East Berlin. Incidentally, the same church had been home to the *Umweltbibliothek* (environmental library) in the late 1980s, an important gathering place for the East German opposition, pivotal in the Peaceful Revolution of 1989. Thirty years later, its board voted in favor of granting Ali church asylum for the six months of his Dublin period. The pastor informed BAMF of the decision to protect Ali, and gave Ali a piece of paper identifying him as a church asylee in case of police controls.

In years past, before the competence to grant asylum was monopolized by European states, religious authorities extended protections on sacred sites, including ancient Greek and Roman temples and medieval churches (Marfleet 2011). In the 1980s, inspired by the sanctuary movement in the United States but also referencing earlier European practices, West German churches began granting church asylum to asylum seekers at risk of deportation. The movement grew throughout the 1990s in response to the Yugoslav Wars and the increased enforcement of deportations, and peaked again in the wake of the 2015–16 refugee crisis. While some legal scholars saw church asylum in the 1980s and '90s as a form of "civil disobedience" (Bohm 2021, 132), its increasing bureaucratization and administrative overhead today defy any such characterization.

Then as now, however, church asylum rests on an "informal agreement" (Bohm 2021, 42) between the churches and the German state— since 2015 the federal government, before then state governments—that protects someone from being deported, but also excludes them from state support. Their accommodation, everyday commodities, and medical care have to be paid for by donations. Dublin and church asylum are both periods of liminality. The Foreigner Registration Office issues serial temporary IDs for asylum seekers who have Dublin, sometimes for only three days at a time. Dublin and church asylum are also liminal periods with regard to jurisdiction. During a Dublin period, the first EU country someone entered is no longer fully responsible, and Germany is not yet fully responsible. For the duration of a church asylum, the state will not deport the church asylee, but also considers him ineligible for any kind of state support. It is as if he did not exist. Dublin and church asylum are thus times when the "boundaries of legality and illegality [are blurred] to create gray areas of incertitude" (Menjívar 2006, 1002).

Ali spent his church asylum first in an Empower volunteer's spare bedroom, then in the donation-funded apartment for asylum seekers with liminal identities, and finally—after being expelled following a fight—in another volunteer's apartment. I helped him move each time, and just as with Samir, whose belongings we had had to collect long before he had a new place to put them in, we would stuff Ali's things into plastic bags and lug them onto the subway into some hazy future. During the six months Ali spent in church asylum, he was unable to focus on school because, he said, he did not know if he would be allowed to stay in Germany. The insistence of various counselors that he had to look at it the other way around—succeeding in school would be his best chance for staying in Germany—did not change this feeling.

During his time in church asylum, I accompanied Ali to a therapeutic facility where psychology students treat uninsured patients free of charge, and he allowed me to attend the sessions with him. One therapist asked whether Ali consumed drugs, and seemed taken aback by Ali's candor when he promptly replied, "Everything but cocaine." Ali said he took the drugs not for fun but out of despair. He usually took them alone, and even when he did so with a group, he would sit apart. The drugs allowed him to become weightless for a while, and to think of nothing. Ali said he was always agitated, always pent up.

"Even now?" the therapist asked.

Ali simply pointed at his right knee, which had been bouncing up and down incessantly. Asked whether he would be willing to seek drug counseling, Ali said that he might do so after his church asylum and Dublin period were over, but that as it stood, drugs were the only reliable thing in his life, impossible for him to give up. The therapist also asked about Ali's level of German, which Ali assessed as "usually intermediate, but beginner when I'm stressed. Then I just forget everything."

While church asylum had initially been intended for a few rare cases of particular hardship, in the wake of the 2015–16 crisis it became a common solution for Dublin cases. In 2018, 1,325 church asylums had been pronounced in Germany, including 1,246 for Dublin cases. In contrast, there had been only 79 asylums five years earlier, in 2013, and only 27 in 2009 (Asyl in der Kirche 2022). In June 2018, when Ali's Dublin period and church asylum were already over, the joint conference of Germany's ministers of the interior therefore decided to stop what they saw as the inflationary use of church asylum (Bohm 2021). If BAMF, to whom the churches send the written justification for a church asylum, found this unconvincing, the person's Dublin period would now be extended from six to eighteen months (an extension previously reserved for people considered to be in hiding). This was meant to deter the pronouncement of church asylum for anyone but the extreme hardship cases for which it had originally been intended. The new law made an impact: while in 2016, 80 percent of proposed church asylums were accepted by BAMF, by late 2019 this number had decreased to 2 percent (*Süddeutsche Zeitung* 2019).

The court orders for Dublin periods also tightened during this time. In spring 2019 the Foreigner Registration Office sent out letters to those who had Dublin, with the directive that they had to specify their whereabouts in advance if they spent a night away from their camp. Even if asylum seekers were lucky enough to have a place other than their camp in which to sleep and avoid their Dublin deportation, they had to return to their camp every third day and swipe their electronic camp ID, so as not to be counted as being in hiding. For those only nominally living in the camp but actually spending the nights at the shelter apartment or with friends, the new order now also required them to post a note on their camp room door every evening with the name and address of their supposed whereabouts. With the help of caseworkers from the shelter apartment and of volunteers, the asylum seekers sought places that were open all night and which they assumed would be unlikely for the police to search. Few places fit the bill. We phoned mosques, but none of them were open all night. One day, I got a call from a young Afghan asking what club would be open through Sunday night. Naively, I asked what style of music he preferred, and we both laughed when I realized that the choice of techno or reggae was not the issue. When he later showed me his schedule for the week—Monday a dance club, Tuesday a porno cinema, and Wednesday the psychiatric ward—he said he did not know whether to laugh or cry about this progression.

When Ali's Dublin period, and therefore his church asylum, was finally over, we went to the Foreigner Registration Office to pick up his first non-GÜB ID in Germany. The Foreigner Registration Office was a large building complex near the center of Berlin. One had to explain the reason for one's visit in a tent in the forecourt, and receive a waiting number for a specific building and waiting room. The waiting times were notorious. On days when the office opened at 8 a.m., a line would form outside by 5 a.m.

In the winter, this meant standing in the cold for three hours. Without a low waiting number, one had to sit on the overcrowded wooden benches all day—or on the stairs, if one was unlucky—staring at the electronic display and posters advertising legal counseling and voluntary returns.

When the clerk saw that Ali had been in church asylum, he ranted: "Ah, the church again. Church asylum should be a criminal offense in itself. It's as though I killed someone and then ran to the church, confessed, and hid there." I said that I found the comparison insolent, since Ali had not killed anyone and church asylum was a legal arrangement, not some shady business, but the man ignored me. When Ali asked for a notice confirming the day's appointment to give to his school to excuse his absence, the clerk mumbled that Ali should ask "his buddy, the pastor" for that. It must have been obvious that I was about to snap, because Ali gestured for me to let it go. Perhaps used to such treatment, the asylum seekers I accompanied to appointments often seemed indifferent to conduct I found infuriating.

Soon after picking up his *Aufenthaltsgestattung* (residence title for specific purposes, usually the asylum procedure), Ali and I were back at the Foreigner Registration Office, this time to trade it in for another GÜB (which was later turned into a *Duldung*). Around the time of Ali's asylum interview, which took place after his Dublin period had ended, Ali's camp closed due to sanitary concerns, and its residents were dispersed to other camps in Berlin. Ali did not know he had to inform BAMF of his new address, did not see his rejection letter, and, as a result, did not appeal within the one-week statutory period. He was therefore unable to use the appeal as a grace period, as other asylum seekers do, and his asylum procedure was terminated. This would not have happened to someone in youth welfare, whose caseworkers would have helped him stay on top of such things.

Back in the office, the same clerk who thought church asylum merited comparison with murder seemed delighted to revoke Ali's *Aufenthaltsgestattung* so soon. "ID!" he barked as Ali put his *Aufenthaltsgestattung* on the table. In its stead he received a GÜB, a white sheet of paper bearing the title "Certificate of Having Crossed a Border." The clerk peered at Ali while summarizing pleasantly: "So, second asylum procedure over. First asylum procedure in Switzerland. Then national procedure in Germany after church asylum. Still no reasons for asylum. Accordingly: Ciao, ciao!"

Outside, Ali folded the sheet to make it small enough to fit in his wallet, and grinned as if none of this seriously concerned him—a reaction I observed often. While officials saw it as disrespectful or taunting, I saw it as a futile attempt to disguise fear and anger. Without a better kind of ID, Ali would not be able to do much besides exist in Germany. He would not be able to start an apprenticeship or seek legal employment, or to rent an apartment or travel outside Berlin, nor could he sign long-term contracts. In fact, when we returned to the Foreigner Registration Office half a year later with a full-time contract of employment Ali had secured with a construction company, the clerk merely reminded him that his *Awful* immigration papers did not permit him to work. Ali stormed out of the office and ripped the contract he had been so proud of minutes ago into dozens of pieces that whirled away in the afternoon wind. He later said, "You go insane when you have ideas in your head for what you want to do with your life but can't act on them. It'd almost be better not to have any ideas at all."

When Samir heard about Ali, he asked why Ali did not go elsewhere. I objected that Ali spoke German and had friends in Berlin. "Yeah, OK," said Samir. "But eating, sleeping, eating, sleeping. No school, no apprenticeship, no job. If that were me, I promise you, I would be gone tomorrow. I would go and find a new country, any country." Samir had not gone to school or sought employment even when his residence papers allowed it. What upset him, I assumed, was not the lack of school or work per se, but the exogenously enforced and indefinite duration of what Sassen (2014) has called a "double expulsion": while some rejected asylum seekers are indeed deported, the vast majority are expelled not from a territory but from basic rights and protections.

Asylum seekers' time in Germany is often not their first period of precariousness, either. Propelled by rejected asylum applications and impending legal adulthood, these "refugees-in-orbit" (Schuster 2005) move from country to country, perpetually stuck in liminal legality—that is, fully belonging in neither one place nor the other. Guled, like Ali, had spent his first years in Europe in a country he eventually had to leave for fear of deportation. His asylum application had been rejected in Sweden when he was fifteen, but his caseworkers encouraged him to stay while he was still protected as a minor, and to hope that the laws might change in his favor. But by the time he turned eighteen the laws had not changed, and so he left for Germany.

Young men who had spent considerable amounts of time in another European country carried with them the traces of that previous life. Ali's German had a Swiss inflection, and he loved to cook *Rösti*, a Swiss fried potatoes dish. Guled translated words from Somali into Swedish, and then from Swedish into German, because the Somali-German dictionary was often wrong. He had decorated his camp wall with a picture of his old Swedish youth soccer team and his German vocabulary sheets—his past and potential past, as he remarked bitterly.

"How do you stay motivated to learn the language and befriend the people of a country you might have to leave soon?" I asked him.

"You don't," he said.

The Illusory Safety of Youth Welfare

As mentioned in the previous chapter, Yakob, who deemed himself safe and should not have been deported, was the only one of my interlocutors to be deported—another testament to the merely liminal protection that even youth welfare provides. After several failed attempts, he was eventually able to return to Berlin, crossing first the Italian-Swiss and then the Swiss-German border unnoticed. Idris and I picked him up from the bus port. The two friends hugged for a long time before Idris started teasing Yakob, like a little brother returning from summer camp. "I see you're Italian now! All new clothes, very stylish! You even got your ear pierced." They both laughed, but later in the evening they grew serious, because neither knew whether Yakob would have a future in Germany. He had been deported three days before his Dublin period was to end, which he compared to being handed a gift that is withdrawn just as you are about to grab it. At the moment, Yakob was simply an illegal returnee; his wrongful deportation had not made his return legal. All summer, he hid in the apartment for asylum seekers with liminal identities. He sometimes went to the nearest subway stop for the public wi-fi, or jogged in a nearby park, but otherwise his life was on hold—in a liminal state of being in Germany neither legally nor illegally. He was not allowed to continue school, or to tell any of his old classmates that he was back in Berlin. Whenever Idris or I missed a phone call from Yakob and could not reach him afterward, especially at night, we panicked that he had been deported again and that we had missed his call for help. Once, as Yakob and I were exiting a supermarket, an alarm sounded. Yakob was about to hurry away, motioning for me to do the same, since he feared the police would be called and that it would come out that he was supposed to be in Italy. But the security guard waved us away, mumbling something about the alarm system being broken.

After Yakob was wrongly deported, social workers put up signs in Idris's hallway citing laws that said deportations from youth welfare apartments were unlawful. They instructed Idris to point to those signs should the police come for him. Even when an asylum seeker is not himself deported, he is always reminded of that possibility. Deportations from Berlin are actually not as common as their ubiquitous specter might suggest.[2] Deportation and the threat of deportation, however, are two sides of the same policy, as Stefan Le Courant (2020, 12) argues, and it is the latter that more immediately affects young asylum seekers' lives in Germany. In this way, Nicholas De Genova has argued that "it is deportability, and not deportation per se" (2002, 438), that must be understood as central to the dynamics of border control and state sovereignty—and which, in Menjívar's (2006) words, adds to the liminality of migrants' legal status.

In fall 2018, a poster campaign by the newly founded Federal Ministry of the Interior for Building and Community (Bundesministerium des Innern, für Bau und Heimat) scared many asylum seekers. They sent me pictures of the posters they had spotted in subway stations and around the city, and asked me what they meant. The posters read, "Your country. Your future. Now!"—insinuating that migrants living in Germany had neglected their responsibilities toward their native countries—and advertised that asylum seekers who voluntarily returned home would receive one thousand euros as a start-up aid. Many asylum seekers interpreted this campaign as a harbinger of mass deportations.

Adam Goodman's (2020) study of deportations from the United States shows precisely that the power of deportation lies not just in the physical act of removing people from their country of residence, but in the day-to-day threat of removal, even if it is never realized and statistically unlikely. Goodman also shows that US organizations that want to help migrants are sometimes inadvertently helping the deportation regime, as they take the threat of deportation propagated by the Department of Homeland Security at face value and inform migrants of supposedly upcoming deportations, thus propelling them to leave or hide. This aids in the removal of people who actually might not have been deported. Something similar happens in Germany when counselors tell asylum seekers who have Dublin that they are going to be caught and returned, and then the asylum seekers hide or go to different countries when that may not have been necessary. Those living in the camps told me about the kind of atmosphere created by the wait for deportations. Ali described the resulting drug and alcohol abuse—"Everyone is just sitting there with their rejection waiting to be deported, it's just too much fear to handle"—as well as the tragedy of men beating up their children in frustration and then, later at night, crying softly in their beds. Radha Sarma Hegde (2016) advocates viewing illegality and irregularity not as a status, a demographic fact, but as something continuously produced by the threat of deportation.

When Different Agencies Recognize Different Ages

Different state agencies often recognize different ages for the same person, which not only gives asylum seekers an opportunity to play agencies off against each other, as Paul did to become a minor again, but also leads to much trouble and biographical paralysis. When you are neither a child nor an adult, neither the agencies geared toward adults nor those geared toward minors feel responsible. This can leave an asylum seeker in a liminal space of total ineligibility. Although I focused my research on male asylum seekers, to demonstrate the chaos that ensues when someone ends up with multiple, contradictory dates of birth, each recognized and applied by some agency, no case is better suited than that of Zeinab from Afghanistan, who has seven different dates of birth.

Zeinab's sister had fled to Germany after her husband tried to kill her. When this man also made threats against Zeinab, her brother organized a fake visa with the birth year 1992 for her to use to leave Afghanistan, which she wouldn't have been allowed to do by herself as a minor. She used this fake visa to travel to Germany via India, but on the visa application form issued by the German Consulate in New Delhi, her birth year was accidentally recorded as 1993. Once in Berlin, she went to the Afghan Embassy and received a passport bearing the birth year 2000, matching her self-stated age. This was also the birth year used by her high school in Berlin. The Berlin Senate Administration, however, ordered a forensic age exam because it considers passports from Afghanistan to be unreliable. This exam determined 1997 as Zeinab's year of birth, which the youth welfare office then used. An employee at the Foreigner Registration Office entered yet another year of birth, 1995, into the computer system after interviewing Zeinab's sister and hearing that she had been three years old when their mother died while giving birth to Zeinab. Finally, two forms exist that different employees of the youth welfare office filled out when Zeinab first arrived in Germany, in which they visually estimated her age. One form reads 2001, and the other 2002.

The family court accepted Zeinab's minority age, so she continued to have a guardian, even though her official ID showed her to be an adult. Zeinab's health insurance listed her as a minor, so her legal guardian had to agree to medical procedures. Her school listed her age as eighteen, but she was not allowed to go on school field trips because her ID showed her to be too old for the youth hostels. After the forensic age exam, the youth welfare office would no longer house her, but the Landesamt für Flüchtlingsangelegenheiten (State Office for Refugees, or LAF), pointing to her minority age, also refused to pay her rent, so Zeinab had to move in with her sister. When a journalist wanted to write about Zeinab's story and asked the youth welfare office for an interview, they asked Zeinab's guardian for permission, even though they listed Zeinab as an adult and should have asked her consent directly.

Being without a settled identity and legal status excludes one from many of life's necessities. Some documents, for example, are stamped "identity not proven," which—unsurprisingly—deters potential landlords and employers. An uncertain identity also prevents one from participating in perhaps smaller ways that are, however, no less important to a sense of belonging and quality of life. Young men with multiple dates of birth, for example, cannot join sports teams, because the coaches need clarity about whether to admit them to the youth team or the men's team. When people have uncertain ages, they also often fall between the spheres of responsibility of various agencies, each of which claims not to be responsible—as when neither the youth welfare office nor the LAF wanted to pay Zeinab and Samir, since each pointed to the date of birth that would make them ineligible for the help. When Paul was "between ages," he could not start psychotherapy, because neither adult nor youth therapists were comfortable taking him on.

Leandre's identity was especially problematic. His mother had left Cameroon for Germany when he was a preteen, and he had spent the next few years staying behind with friends and relatives and taking care of his younger sister. His mother had married a German woman to obtain a residence permit, and eventually brought over Leandre and his sister on fake visas. Leandre was, according to himself, seventeen when he came to Germany, but the visa he had traveled with belonged to a twelve-year-old, and his fingerprints were now permanently linked to that age. Leandre was an exceptionally smart, motivated young man who had taught himself intermediate German within only a few months. He wanted to study medicine or at least do an apprenticeship in nursing. Yet even though he was visibly not twelve, he was not allowed to study, start an apprenticeship, or even work or do an internship as a twelve-year-old. Several apprenticeship interviews had gone well, but as soon as the firms asked to make a copy of his ID, they retracted their offers, as they were not allowed to employ children. He also could not enroll in a regular school, because as a twelve-year-old he would have to be enrolled in the sixth grade, but no sixth-grade teacher would allow a grown man in her class. When Leandre visited a friend in another German city, he got into a stop-and-search, and the police sneered, "Twelve, huh?" when they saw his ID. He tried to explain to them that this was not his real age, but they took him back to the precinct and called the Foreigner Registration Office in Berlin, which confirmed that Leandre was indeed twelve. The police then issued a caution, because a twelve-year-old is not allowed to travel without the permission of a guardian.

Leandre could not live with his mother, because she lived in a community project exclusively for women, which allowed boys but not men on its premises. He also was too young for youth welfare (which starts at fourteen), let alone a room at a camp for adults. He also feared that if he were to apply for children's welfare, they would investigate why he could not live with his mother, and find out about her fake marriage. He also could not file for asylum because as a twelve-year-old, he needed a guardian to do so for him. His mother was not officially his guardian, and he did not want to alert the family court to this situation, lest it jeopardize his mother's residence papers. Leandre, like Zeinab, thus experienced extreme legal precariousness because of his disputed age. Their cases show that not only young adults, but also those with liminal ages—classified as both minor and adult, and therefore neither—suffer from liminal legality.

And even when one date of birth is recognized across various agencies, those agencies might interpret its meaning differently. Social worker Julian told me about unaccompanied minors from Senegal who, once they turn eighteen in Germany, are adults as far as their residence is concerned. Yet because minority age in Senegal ends only at twenty-one, they can sometimes keep their legal guardians in Germany until they turn twenty-one. Thus, depending on the issue, they are treated either as minors or as adults. Without the signatures of their guardians, they cannot get gym memberships or open bank accounts; yet they can be deported and receive their money from the office for adult refugees, not the youth welfare office.

Trauma and Illness

Many asylum seekers must deal with trauma, illness, or addiction; but those living in youth welfare have better health insurance, as well as the support of social workers who push them to get the care they need. Tending to health issues is even prerequisite for remaining in youth welfare. While minors are thus legally and socially well equipped to address their physical and emotional ailments, for their young adult peers this is often an insurmountable challenge, as a comparison of Paul's relatively easy access to medical care with the much more problematic treatment of Samir's tuberculosis will show.

Paul had what he described as unbearable pain in his knees. On the insistence of his caseworkers and often accompanied by them, he went to dozens of surgeons, orthopedists, and physical therapists. He was examined through X-rays and MRI and CT scans. He received hours of massage, as well as creams, pills, and even injections with radioactive liquids. But nothing helped. Sometimes he could not walk, despite every expert insisting that there was nothing physically wrong with him. One physician laughed out loud when Paul told him he sometimes woke up "paralyzed." Such mysterious pains were common among the asylum seekers I knew. Despite studying young, healthy men, for the years of my fieldwork I would spend at least a few mornings or afternoons a week at a doctor's office, and countless nights at emergency rooms. The asylum seekers complained about head and stomach aches, chest pains, nausea, and pains in their legs and backs for which there was almost never a discernible physical reason. Physicians were unnerved by what they perceived as unnecessary visits by perfectly healthy young men.

In an attempt to better understand and help, I read about the psychosomatic expression of trauma and found that pain without apparent medical cause could stem either from a constant tensing of the muscles or from a "physical memory"—that is, a physical injury incurred during the traumatizing event that has healed, but through whose locus the body was still signaling the painful memory. Since Paul had been beaten on his legs in a Libyan labor camp, I suspected that his pain could be such a physical memory, and suggested he start psychotherapy—which, once officially a minor, he was able to do, and did.

Few physicians recognized that such ailments were real but perhaps not in the way described by the patient. One exceptionally empathetic doctor who treated anyone, insured or not, and whose waiting room had been crowded with drug addicts, sex workers, and homeless people since the 1980s—and with asylum seekers since 2015—asked Samir about his sleep. When Samir said he could not sleep at night, the doctor, instead of giving him pills or brushing him off, said, "That's completely normal. It's your soul that has to heal from everything you have seen."

"How much longer?" Samir asked laconically.

"That's different for everyone," the doctor said.

"Two weeks? Two months?" Samir asked.

"Or two years," the doctor admitted. "And for some, it takes a lifetime."

Samir simply replied, "Fuck that." And the doctor nodded tenderly.

Unlike Paul, whose caseworkers insisted that the pain in his knees be examined and addressed in every possible way, and who eventually found relief in psychotherapy, Samir displayed signs of advanced tuberculosis for months without anyone noticing. And even when his tuberculosis was eventually discovered, his health insurance only covered basic emergency care, and his daily routine at the camp turned out to be incompatible with the antibiotics regimen ordered by his doctor.

Only a few months after I met him, Samir began coughing up blood. I urged him to go to the doctor, but he refused. I nudged him every week or so, each time in vain. Genuinely worried, I decided that Samir's bloody cough could not go untreated. The next time we were at a hospital for something else, I mentioned to the doctor that Samir had been coughing up blood for a while, occasionally had a fever, and had lost weight off his already thin body. The reaction was as I had hoped: the doctor ordered us to go to the emergency room immediately, and after Samir's TBC test came back positive, he was put in a quarantine room where he would stay for two weeks following surgery for lymph node removal. He had had painful walnut-sized bumps all along his neck for more than a year; they turned out be severely infected lymph nodes.

For the next two weeks, I visited Samir once every day. He was not allowed to leave his room, and I had to cover my body with plastic overalls, gloves, and a mask during visits. Each day, Samir insisted he could not stay any longer, and that he felt suffocated and lonely and was going to leave. One night, he sent me a selfie with a sky full of stars behind him and simply wrote, "I left." I called and tried to convince him to go back to the hospital. He finally burst into laughter and told me not to worry, that he had staged the starry-sky selfie by his hospital room window. Samir was initially angry at my having taken matters into my own hands and told doctors about his hemoptysis—through which, I know, I had violated his autonomy—but he later thanked me when doctors said it had been a matter of life or death.

When we returned to the hospital ten days after the surgery to have the stitches removed, as the surgeon had instructed, Samir was again reminded that his existence in Germany was legally liminal, hovering somewhere between in and out. When the nurse realized that Samir was an adult asylum seeker, she informed us that his insurance only covered medical emergencies. While his infected lymph nodes had been such an emergency, the removal of his stitches was not, and she told us to leave. Exasperated, I asked whether she expected me to pull the threads, but she just shrugged and said that we could return if the stitches became infected, because that would count as an emergency and again be covered by his insurance. We then returned to the doctor who had been unusually sympathetic to Samir's insomnia, and he, thankfully, pulled Samir's threads for free, while cursing the hospital nurse who had refused to do so.

While the lymph node surgery was successful, the actual TBC treatment required Samir to take eleven antibiotic pills daily, at specific times each day, for half a year. For the first few weeks, Samir tried to take the groups of pills I had sorted into individual boxes for him each day; but even then I could tell from the leftovers and his confusion about the times and amounts that he was not keeping up. His life was not conducive to taking pills at prescribed times. He often worked all night, slept a few hours here and a few hours there, and sometimes did not return to his camp room for days. He initially hid his failure to take the medicine properly from the responsible doctor, whom we saw every week for follow-up appointments. Eventually, however, the doctor realized Samir was not taking all his medication, because he had many pills left when he should have long run out of them, and could not correctly answer the doctor's questions about when he should be taking which pill. For a few months, every time we returned, the doctor threatened to call the public health department, explaining to Samir that tuberculosis was the only illness in Germany for which patients could not opt out of treatment, and for which they could even be confined to a prison hospital and force-fed their medication.[3] Samir eventually refused to go to the hospital, despite my begging, because he was afraid that the doctor would make good on his threat. When he entered youth welfare, however, Samir had to resume checkups, because staying on top of health issues is a prerequisite for being in youth welfare.

Paradoxically, though it is more difficult for young adult asylum seekers to access medical care, their particularly precarious legal situation at the same time often forces them to evaluate diagnoses for their potential as deportation impediments—to "sell their suffering," as Miriam Ticktin (2011, 45) has put it. When Farid, a young Afghan, was diagnosed with a facial tumor that pushed against his ear drum and threatened to make him deaf, his horror was mixed with hope that becoming deaf would allow him to stay in Germany. When he submitted his doctor's letter to BAMF, they indeed issued him a deportation impediment—although they retracted it a few months later, when his tumor was successfully removed and his hearing saved. Sometimes the assumption that asylum seekers would exaggerate medical conditions in the hope that it would help them remain in Germany led to the dismissal of real and serious afflictions. Mujtaba, for example, had repeatedly told his caseworkers that he was severely depressed and suicidal, but given that he had Dublin, they assumed he thought he had to play this role to evade deportation. When his Dublin period was over and he still appeared suicidal, they responded with a wink: "It's over. You don't have to say that anymore." Mujtaba, confused, repeated how he felt, and it dawned on his caseworkers that he was not acting. He was eventually admitted to a psychiatric ward, where he stayed for several weeks and his condition improved. Ironically, his roommate at the hospital was a former camp roommate, who indeed had asked to be hospitalized because he feared a Dublin deportation.

Vulnerability to Exploitation

Besides finding it more difficult to deal with illness, young adult asylum seekers, because of their liminal legality, are also more vulnerable to being exploited by supposed helpers, employers, and lawyers. Several times during my fieldwork years, the case of young male asylum seekers selling sex in the Tiergarten, Berlin's largest park, received some media attention. Volunteers also sometimes eyed each other suspiciously, trying to identify other volunteers who might use their position to get sexual access to unaccompanied minors. Young refugees, the volunteers feared, would be too ashamed to admit they had been approached sexually. Moreover, many were in such a precarious legal position that they might imprudently accept if a stranger offered them some money or a place to stay, realizing too late that such gifts came with the expectation of sexual favors. There had even been cases of social workers, not just strangers, starting sexual relations with asylum seekers. Even when the asylum seekers were over the age of eighteen, guardians and other social workers perceived such relationships as inappropriate because, they argued, the young men may not have dared reject the caseworkers, or may not have fully understood that the caseworkers were being paid to help and should not expect any further reward.

Young adult asylum seekers who are not allowed to be legally employed often seek out other sources of income, particularly during periods when state agencies stall their payments. Illicit work is usually underpaid or not paid at all, and exposes the worker to physical danger. Ali, for example, was working in a car wash when his boss told him he was fired and would not be paid. The boss counted on Ali having too precarious a legal status to dare go to the police. Ali then stole his boss's car keys, counting on him not to go to the police so as not to get in trouble for employing rejected asylum seekers without a work permit, an act penalized with a large fine. Indeed, the boss exchanged Ali's payment for his car keys, albeit while cursing. On weekends, Guled worked in the garden of a German man he had met at the camp. For a few euros and without safety precautions, he cut branches off tall trees and performed other dangerous work.

Samir sold drugs during most of the time I knew him. He would spend the night dealing by a subway station and in the morning join his colleagues in a park to celebrate the successful shift. I would occasionally join him for his work nights. When the police appeared, he would quickly put his arm around me so that, he said, the police would think he was someone hanging out with his girlfriend, not a dealer. When there was conflict with other dealers, he would always tell me to leave, and I would wait a block or two away until he motioned for me to come back. While he often talked about wanting to stop dealing because he was sick of running from the police and neglecting every other aspect of his life, the money he earned enabled him to live what in some ways he envisioned as a respectable life. Not only could he send his state welfare money to his family; he used the drug money to finally buy a monthly pass for public transport, instead of dodging the fare and running from ticket inspectors.

He also purchased a blender with which he mixed nourishing smoothies before work. He even offered to help me out financially—an offer I declined with amusement.

It is important to note that most of my interlocutors had no involvement with drugs whatsoever, despite having similar opportunities. Paul had many friends who dealt, and was himself occasionally mistaken for a dealer by customers, other dealers, and the police, simply by association. But to my knowledge, he never got involved, despite always complaining about having considerably less money than his friends. That Paul only spent a few months at a camp, and then lived in youth welfare with caseworkers keeping a close watch on him, surely played a big part in this. When Samir entered youth welfare, one of the first things his caseworker did was sign him up for weekly mandatory drug counseling. He initially went with great enthusiasm. I joined him most weeks; sometimes he wanted me to be present during the session, and at other times he asked me to wait outside. He liked the sympathetic approach of the counselor who told him that his goal should be not to stop taking drugs altogether, but to learn why he was consuming and to gain control over when and with what intention he did. For a while, Samir tried to meet the goals he and the counselor had set together: consuming drugs only after 6 p.m. and never alone, for example. When Samir left youth welfare, however, he also stopped going to drug counseling.

Besides being exploited by alleged helpers and employers, young asylum seekers were also frequently exploited by their lawyers. Asylum seekers can write their appeals themselves, usually with the help of caseworkers or volunteers, or they can hire lawyers to do so. Those who decide to hire lawyers often find that the lawyer does little, for a sum that will keep them in debt for years. Appealing the rejection of an asylum application with the help of a lawyer usually costs 975 euros, 200 of which are often paid upfront and the rest in installments of 30 euros a month, amounting to more than two years of payments. Some lawyers even keep the legal aid money they receive from the state. One such lawyer wrote privately to a colleague, who then showed me a screenshot of the remark, "The Afghans wouldn't notice anyway."

Ali's lawyer did nothing, not even requesting access to Ali's BAMF records, despite collecting payments every month. He also failed to respond to emails or answer the phone. He had come recommended by Ali's friend, and Ali suspected that asylum seekers lied about how competent their lawyers were, just as they lied about their legal status, because they did not want to seem pitiful. Ali and I decided to go to the lawyer's office and talk to him in person. The sign on his door read "Tax Law and Tenancy Law." I assumed he had to be one of the countless professionals who had moved their focus to asylum when it promised to become an inexhaustible trove of clients and state support. Although we were "on time like the Swiss," as Ali said with an annoyed grin, an assistant ordered us to wait in the foyer, where for the next hour I inspected with incredulity the ramshackle condition of the room: gray faded carpet with stains and burn holes, plants in soil blanketed with mildew, wallpaper rolling up from the bottom of the wall until it eventually hung from the ceiling like curtains.

When the lawyer finally called us in, he turned out to be a middle-aged man in his stocking feet. He never once looked Ali or me in the eye. He had not read Ali's file, and knew nothing about his case. When Ali announced that he would only continue his monthly payments once the lawyer had at least requested access to his BAMF files, the lawyer said he did not need Ali's files, that it was Ali's job to explain his situation to him. When Ali objected that it was emotionally difficult for him to recount his personal story, and that the files could explain his legal journey much better than he could, the lawyer started a tirade as though Ali and I were naughty children who needed to be put in our place: "He thinks he's all that, and is too lazy to explain his situation. It's not my job to read; it's your job to tell! You have to know your life, not me! I've never been to Afghanistan!"

Adulthood, Liminal Identities, and Liminal Legality

Cawo Abdi (2015) notes that anthropologists focus on issues of identity and belonging, while sociologists focus on settlement and integration; both should be brought together, however, as the two are intrinsically connected. Bureaucratic categories and legal status profoundly shape young asylum seekers' opportunities for belonging, and in turn the desire to belong frames their pursuit of categories and status. Irrespective of the actual motivation for moving or of the outcome of an asylum case, being an asylum seeker or an unaccompanied minor reifies a migrant's status in their own mind and in the eyes of society—even if it cannot erase the discrepancy between their bureaucratic label and their actual experience. The context of a migrant's reception in a new country is, moreover, often ambivalent, precisely because the migrant occupies multiple categories: for instance, the condition of being both a minor with the right to protection *and* a rejected asylum seeker with the obligation to leave Europe. Such ambivalence is central to their experience of migration.

Young asylum seekers live in a state of liminal legality, or betweenness: between the jurisprudence of one country and that of another, between inclusion and expulsion, and between minority and adulthood. Liminal legal statuses intended to be temporary are renewed so often that one might almost call them permanent—though of course they lack any of the stability implied by permanent residence. There are also clear and observable connections between being an adult, living in liminal legality, and dealing with other forms of precariousness. This includes the peculiar circumstance of having been classified as a minor *and* an adult—and thus being neither. Many young adults "have Dublin." The resulting constant ID renewals at the Foreigner Registration Office make it impossible to master school, an apprenticeship, or a job, as teachers and employers have little patience for frequent absences. GÜBs and other precarious IDs such as the *Duldung light* prevent a person from working, doing an apprenticeship, or signing long-term contracts, such as rental contracts. The new Law of Orderly Return punishes people without a settled identity—"those persistently refusing to have an identity," as the German legal definition goes.

Some try to pass their Dublin periods under the tenuous protection of church asylum, while others count on the fact that deportations should not occur from youth welfare, even for young adults—though, as Yakob's case shows, they sometimes do. Without youth welfare, one has no help in navigating Dublin or the appeals process, and even seemingly trivial things, like forgetting to report an address change to BAMF, can have disastrous consequences. The legal liminality in which all asylum seekers live is thus even greater for adults, because certain laws that produce precariousness, such as the Dublin III agreement, apply only to adults, and others that provide stability apply only to minors. For Idris and Paul, for example, the rejection of their asylum application did not matter as much, because they were embedded in extensive support and compensatory structures on account of officially being minors. For Ali, on the other hand, rejection had severe consequences, largely because he lacked the social support and legal alternatives that minors—and even former minors—have. Finally, legal adulthood impedes one's ability to address illness and trauma and to avoid exploitation. In the next chapter I will discuss the necessity to prepare mentally and practically for two different futures—being able to stay in Germany, and having to leave—which stems from an asylum seeker's liminal legality.

6 * *Imagining the Future*

At any given moment, humans hold multiple temporal orientations: they move "beyond themselves" (Emirbayer and Mische 1998, 984) into the future, drawing on identifications with the past and experimentations in the present. Youth and migration are particularly intense periods of future projection, of unsettled identifications with the past and of cautious or bold but always high-stakes experimentations in the present. They are times in which the life to come seems to be uniquely brimming with distinct possibilities, and one's "rays of attention" wander excitedly across a horizon of "overripe fruit" ready to be plucked (Schutz 1967, 67–68). Negotiated ages, however, inhibit young migrants' ability to project themselves into the future because the negotiation of one's age makes time itself an object of contention.[1] For instance, before Paul's appointment with the family court, where he hoped to reestablish his minority age after two conflicting age exams, he suggested with a smile that we spend one last weekend as adults: order a drink, go to a club. I told him the story of *Through the Looking-Glass*. In Lewis Carroll's novel, time passes backward, and Alice observes with astonishment the White Queen complaining of pain before pricking her finger, and remembering what would happen in two weeks.

Paradoxically, it also often seemed that people who claimed to be younger than their real ages actually ended up being declared older than their real ages. Those who claimed to be eighteen were usually believed, while those who claimed to be under eighteen were often given age exams and deemed several years older than eighteen. With what seemed uncanny timing, state offices often accepted someone's minority age just when their self-stated date of birth would no longer officially make them a minor, and had therefore lost its importance.

How can young migrants imagine and plan the future when not even the elapsing of time is predictable? When we think about human experience, we need to consider its temporal nature and what enables, impedes, and generally shapes people's ability to meaningfully engage past and future in the present. In this chapter I examine how young asylum seekers imagine the future in the face of great uncertainty, which stems from liminal ages and precarious legal status and is compounded by the uncertainty that simply comes with migration and adolescence, a stage of life that tries to differentiate itself from both childhood and adulthood. The asylum seekers' view of the future oscillates between defiant optimism and despondent pessimism, between hope and resignation. They try desperately to understand their complex legal situation, then resign themselves to the fact that their asylum applications will be rejected regardless. They feed their families stories about how well their lives in Europe are going, then break off contact to evade their questions and requests for help. They make fun of the German state and its rules, then turn the joke on themselves, mocking their own impotence toward it. They put great effort into settling down, then threaten to leave Germany forever. They greatly desire security, then reject the coveted apartment or residence title because they feel the price is too high. I will examine these aspects of alternating hope and resignation and how they relate to young migrants' imaginings of the future.

Understanding One's Situation and Playing to Lose

The German asylum system is complicated. Even professionals and experienced volunteers often disagree about laws. Not only are the laws complex, but contradictory laws exist at different levels of government. Some are merely recommendations, some are almost never enforced, and in the end, much depends on the discretion of individual bureaucrats. This means that asylum seekers ostensibly in the same situation often see different outcomes, which makes it hard for them to understand their own situations in comparison to those of others. Hence, they come up with extralegal explanations to make sense of an environment that seems erratic: chance, divine destiny, and their own moral character and conduct.

Ali, for instance, referred to what social scientists call the discretion of street-level bureaucrats as "chance." He explained to me why one's treatment at the Foreigner Registration Office differed from day to day and from employee to employee: "They could be happy or sad. Be hungry. Or their wife left them. Or they got fucked up at a party the night before. And all that goes into my paper." An occurrence a few months later seemed to prove his point. Ali and Guled had appointments on the same day for the very same issue. Both had their asylum applications rejected, and they should each have received a *Duldung*. While the employee who happened to attend to Guled's waiting number correctly issued him a *Duldung* with all the attendant restrictions on residence and employment, the employee responsible for Ali's waiting number mistakenly issued an *Aufenthaltsgestattung*, the slightly less restrictive ID one keeps and uses *during* the asylum procedure.

Most of my interlocutors were religious and believed in divine destiny. They held that everything was already written and that their current situation was a result of God's mysterious plan. Especially in scary situations, the belief that everything was foreordained seemed to help them persevere.[2] Guled, for example, insisted throughout his Dublin period that he was not afraid of a deportation, because if he was to be deported, it had already been decided by God and there was nothing he could do. I found it difficult to reconcile this ostensibly passive outlook on life with asylum seekers' determination and mobility. How did leaving your home on your own as a very young person, taking the dangerous journey to another continent, and literally constructing a new identity for yourself fit with the idea that "the pens have been lifted and the pages are dry," as a famous hadith, or Islamic tradition, states? Idris explained it this way: God had written the hardships he had experienced in Ethiopia, but taking those hardships as reasons for leaving had been Idris's own decision. God grants everyone livelihood (*rizq* in Arabic), but it is the task of humans to find where their livelihood lies, like the migratory birds who will survive as long as they fly to the place where God has provided for them.[3] And to lie about his age was Idris's fault, too. The rejection of his asylum application was now a test from God.

Third, asylum seekers explained their situation in light of individual character and conduct. When Paul's friend Bouba received a *Duldung* with a red line through it—meaning he could not leave the city limits of Berlin — Paul assumed it had to be because of Bouba's belligerence. When Yakob was deported to Italy, Idris said incredulously: "But he didn't do anything. He never got in trouble with the police or anything like that." Of course, neither Bouba's limited mobility nor Yakob's deportation was due to their public conduct. Similarly, Guled regularly told me about friends who had supposedly received asylum when they offered to do their interviews over in German and the interviewer was impressed by their language abilities. And when someone had received a good ID, Idris referred to the Foreigner Registration Office as having "forgiven" that person.

When I first began my research, I assumed that the days when my interlocutors' asylum applications were rejected would be among the most dramatic during my time in the field. I could not have been more wrong. Despite the enormous amount of energy they put into "getting papers," by the time their asylum applications were rejected—usually years after the initial interviews—they had come to expect rejection. Paul, for example, did not know anyone whose asylum case had been decided positively.

By the time of his interview, he had realized that "Guineans are always rejected anyway," and no longer even cared about telling a compelling story. When his asylum application was rejected on the same day as his application to a professional soccer team, he was much more upset about the latter. And more than three years later, he decided not to even attend the court hearing on his appeal, because he was certain he would lose and had a soccer match the same day, which he deemed more winnable.

Despite wanting to understand their own legal situations and contriving explanations for seemingly inexplicable status, nearly all asylum seekers from countries with low protection rates eventually understand one thing: they are playing to lose, and their only possible triumph is to lose as slowly as possible. Even as counselors advised asylum seekers how to prepare for interviews, they would tell them that their applications would almost certainly be rejected. I often wondered why young asylum seekers were urged to tell the truth, to practice telling it, and to prioritize the preparation of their asylum interviews above school commitments, when at the same time they were being mentally prepared for rejection and urged to find alternative paths to residence, particularly apprenticeships for which continuous school attendance would have been the best preparation? In other words, why do you play a game you will lose? Why do others encourage you to play a game they think you will lose? In chapter 4 I described helpers' "emperor's new clothes" approach to asylum seekers' identities, which creates a fragile reality through collective pretense. Similarly, the asylum system is a game young migrants are encouraged to enter and move through both for the sake of the game itself and to attain the social category of "refugee," if not the legal one. In addition, in the wake of the 2015–16 refugee crisis, vast state and nonstate infrastructures were built around asylum seeking, with counselors telling virtually every migrant who happened upon their services to apply for asylum.[4] Seeking asylum also confirms in one's own eyes and in the eyes of others that one has had no choice but to leave one's home country. It gives one years in which one cannot be deported, and time to pave other legal pathways to residence. Even playing to lose thus lays important groundwork for a better future. It legitimizes migration, embeds the migrant in helpful infrastructures, and buys time. Playing is not a path to victory, but a time to prepare oneself for losing.

Appeasing Parents' Worries and Avoiding Contact

The UNHCR defines "unaccompanied" minors as those who have entered a country without their parents or legal guardians (UNHCR 1997). Because of widespread information and communication technologies (ICT), however, families often figure prominently in the lives of their unaccompanied asylum-seeking children. On the one hand, being in close contact with family and friends can be a source of joy. For example, when Samir talked to his mother on the phone, he would afterward text me proudly about exactly how many hours and minutes the call had lasted, and adorn his message with a blast of heart emojis. During Ramadan one year, as Idris, Guled, and I were preparing food for *iftar*, the evening meal after a day of fasting, Idris abruptly put down the wooden spoon and picked up his phone. He opened a WhatsApp chat with his best childhood friend Heydar, started recording a voice message, and sang the popular Ramadan song "Ahlan wa sahlan ya Ramadan" (Welcome, oh month of Ramadan). He then eyed the chat window until he saw two blue checkmarks and smiled, knowing that Heydar was now listening in Ethiopia.

On the other hand, being in frequent contact with family and friends back home and having access to news and social networks from one's origin country also means being confronted with disturbing political developments there. When Guled learned about bombings in Somalia, Paul about the government brutally striking down street protests in Guinea, Idris about interethnic violence in Ethiopia, and Ali about the Taliban's return to power, they were devastated by these events but also knew that they could bolster their asylum case. The worse things got in their home countries, to put it bluntly, the less likely Germany was to deport them. When Idris and I attended a party at the Ethiopian embassy to celebrate the awarding of the Nobel Peace Prize to the Ethiopian president, Abiy Ahmed, Idris felt both proud of his country and worried that its new peaceful image would shatter any hope for Ethiopians to receive asylum.[5]

Besides news of political crises, asylum seekers are confronted with emotionally burdensome calls for help. Just as Idris, Samir, and Paul once did, their peers back home imagine Europe as a prosperous paradise. A girl whom Idris had grown up with, and who had had a crush on him, sometimes wrote to him. She was by now married with two children, but in her sentimental messages to Idris she imagined how different her life would have been had he reciprocated her feelings and taken her with him to Europe. Only once you are in Europe, Idris said, do you understand that those living here cannot help people elsewhere with their residence papers—and that, in fact, they usually do not even have papers themselves.

Ali's mother, similarly, had fled from Afghanistan to Iran and was waiting there for her son to bring her to Europe via family reunification. Every time she talked to Ali, she asked him when he would finally finish all the paperwork for her to come. He did not dare tell her that his asylum application had been rejected, and that he would not be able to bring her over. He eventually felt so guilty about lying that he stopped calling her altogether: an avoidance of contact not uncommon among migrants who feel they have disappointed their families' expectations (Belloni 2020).

Some young men also dreaded calling their relatives because they knew the relatives would ask for money.[6] Paul said he hated talking to anyone from Guinea, since they only talked about how badly they were doing, in the hopes of guilt-tripping Paul. They did not understand that he was in youth welfare with barely enough money for himself. Idris also frequently received messages and calls from Ethiopians he barely knew who told him stories about their desperate situations, which only money could solve. One young man told him his wife was pregnant but was too sick to give birth and desperately needed money for an abortion. He kept repeating this story until Idris eventually yelled that by now it must surely be too late for an abortion. Some sent pictures of their emaciated children—uncannily similar to the images of Ethiopian children shown to Westerners in the 1980s. One time, unnerved, Idris simply responded with a screenshot of his bank account statement which showed him to have all of twenty euros.

Some did send money home. As Filomeno V. Aguilar has pointed out, remittances by migrants who have themselves made the decision to migrate "actually may represent a mechanism for acquiring legitimacy"—in the migrants' own eyes and those of their families—"for the journey which, in the first place, was undertaken without parental or familial consent" (1999, 103). Remittances may not so much be an assertion of belonging to former social structures as an assertion that one is finally separate and independent—an adult, a man. Samir, who kept his savings at my apartment for fear of spending them all or being robbed of them at his camp, asked me to store his money in two separate envelopes. One he labeled *haram*—money he had earned illicitly and was careful to spend only on himself, the sole person for whom such money was good enough. The other he labeled *halal*—the money he received from the German state. When he needed money, he would tell me, "I need twenty *haram*," as if *haram* were a currency. As soon as the *halal* envelope had grown to 150 euros, we took the money to a Sudanese restaurant whose owner regularly traveled to Sudan to distribute remittances—an informal money transfer system known in Arabic as *hawala*. Although he kept 10 percent, this was an attractive offer for families like Samir's, who, without IDs, could not use Western Union or MoneyGram.

Besides expecting help or remittances, friends and family at home also simply ask how life in Europe is going, which often puts young asylum seekers in a position where they feel they must portray their life in a certain way so as not to displease, disappoint, or worry their loved ones. Paul avoided telling his parents anything that could cause them pain or worry. Upon arriving in Italy, he had told them of a leg injury he had sustained crossing the ocean. His older brother later scolded him for having made his parents cry, and commanded him never to upset them with "sad stories from Europe" again. Paul heeded the command. Even when he became a father, he did not tell his own father, who, according to Paul, had "no tolerance for children out of wedlock." The reactions and judgments of those left behind have an important impact on the psychosocial well-being of migrants (Wiesinger 2018, 431).

Whenever Samir was on a video call with his parents, he wore a baseball hat so as to hide his un-Islamic hairstyle from them. He often made these calls from my apartment, so that he could use my wi-fi. One time, he realized he had forgotten to cover his head; and as the phone rang, he hastily stuffed his dreads under a straw hat I had lying around. He would tell his family he was doing well, going to school, learning German, and would soon start an apprenticeship as a car mechanic. He did not tell his family that he had not attended school in months, had given up prayer, and was dealing drugs so that he could send his state welfare money to them. "If my parents knew what I was doing here, they would say, 'Fuck the money, fuck Europe, fuck everything. You're coming back to Africa.'" Like Ali, Samir eventually began to avoid calling his parents, because every phone call made him feel guilty for lying, and caused him to mourn the discrepancy between the life he was inventing and the one he was leading.

While being unaccompanied in a new cultural environment can be a tremendous opportunity for personal freedom, reflection, and growth, many young asylum seekers instead feel guilty for not living up to their parents' expectations. Thus they invent stories about life in Europe that bear little resemblance to the precarious existence they really lead. Digital information and communication technologies, then, are a mixed blessing for young migrants: while they allow a continued connection to one's homeland, such a connection also carries disturbing news and unrealizable appeals for help and money, and may even become a magnifying mirror for one's own failings and disappointments in Europe. By inventing tales of success, young asylum seekers are bucking the odds—teetering between a future in which they might at last live up to their families' expectations, and one in which they will have to break their family ties so as not to be exposed as failures and frauds.

Mocking Germany and Mocking Oneself

Just like success stories told to parents prematurely, jokes too can reveal the contradictions and vulnerabilities of lives caught in limbo. Asylum seekers often make fun of Germany and its rules and norms. Their jokes mock the state while at the same time mocking their own failures—the ultimate laughingstock is not always clear. Some jokes I heard concerned the absurdity of negotiated dates of birth. Asylum seekers quipped that they could celebrate their birthdays together, since so many had been given January 1 as their birthdate. Others, who had been given their age exams in groups and had received the date of the exam as a common birthday even if their new birth years differed, would later joke that "those who are examined together, party together," since they would be able to celebrate their future birthdays together. When I first met Samir, whenever anyone asked how old he was, he would say, "Ask my lawyer!"—to which Franka once replied, "She was hardly your midwife." And whenever Idris said he didn't know what he wanted to do with his life, I would say, "It's OK. When I was eighteen, I didn't know either." And we both laughed.

Some made light of their legal status. Ali liked to joke that he enjoyed getting ticketed for dodging the public transportation fare, because it was the only time Germany readily issued him documents. When Afghans who were supposed to be returned to Sweden went to the IKEA store, they wondered aloud whether they would be allowed to leave it. I once went to the Foreigner Registration Office with Guled and a young Afghan named Omar. I kept going back and forth between their different waiting rooms, hoping they would not both be called at the same time, so I could join each of them during their appointments. Guled was up first, and when we were finished with his appointment, we received a text from Omar: "I have to go to Sweden. Thank you for everything." We ran downstairs and found Omar outside, having a smoke and laughing. "I'm just kidding," he said. "Everything went fine."

Idris regularly called me to have some version of the following conversation.

Idris: "The court sent a letter. They're giving me papers."

Me (playing along): "Cool! Without a hearing, yeah?"

"Yup."

"Amazing. Have you already picked up your new ID?"

"No, I thought we could do that together next week. I thought it could be interesting for your book."

"Hey, yes, thanks, I really appreciate that."

When Yakob and Idris were both hospitalized for tuberculosis and I visited them at the hospital, we invented "vampire" stories in which they would infect the people who needed deportation impediments. "Guled first," Idris said. "And then I'll set up shop in front of BBZ [asylum counseling] and smooch anyone who has Dublin."

In one instance when Idris was talking to a childhood friend on the phone, the friend asked when he would finally come visit Ethiopia. I was present during the call, and I asked Idris afterward what he had replied, since I do not understand Amharic.

Idris replied, "I said, 'Brother, I'm in prison here. Paradise-prison. It's beautiful beyond words, but one cannot leave.'"

"Really, that's what you said?" I asked skeptically.

"No," Idris laughed. "I just said, '*Inshallah* we'll see each other soon.'"

The prison theme appeared often. Yakob told me one day that it was the two-year anniversary of his arrival in Germany. I asked if he had celebrated, and he replied, "Here in prison, we celebrate with bread and water."

Some asylum seekers used humor to diffuse their feelings about the racism and discrimination they perceived. The nursing home where Idris interned had one Black resident. When he told Yakob about this man, Yakob joked, "Maybe he got rejected." When I had my German passport renewed, Idris quipped: "You got ten years. Congratulations!" Another time, Idris accompanied me to a public round-table discussion among academic and activist experts on the digital surveillance of refugees. The room was filled with German refugee rights activists, and Idris was the only audience member from the population the discussants were talking about. "I think refugees are not welcome here," he whispered to me with a giggle.

Some jokes targeted the offices and agencies whose rulings over their lives asylum seekers perceived as nonsensical and capricious. The surest way to get a single room at the camp, it was rumored, was mental illness. Samir imagined asking for a single room with the argument that he was "crazy" and could not be trusted around another person:

"You crazy, yes?"

"I'm crazy, *W'Allah*."

Parodying the asylum counselor's instruction to show emotion when recounting his story, he began sobbing when I asked for his name during our practice interview. When I joined Idris for an appointment at BAMF, we noticed the many babies in the waiting room, and Idris imagined how BAMF would interrogate them: "Why are you here? Why can't you go back to where you came from [i.e., your mother's womb]?"

In some jokes, asylum seekers fantasized about ways out of their situation. One day, Samir sent me a selfie from a room that was not his. I asked where he was, and he said France. I was in New York at the time for a conference, and I said I wished he had said goodbye. "I know, I'm really sorry," he replied. A few hours later he texted me again: "Hey, you know I'm kidding, right? I'd never leave *habibi* Berlin."

One evening, as we did so often in the warmer months, Samir and I were sitting by the river near Oberbaumbrücke, where former industrial buildings had been converted into lofts, and empty space had been filled with townhouses. Samir pointed to the upscale apartment buildings across the water and said, "I'm moving in there next week."

"Yeah, I know," I said. "What floor was it again? Second or third?"

"Second."

"That's right." I nodded, looking at the terrace from which he would be able to see people like us sitting by the water.

Another time, as we were walking down the street, Samir pointed at a few windows of an apartment building and said, "That's my place." Then he added, "Just kidding. I have nothing, just a bike." He hit the saddle of a parked bike we walked past. Then he said, in a serious tone, "I don't even have a bike. I have nothing."

Jokes allow asylum seekers to regain at least some oratorical control of their precarious situation, but the state whose order they mock usually has the last laugh. A "paradise-prison" where even an IKEA store or nursing home might be repurposed for confinement, and where asylum seekers must justify leaving their mother's womb, is undoubtedly a ludicrous place, but it entraps young migrants nonetheless. A world where one must be demonstrably crazy to have some privacy and where a tuberculosis infection is a blessing to be generously shared with friends is indeed "crazy," but power is not weakened by nonsense. As asylum seekers mock the German state and its ways, then, they become the targets of their own jokes. What at first seems derision of bureaucratic lunacy often turns out to be missing a punchline—another testament to the indeterminateness and inconsistency of liminal lives.

Settling Down and Threatening to Leave

Another instance where hope and resignation express themselves together is in the question of whether to try to make a home in Germany, despite not knowing that one will be allowed to remain, or whether to give up and leave, to preempt a possible deportation. Early in my fieldwork, a social worker mused that while others with personal or family histories of migration, such as the children and grandchildren of former guest workers, were often neither here in Germany nor back in their families' countries of origin, these newly arrived asylum seekers could be fully here in Germany, for several reasons. They had wanted to leave their countries, which lacked large diasporas in Germany, and now they could not travel freely between those countries and Germany. They were also young, and thus adaptable. While these factors may indeed encourage full presence in Germany, the young asylum seekers I knew often seemed stuck in a "chronified transitional period" due to their uncertain legal status, which solidified their "inability to arrive as a way of life" (Wiesinger 2018, 433).

Because they do not know if they will be able to stay in Germany—an uncertainty captured by the German word *Bleibeperspektive*, or long-term prospect of remaining—asylum seekers constantly ask themselves whether plans will become disappointments, and efforts wasted energy. They make connections to German helpers, build friendships, and even form romantic relationships—but they are also prepared to leave everything behind. This is why I overcredulously believed that Samir had gone to France without saying goodbye. I thought we were close, and would have expected a farewell, yet at the same time I knew that sudden departures were common among his peers. Samir repeatedly told me that the scenario he most feared was that of staying in Germany for several more years and then being told to leave—after having learned German, formed relationships, and made the sacrifice of not seeing his family in order to get a residence permit to eventually visit them. He often wondered whether it would be better to just try his luck in Great Britain before wasting any more time in a country that might eventually send him away.

Patience and the ability to cope with indefinite periods of "stucked-ness" (Hage 2009) are an essential survival strategy for migrants (Brigden and Mainwaring 2016). They have to navigate the contradiction between an exclusionary national context and an inclusionary local one. That is, they have to reconcile the prospect of rejection and deportation with the support of social workers and volunteers who encourage them to settle down, learn German, go to school, and get wi-fi contracts and gym memberships. This "mixed message" (Wiesinger 2018) or "ambivalent receiving context" (Galli 2020) leads to rejected asylum seekers deeming it necessary to "ambivalently orient themselves to multiple futures at once" (Tavory and Eliasoph 2013, 909): one in Germany and one elsewhere. I will discuss each of these futures in turn.

Young asylum seekers put a lot of energy into settling down by finding apartments of their own. Living in one of Berlin's refugee camps, even for years, has always had an air of temporariness about it. Guled lived in a container village erected on the edge of Tempelhofer Feld, formerly West Berlin's airport and now a large, open green field Berliners use as a park. In 2016, several hundred white construction site trailers were assembled side by side in rows, to accommodate asylum seekers. Each set of three containers housed four people: the middle trailer contained the shared kitchen and bathroom, and the trailers on either side of it were bedrooms for two people each. I spent many afternoons and evenings in Guled's container. Looking out the window onto Tempelhofer Feld, where Berliners and tourists flew kites and held barbecues with the wind and weather unusually near, always felt like camping to me. Although the view from the window seemed romantic, a glance inside the container revealed true precariousness. Guled's suitcase was always visible on top of the locker, and for months his former roommate's belongings had sat in a corner, stuffed into two giant blue trash bags. The camp employees said they had to keep the bags there in case their owner came to pick them up—a mere formality, since he had been deported to Sweden. Most things that would have made the container feel homey were forbidden; even prayer rugs were banned for "hygienic reasons." Despite the heat, fans were not allowed in the summer because they used too much energy.

When Samir finally moved into a youth welfare apartment after years of living in such camps, furnishing and decorating his room was of the utmost importance to him. The day after he moved in, he gathered most of the cleaning supplies in my kitchen, and we went to his new place. For hours, we cleaned every bit of the room, which was empty except for a bed, a small chest, and a glass table, which Samir broke while jumping up and down on it with a broom, trying to get rid of dust he claimed to see on the ceiling. Meticulously, Samir cleaned the windows, window frames and sills, and every crease of the heater. We vacuumed and dusted the walls, and Samir only agreed to stop once he was sure he could start his new life on clean surfaces. We sat on the bed, and Samir fantasized about the furniture he would buy with his first youth welfare payment: a white leather couch and a large TV. His caseworker, Nelly, later told me with amusement that she used to give every teenager a plant as a move-in gift, but that after a month or two she would always find the plant withered in the corner. She concluded that teenagers did not care for houseplants, and stopped this move-in tradition. To her surprise, soon after moving in, Samir asked when the furniture money from the youth welfare office would finally come, because he wanted to buy a plant. He was serious about making his first room a home.

When we looked for used furniture on eBay, Samir insisted that he needed something sturdy, something that would last years. He was also fixed on the idea of making his walls look like red brick. A caseworker purchased wallpaper with a printed brick pattern, along with a water sprayer and scrapers to remove the old wallpaper, and paste and brushes to put up the new wallpaper. Throughout Samir's ten months in youth welfare, we worked on this wall little by little. We would remove a few square meters of the old wallpaper, or take measurements and put up one length of wallpaper at a time, transforming his wall first into a raw building surface and then into a construction site with ever more brick wallpaper on the walls. Sometimes his friends came over and joined us in the work. Once, a friend who was going to try to move to Great Britain the next day helped. Leaving and staying, detaching oneself and settling down, always occurred side by side. Progress on the brick wall came to reflect Samir's emotional state. During times when he insisted he was practically on his way to Belgium or France or England, we made no progress at all, the half-finished brick wall a reminder of the home he was unable to make. When he was more optimistic about his future in Germany, the brick wall unfurled steadily, every strip bringing him closer to the protective long-term home he envisioned.

Outside youth welfare, it is extremely difficult for young asylum seekers to find apartments. Berlin's ever-tightening housing market has made finding an apartment difficult for anyone. And for someone whose ID is never valid for more than another few months (in any case, less than a typical one- or two-year lease); who lacks the linguistic, social, and cultural capital required on the housing market; who can only pay the amount of rent covered by the State Office for Refugees (LAF); and who may also face discrimination, it is nearly impossible. Not only does youth welfare provide housing, but caseworkers are supposed to help someone find a regular apartment when youth welfare ends, so that housing is another example in which the positive effects of minority last well into adulthood.

Guled searched unsuccessfully for an apartment for much of the time I knew him. He had no demands besides the price limit set by LAF. Living in any apartment—however run-down, small, or inconveniently located—was more appealing than living in the camp. We sent out hundreds of inquiries and applications, but usually did not even get a reply. Guled's WBS application was rejected with the explanation that a WBS—*Wohnberechtigungsschein*, the certificate needed to rent a state-subsidized apartment—was not for people who were "only in Germany temporarily." To qualify, one needed a residence permit valid for at least a year; paradoxically, one's arrival was impeded if one could not prove that one would stay. Desperate, Guled several times almost fell for fraudulent schemes in which alleged landlords advertised affordable apartments online and insisted on receiving a deposit before the prospective resident had seen the apartment. I was able to talk Guled out of this on multiple occasions, but always felt guilty for crushing what little hope he had in ever leaving the camp.

Ali was the only one I knew who successfully found an apartment on his own, and he did so by altogether foregoing the official path of applying for apartments. Not being allowed to seek legal employment, he had worked clandestinely for a year, saving enough money to pay the 1,500 euros an Iranian landlord demanded from each of the two roommates for a small two-room apartment at the Western outskirts of Berlin. In turn, this man refrained from looking at their residence papers or asking for a formal application. The rent was then paid by LAF. The apartment was tiny and sparsely furnished, but it was not a camp, and that was the most important thing. I often visited Ali and, together with his roommate, Doctor—whose nickname was the only remaining token of his former career—we would sit on a large rug in the kitchen, eat the Afghan vegan food they had cooked for me, watch Bollywood movies or the television show *Afghan Star*, smoke shisha, and in summer turn on a fan—in other words, all the things that had not been allowed at the camp. The camp had never felt like a home, Ali said, but this apartment did.

Despite putting so much energy into settling down, many asylum seekers also found the possibility of leaving Germany voluntarily to be a source of comfort. I was always told stories, which were factually false, about how easy and bright life in other European countries supposedly was. Idris told me that his friends in England had been given asylum within a week of their application and were allowed to attend university without showing high school diplomas or paying tuition. I also heard rumors that Canada gave every asylum seeker a passport with which he could travel, and even that England picked up asylum seekers from France so that they would not have to risk their lives crossing the English Channel. Idris and his childhood friend Kadir, who lived in southern Germany, had agreed that if their asylum applications were rejected, they would go to England together. But when both received rejections, they stayed. "My heart is here," Idris said.

A few times, however, Idris seemed to be more serious about leaving. He called me one day, asked me some questions about England, and said he was packing immediately and leaving on the weekend. I asked why, if he was leaving, he had just started an internship, and if he still wanted me to join him at the Foreigner Registration Office the next day to renew his ID. Seemingly irritated, he asked why I would ask him those questions. I later realized I was meant to play along with his plan to go to England without calling him out on the fact that his actions revealed it to be just talk. Another day, Idris texted me to say he was at Berlin Central Station and was leaving Germany. I quickly rode my bike there and saw him waiting on the platform holding a coffee to go and a paper bag containing two croissants, and with a medium-sized, crammed-full backpack on his back. I asked where he was going, and he said he didn't know or care—just away from Germany. He got onto the next train, toward Frankfurt, but must have gotten off at another stop in Berlin, because that same evening he texted me to say casually that he was at home watching television.

He offered no explanation for why he had exited the train or for why he had boarded it in the first place, and I did not ask for one. A few days later, he just remarked, "I went crazy there for a second; just don't tell anyone." And we left it at that.

Although Michael was the only one of my interlocutors who actually left Germany during my research, nearly everyone else talked about leaving. Every year, thousands of unaccompanied minor asylum seekers simply disappear from Germany. Most probably go to other European countries, never having fully "arrived" in the first one.[7] Samir always said he would like to go to Great Britain, where friends of his had already gone. Since he announced his plans so frequently, I stopped taking the announcements seriously. I concluded that announcing that one was going to leave was simply part of staying put in Germany.

Three times, however, I thought Samir actually would leave. The first time, he told me we should say goodbye since he was leaving for England via France in the morning. I did not believe him, but he showed me on his phone that he had already planned a route. He asked me to go through his documents with him and help him decide which he should take. He said he feared that he would be kicked out of the youth welfare apartment and be forced to live in a camp and start dealing again. He also feared that his appeal to his rejected asylum application would itself be rejected, and that he would have waited all these years in Germany for nothing. I told him that after four years in Germany, he would soon be able to apply for a residence permit under section 25a of German residence law. "What if not?" he asked skeptically. "What if the laws change?" I pleaded with him that I had heard again and again of asylum seekers dying on their way to England—suffocating in the trucks they hid in, or getting run over by vehicles. "Yeah," he admitted, "but of a hundred people, maybe two die, and that's a good enough chance for me."[8]

The second time, Samir called me late in the evening and asked if I could come to his apartment. I said I was about to go to sleep and would go there the next day. He said he would be leaving for Belgium the next day and wanted to say goodbye and give me some of his things. I was skeptical, but when he began swearing by everything I knew he cared about, I got dressed and headed over. When I got there, Samir and a friend were sitting in the living room, the coffee table littered with cigarette filters, rolling papers, crumbs of tobacco and cannabis, and empty cans of alcoholic mixed drinks. Samir was crushing ecstasy pills on the IKEA catalog his caseworker had given him for inspiration in furnishing his still largely unfurnished room. We spent the evening reminiscing about Samir's three years in Berlin and discussing his plan of going to England. He said he wanted to start over, that in Germany he had messed everything up: he had skipped school, received a rejection, become addicted. England was going to be a fresh start. And while he would miss Berlin, he could always visit once he had residence papers from England. "Berlin will always be my true love," he said, "but she didn't want me and so I have to find a new love." Before I left, Samir handed me a small plastic bag containing his most precious possessions, and said he would give my phone number to his family for safekeeping in case he lost his phone. He also asked if I would accompany him to the German-Belgian border, and I said yes. But we never went. When I later returned the bag with his possessions to him, he took it back casually, like an irrelevant loan, and neither of us mentioned the failed plan the exchange signified.

The third time, Samir left me a voice message listing the furniture in his room, and asking if I knew anyone who wanted it, since he would be leaving the next day. When I told Idris that Samir was giving away his furniture, asked if he wanted any of it, he commented drily, "That's all blah-blah. How many times have I said I'm leaving? And I'm still here." Yakob and Idris had explained to me, in fact, that the best way to test whether a German girl really liked you was to tell her you would leave and then observe her reaction. I assumed that showing oneself and others that one had not given up on finding a better country largely served a psychological purpose. Ironically, both settling down and threatening to leave made staying more bearable.

Desiring Security and Finding the Price Too High

Asylum seekers living in legal precariousness unsurprisingly desire a more secure legal status—one that will allow them to work, rent an apartment, visit their family, and plan the future beyond the next few months—as well as housing more permanent than a camp. Yet when they have the possibility to leave the camp, or to secure their residence in spite of a rejected asylum application, they sometimes refuse, because regardless of the stability they offer, such legal pathways—most notably apprenticeships, marriage, and children—are at odds with the authentic life and self they envision, and not every private apartment is actually more dignified than the camp. I will first describe why Samir rejected a private apartment, and then why asylum seekers in legal precariousness sometimes reject pathways to obtaining residence papers.

DECIDING AGAINST AN APARTMENT

Like many people in precarious circumstances, migrants look to other migrants for glimpses of what the future might hold. They observe them to glean aspirations or warnings for their own lives. Not only does the fact that asylum seekers all follow more or less the same legal steps create a timeline against which they can compare their progress in the present and near future, but older migrants who have come to Germany decades earlier also provide ideas of what a life in Germany might look like in the long term. At the park, Samir and I often chatted with drug dealers who had been in Europe for many years, moving from country to country in a futile search for residence papers and eventually just succumbing to a life without them. Yet Samir also saw in the lives of others that papers, just like being seventeen, were neither a panacea nor a guarantee of happiness.

About half a year before turning seventeen and entering youth welfare, Samir met someone who had the residence permit he dreamed of. He wanted to introduce me to Abdullah, a Sudanese man who, Samir claimed, was over seventy years old. To my confusion, only a few days later, Samir already owned Abdullah's house keys. Before he opened the door to the court-side apartment on the ground floor, he theatrically pinched his nose with his thumb and index finger, signaling to me to do the same. But when the door opened, the place only smelled like stale smoke. A friend of Samir had agreed to move into Abdullah's bedroom— Abdullah slept in the living room—but had backtracked after seeing it. Samir, however, was so desperate to leave the camp that he was willing to see past the shortcomings of Abdullah and his apartment. Abdullah was hardly seventy, but he looked frail. He smoked without pause, watched TV, and sometimes grabbed one of the drums near his daybed, which he beat for only a few minutes before falling back limply into a more restful position. Several times per minute he spit into a large bucket beside him.

Abdullah told me that Samir was like a son to him, that he reminded him of himself when he was young, and that he would be happy if Samir moved in to keep him company. Abdullah had moved to Berlin in 1980. Like Samir, he had left Sudan to escape the violence and poverty, and to see if there was a better life for him elsewhere. He had made music, smoked, and met a few women.

Samir said, "He has papers and everything."

"I'm German now," Abdullah added. Because of his health, the German state had even assigned him a caregiver who came every day to help with personal hygiene and grocery shopping. "My Ulrike," he joked.

The apartment had a long hallway whose walls were entirely mirrored. To the far right it led into a living room and a kitchenette. Immediately to the left of the apartment entrance was the tiny bedroom that was for rent. The living room was full of furniture and various walking implements: a folded-up wheelchair, several pairs of crutches, and a walking frame. The walls were covered with nails, screws, and hooks which held hats, animal skins and furs, paper cutouts of birds, and more mirrors. I wondered if Abdullah used the mirrors to peek into the hallway and bedroom without having to leave the pull-out couch to which he seemed eternally glued.

The bedroom Samir wanted to move into had a small, barred milk glass window overseeing the communal trash cans outside. There was an old dark brown chest and a twin-size bed with bedclothes that had the logo of the Berlin hospital chain *Vivantes* printed on them. The floor and the top of the chest were littered with empty beer bottles and takeout containers. Samir assured me that he would pull out the stained carpet and throw away the bed and chest as soon as he moved in. Whenever a neighbor threw trash into one of the trash cans outside, Samir yelled through the window bars, "Fuck off, bitch!" I interpreted it as a sign of pride in his new space, and of a desire to defend Abdullah. It became increasingly clear that he saw in Abdullah not only someone who had what he himself longed for—residence papers and an apartment—but also what he was afraid of: the long-term effects of addiction.

In the following weeks, Samir spent most evenings at Abdullah's, and a few nights in the bedroom with the barred windows. They watched the Soccer World Cup together, and smoked weed or even crystal meth—"ice," as Samir called it. While Samir flew high, Abdullah sometimes passed out and fell off the couch. When Abdullah had to go to the hospital for a few days, Samir took his place on the couch facing the TV. Despite spending more and more time with him, Samir did not want to move in anymore, and increasingly spoke with disgust of Abdullah and his apartment. Whenever I asked him how Abdullah was doing, he would say, "He'll be dead within a week." He said it without sadness, just the way he anticipated his own death time and again. After one of the dozens of tuberculosis appointments during which doctors scolded him for not taking his antibiotics, or in the middle of yet another excruciating hangover, he would routinely tell me, "I think it's another three days before I die," or "You have maybe sixty more years; I have twenty."

Samir talked about Abdullah constantly, appearing at once empathetic with his misery and repulsed by it. He told me that he was afraid he would find Abdullah dead when he entered the apartment, or that Abdullah would die while Samir was with him. He would not dare call the police, because they might conclude that he had killed Abdullah. In the end, though, it was not Samir who had to rescue Abdullah. Abdullah called me one night and said that Samir had passed out and that he had called an ambulance, which should arrive soon. I took a cab to the hospital closest to Abdullah's place and, by chance, pulled in just as Samir was staggering out of the back of an ambulance. His small black pouch with the Ellesse brand logo dangled around his neck over his open tracksuit jacket, and his worn-out shoes were only loosely tied.

We sat down in the waiting room, which was crowded with people whose injuries were easily visible. Samir was quiet for the first half hour, staring at his shoelaces. Then, suddenly, he said that come fall, he would re-enroll in school. He would smoke weed only once a week, and no more of that other stuff. His favorite sister, Samar, had texted him the previous day and asked why he never called anymore. "I have to leave the camp," he repeated. "I have to go to school. I hope that I can be seventeen again. I need papers. I hope that God forgives me."

After several hours in the emergency room's waiting area, Samir grabbed my arm. "I'm tired, you're tired," he said. "Let's just go." He walked me to the night bus, and I waved from my seat on the top floor. Later at home, as I tried to fall asleep, my phone lit up. It was Samir, with a picture of a sloping horizon, flowing water still gray at the break of dawn, and the drooping branches of a weeping willow. A paper cup, and a gleaming cigarette resting on the stone wall bordering the water. After we had said goodbye, he had bought coffee and sat down by the canal near the hospital, where we often idled after school.

"Hey, you need to get some sleep. Go home!" I replied.

"Home?" he wrote, followed by the emoji of a face laughing with tears.

DECIDING AGAINST PAPERS

Just as Samir decided in the end against leaving the camp for Abdullah's apartment, asylum seekers sometimes decide against secure legal statuses. Doing an apprenticeship (*Ausbildung*) can secure one's residence, while going to school cannot. Pro Asyl, Germany's largest refugee advocacy organization, has thus called this quasi-compulsion to start an apprenticeship an "aid program for dropping out of school and university" (2018). No one can predict exactly how long the appeal of a rejected asylum application will take, so asylum seekers try to stay in school as long as possible—to improve their German, accumulate years that later count toward residence, and, ideally, graduate—while also being careful to start the apprenticeship before the appeal is decided in the negative. This often means dropping out in the middle of the school year.

Young asylum seekers are constantly told that Germany needs nursing staff, and that doing an apprenticeship in a nursing home or hospital will secure their residence papers. Made to feel insecure by the constant prodding in this direction by teachers, counselors, and caseworkers, Idris initially decided to give up on his dream of becoming a car mechanic, and interned at a nursing home. He loathed his work there but felt he had no choice, given that his asylum application had been rejected, and that in all likelihood his appeal would be rejected too. When I visited him at the nursing home, I found it easy to understand why he hated it there. Not only was he expected to do difficult work for which he had not been trained, but the elderly residents were also openly hostile: accusing him of stealing, ranting that nothing but coffee should be coming to Europe from Ethiopia, and even calling him a monkey without a tail. Although the nursing home offered him an apprenticeship, Idris declined and decided to stay in school for another year, which would allow him to graduate, even at the risk that his appeal would be decided before he had started another apprenticeship.

A week after Idris had resumed school, his caseworker intervened and introduced him to a company producing commercial sanitary and bathroom equipment that needed an apprentice. Idris was to do a two-week internship there, which he halfheartedly did. Afterward he again returned to school, but had now missed so much material that it was difficult for him to catch up. At the same time, his caseworkers were still urging him to drop out and begin an apprenticeship at the sanitary facilities company. He did; but then he left again, and returned to school once more. At that point his teacher scolded him for not having his priorities straight, and I could not help but marvel at this upside-down world in which teachers reprimanded their students for wanting to stay in school.

Idris was extremely unhappy during this time and unsure what to do. He had already missed so much school that it seemed unlikely he would pass the semester, but he also hated the idea of spending years fixing toilets. One evening, as we sat on his couch, he kept saying, "I love school," while resting his forehead on his palms and shaking his head. I remembered how he had cursed school throughout the past school year, but— just as with Samir's remarks about Ali's forced stagnation—I concluded that it was the exogenous shaping of his life that bothered him. Then Idris suddenly lifted his head and said defiantly, "I'm going back to school. If God has written that I will be deported, I will be deported anyway. I want to finish high school."

By chance, he heard the next day from a friend about an organization that offered apprenticeships for "problem kids"—German teenagers who had dropped out of school, had behavioral or substance-abuse issues, or had even been to juvenile prison. With the refugee crisis, such programs were opened to young asylum seekers, even those without behavioral issues. The organization offered an apprenticeship as a car mechanic, which Idris applied for, got, and took. While the organization's low expectations of its apprentices made him feel less nervous about his nonnative German and lack of formal schooling, he resented the fact that he was now associated with young men who skipped school and smoked cannabis at work, and who posted racist and sexist memes in the apprenticeship group chat, making Idris feel alienated and uncomfortable. He distanced himself verbally from this organization, assuring himself and others that if he were a native German he would be doing an apprenticeship with a regular company, not an organization for special-needs youth.

Ali was in an even more precarious legal situation than Idris, because he lacked the protection of youth welfare and had not appealed his rejection. His dream was to become a social worker, but every counselor told him that it was impossible without a high school diploma and that he should aim lower. "You will never work in an office," a particularly blunt counselor said. "Why did you not pass the school year?"

"I missed too many tests," Ali said truthfully.

"You missed tests?" said the counselor, her voice rising.

"Yeah, I had too many appointments with Dublin and my church asylum."

"Are you not aware that school should be your top priority?" said the counselor. "That school is your one chance in Germany?"

Neither Ali nor I responded, but I thought of the many times counselors had told him that his asylum case came first, even before his education.

Since so many counselors had told him to give up on his dream of becoming a social worker, Ali eventually started saying, "Don't care" when asked what apprenticeship he would like to do. He would take just anything to secure his residence. When it came time to write applications, however, he decided against accepting an apprenticeship he would not enjoy. Explaining his decision over tea at my kitchen table one afternoon, he said, "I'm not going to do an apprenticeship I don't want to do. Afterward I'll be years older with a job I hate, and then they can deport me again. I'm not going to make decisions based on papers anymore. I'm just going to do what I want, and if they deport me, so be it." He told me about the many people he knew who tormented themselves with work they hated just to have residence papers. He did not want his papers to be "made of unhappiness," as he put it.

Contrary to the stereotype of rejected asylum seekers marrying German women for papers, I never heard any asylum seeker approve of this possibility. In fact, whenever a well-meaning helper proposed it or it otherwise came up, Samir, Paul, Idris, Yakob, Guled, Ali, and others protested that they would never do that. Yakob said, as Idris nodded in agreement, that they finally wanted a "real life" and not more of the fake stuff. If they had a German girlfriend, both insisted, they would not marry her until their legal status was secure, so that no one could doubt they had married for love. Guled once texted me asking whether he should just marry a German woman instead of worrying about an apprenticeship, and was offended when I did not immediately recognize his question as a joke and candidly responded with the pros and cons. "*W'Allah*, I would never do that," he wrote.

Paul was in the same situation as Idris, and had already signed an apprenticeship contract in spite of his wish to stay in school. Then his German girlfriend became pregnant. Although the situation was less than ideal—they had separated, and she was even younger than him—becoming the father of a German child would give him the freedom that the rejection of his asylum application had taken away. He no longer depended on an apprenticeship for residence papers, and therefore decided to call it off and finish high school instead. Despite this propitious development, Paul insisted that a child was a blessing in itself—not a means to an end. He told few people in his life about his fatherhood, and got angry with friends who congratulated him on his acquisition of residence papers instead of the birth of his son. Paul did not want anyone to think that he was happy about his child for the sake of his legal status, let alone that he had become a father in an attempt to get a residence permit. The biggest fight he and his baby's mother had was when she yelled at him that he only wanted papers. After that, any hope of being friends, let alone lovers, was spoiled permanently by those words.

Paul named his son after his best Guinean friend, Aliou, manifesting his emotional connection to his child. Aliou and Paul had grown up together and had become the two best soccer players in the Bambeto neighborhood of Conakry, the Guinean capital. Together they had decided to go to Europe and become soccer stars; but after a car accident, Aliou walked with a severe limp, and the journey would have been too strenuous for him. Naming his firstborn son after Aliou, Paul felt, was the least he could do to commemorate their friendship and Aliou's failed European dream.

Just as asylum seekers have a moral ranking of lies about their identity—Idris, for example, found lying about his age justifiable but considered lies about one's nationality much more grave—they also have a moral ranking of ways to obtain residence papers. Getting asylum is the best way, not only for practical reasons (it happens sooner, saves one the trouble of appealing and seeking alternative paths, and allows one to travel) but because it acknowledges the difficulties in a migrant's past life and validates their decision to leave their country of origin. When a person has experienced hardship or even violence, the denial of that experience by immigration officials can add to the initial trauma (Beneduce 2015). Getting papers through an apprenticeship is the second-best option. One cannot travel with an *Ausbildungsduldung* ("status of being tolerated" for the duration of an apprenticeship); it is only valid for a few years and denies the suffering in one's past, but at least the apprenticeship is received on one's own merit, and upon successfully completing it, one can feel proud of the accomplishment.

The least desirable, even unethical, way to receive residence papers—in the eyes of most asylum seekers I knew—is through marriage or parenthood. I met no one who openly considered this option. In fact, most vehemently condemned this step, seeing it as an unwarrantable instrumentalization of the sacred institutions of love and family. Moreover, receiving papers through a romantic relationship makes one dependent on another person. As Damani Partridge has argued, European women who marry Africans "exercise intimate forms of bureaucratic judgment and state power" (2008, 660). They are informal street-level bureaucrats with the discretionary power to "make an exception to the rule of exclusion" (667). When street-level bureaucratic power is exercised by private citizens and entangled with emotion and attraction, it is perhaps more humiliating than when a BAMF adjudicator simply does their job. Opportunities for securing legal residence outside asylum are thus another site where asylum seekers oscillate between security and precariousness, between one future and another.

A Future Between Hope and Resignation

Young asylum seekers vacillate between different kinds of imagined futures and orientations toward the future. They are caught between trying to make sense of their legal situation and assuming that their request for asylum will be denied—between painting their future in bright colors for their parents and avoiding their questions about life in Europe. They shift back and forth between mocking the absurdity of the German migration bureaucracy and being unable to escape it, between settling down and packing up to leave, and between desire for future security and unwillingness to compromise future selves.

Why such wavering? Perhaps because asylum seekers see the future as being at once near and distant, pliant and fixed.[9] For instance, when thinking of the near future, migrants may focus on better understanding their legal situation; but when reminded of the far future, they may conclude that understanding or not, they will end up rejected and *geduldet* (tolerated). Reflecting on their current situation, they may be able to see its bureaucratic absurdities; but when projecting themselves into the possibility of enduring future failure, they may decide that the joke seems to be on them. In phone conversations with their parents they may embellish their life in Europe, knowing how much more pleasant that will make the calls in the present and near future, but then realize with dismay that they will either have to live up to their claims or risk being exposed as disappointments. Young asylum seekers may desperately want to settle down, but may also fear a future in which they will regret having waited too long for legal security in Germany, or will regret not having tried anew in another country. They want legal security in the short term, but also a future self they can live with, one that does not compromise values and aspirations for acquisition of residence papers. When the future is imagined to be uncertain and expansive, it pays to figure out how to affect it; but if one is doomed to end up in a future of legal precariousness, comprehension seems pointless. When someone can still affect the future, he might become what he has long told his parents he is; but if the future is already fixed, he will be a lifelong fraud, forging only stories and not his destiny. Young migrants' ambivalences and oscillations can thus be explained in terms of how migrants are able to orient themselves toward the future at any given time.

Such future projections are externalized through attitudes, narratives, performance, and material forms (Mische 2014)—through despondency and the inability to escape an allegorical prison-paradise, through boarding trains and hanging brick wallpaper. Although it is difficult to determine the exact impact of imagining the future, projection and hope do have real social effects (Desroche 1979; Mische 2009). How Idris, Samir, Paul, and other young migrants dealt with the changeability of their ages and the uncertainty of whether they would be able to stay in Germany became, in a bit of twisted logic, an important predictor of their ability to stay in the country at all. Illuminating the matter, Iddo Tavory and Nina Eliasoph distinguish between trajectories and temporal landscapes. Trajectories are imagined biographies and histories in the context of which events, as well as our own actions, take place, and in accordance with which we interpret them. We have agency over the trajectories we perceive and pursue, and over our resultant interpretations of the world—which is why the same events may be interpreted very differently by different people. Temporal landscapes, in contrast, are "overarching temporal orientations that actors experience as inevitable and even natural" (2013, 909). After twelve months, a new calendar year begins; after a set number of years, a legislative period ends. For asylum seekers whose ages are negotiated, however, trajectories are not performed on naturalized and predictable temporal landscapes, but on ones that are continuously negotiated, constructed, and unstable. Consider, for example, the practical as well as philosophical question of whether someone's age can change retroactively. Had Samir been eighteen, nineteen, twenty, and then seventeen in Germany, or fifteen, sixteen, and seventeen all along? Had he really wasted his nineteenth and twentieth years, as he seemed to fear, even though he would be able to relive them?

Jacqueline Bhabha points out that permanency planning (2019, 379) is particularly important in adolescence. But with negotiated ages, and amid frequently changing asylum and residence laws, planning one's future in Germany is difficult. As Bourdieu describes in the empirical context of colonized Algerians, they "oscillate between fantasy and surrender, between flight into the imaginary and fatalistic surrender to the verdicts of the given" (2000, 221). Many of my interlocutors talked about lost time— lost during the journey, lost learning German, lost even just growing up in their countries of origin rather than in Europe, where time, it seemed to them, could be better used. They appeared to be almost obsessed with the idea of making up for all that time, of catching up with some imagined normality. The ability to imagine their future as something they could yet affect—as one that would, however roughly, at least correspond with their efforts and decisions today—proved time and again to be a potent weapon against a past that seemed wasted and a present that seemed erratic and precarious.

7 * *Was It All Worth It?*

Samir and Asim had been neighbors as children, and had grown up to be best friends. They had left Sudan together but decided to get on separate boats in Libya, agreeing that if one of them died, the other would provide financially for both of their families. Samir took a boat first and waited for Asim in Italy, but after a few weeks Asim still had not arrived, so Samir decided to continue to Germany alone. Asim got in touch a few months later. He was now in Italy and about to make his way to Germany. After that, Samir did not hear from him again.

Asim's parents regularly called Samir to ask if he had any news of their son, and Asim's mother began assuming her son might have died since no one had heard from him in months, his phone numbers had stopped working, and he had been inactive on his social media accounts. Samir lied to her, saying that the last time he had heard from him, Asim was headed to England, that he must have lost his phone on his way there, and they would surely hear from him soon. By chance, Samir then ran into an old friend one day who told him that Asim had been in prison in a small town in Bavaria for the past six months.

Samir was overjoyed when I scheduled a visit to Asim in prison. He used his weekly youth welfare allowance to buy a supply of tobacco, filters, papers, and Nutella as a gift for Asim, despite my caution that we would probably not be allowed to take it into the prison. The night before the visit, I found Samir slumped down on his bed next to Asim's care package.

"Ulrike, I am so high and sad," he said. "Asim came all this way, such a long way, and to go to prison. Two and a half years to get to Germany, and he's been in prison for six months. Three years of his life—gone. Imagine being in prison in a foreign country where you don't speak the language. And his mother always called me and asked where her son was, and I knew nothing. And I said he's probably in Belgium trying to get to England. And now I know. When she calls now, what am I supposed to tell her?"

Samir was unsure whether he would be able to go to Bavaria with me in the morning. As sad as he was, he would not be able to go to sleep. And if he smoked enough cannabis to fall asleep, he would sleep through his alarm. He finally settled on a compromise: he would knock himself out with weed and give me his house and apartment keys, so that I could force him out of bed in the morning. I did as he had asked me, and we made it to Berlin Central Station just in time for our train.

In the prison waiting room, I showed Samir my lightly trembling hand. I had never been to a prison and did not know what to expect. Samir said, "If your hand is trembling, guess how I'm feeling. Asim is my best friend." Finally, we were called into the visiting room and sat down at a round table with three chairs. Asim walked in half a minute after us: a lanky young man in a roomy olive green parka that made him appear even thinner. His eyes twitched nervously in his boyish face, and kinks were just barely hinted at in his short hair. Asim embraced Samir with his long arms, like a baby brother. For an hour, the two tried to catch up on the news of each others' recent lives. Asim told Samir that he was in prison for multiple accounts of stealing groceries and possession of cannabis, and that he had another eight months to go. He instructed Samir to tell his mother that he was in England but did not have enough money for a phone right now. They laughed giddily, but Samir also had tears in his eyes.

A few days after we returned to Berlin, Asim's parents called and asked Samir if he had any news of their son. Samir dutifully reported that Asim was in England and had no money for a phone but would call soon. Asim's mother interrupted Samir: "You think I'm stupid? I can tell you're lying." I could hear her sob over the phone, which Samir had put on loudspeaker for me. Samir finally conceded that Asim was in prison for dodging the public transit fare. He later explained to me that it would break Asim's parents' hearts to hear that their son was a thief and drug user. Asim's mother cried—and, as if to balance out her tears, Samir lifted his own voice to a cheerful trill and concocted for Asim's mother a universe in which her son had lucked out.

"It's good that he's in prison," he said. "They have really good German classes in there. When he is released, he will speak German and he will also get papers. Look at me: I'm free, but I don't have papers and my German is terrible. I'm outside doing nothing, wasting my time."

For weeks after our visit, Samir was blue. Asim had told him that he had been looking for ways to end his life, and that our visit—the first time in six months he had been able to speak to anyone, since he did not speak German—had been the only time he felt any will to live. For asylum seekers, what happens to other asylum seekers seems to foreshadow their own potential future. When someone says that he made it to England or got residence papers for giving a wrong nationality, others see their own chance in that path. When an asylum seeker goes to prison, particularly for something other asylum seekers have done countless times, the others begin to imagine themselves in that place. I could not tell whether Samir's sadness stemmed more from his own fear of being incarcerated or from the question of why he had been spared and his best friend caught. This was akin to another question I heard so often: Why some migrants never made it out of the Sahara or the ocean, while others made it to Europe, alive and safe—even if Europe was no paradise.

From prison administrators and from his lawyer—whom Asim had given permission to speak with me—I learned that Asim had the option of being released on parole if he agreed to be deported to Italy. Samir was elated to hear about this option, sure that Asim would take it. We visited Asim one more time to tell him about the possibility of being deported to Italy and to say goodbye. As Samir had predicted, Asim said he would take the deal. The two hugged for a long time. Asim assured Samir that, once in Italy, he would leave that country as soon as possible and head to England. Samir promised he would meet him there within the year.

As I finish writing this manuscript in the spring of 2022, it has been six years since Idris shaved on the boat, five years since Paul was referred to Empower, three and a half since Samir became a Sagittarius. Has minority kept its promise? And how have those fared who were unable to turn seventeen?

Ali still shares a small apartment with his roommate. After the Taliban's takeover of Afghanistan, he is not too worried that Germany will try to deport him anytime soon, despite his only having a *Duldung*, and he no longer feels the pressure to start an apprenticeship to secure his residence. But he would still like to study, to strive for something. Working at a burger restaurant, he says, is "decent money but not a decent life."

Yakob did start an apprenticeship at a nursing home. He is still registered in Germany as an Eritrean, but has never dared apply for the Eritrean passport he would need to get a residence title as an Eritrean, or even for just an *Ausbildungsduldung* ("status of being tolerated" for the duration of an apprenticeship). So he lives with a simple *Duldung*. Although he is officially twenty-three, he has until now been allowed to remain in youth welfare—a grace period while the covid-19 pandemic makes life in a camp risky, and apartment searches even more difficult.

Difficult, but not impossible: After hundreds of applications, Guled has finally signed the contract for a tiny apartment in Berlin's outskirts. He has also started an apprenticeship with a moving company, and hopes it will secure his residence. But he still needs a Somali passport, which he fears would simply make it easier for the German state to deport him. So, at least for now, he will continue to live with a *Duldung* and wait.

Samir, once again, has decided to stop waiting. He has been living on the "schtraser"—as he still spells *Straße*, the German word for street, in WhatsApp messages—for so long that he assumes he must by now have missed an invitation letter to his final appeal hearing. I convinced him that we should call the court to find out for sure. When we did, the clerk informed us that the court had not yet sent out an invitation. Samir's appeal was still somewhere on the judge's shelf, amid high piles of others like it—five years after his asylum application, four after his interviews, and three after his rejection and appeal. As though for the first time, Samir asked me what I thought of the idea of going to England. Although he still called Berlin his great love, he said he did not know how much longer he could "fight for love."

Paul will not be leaving Berlin anytime soon. He has a permanent contract of employment with a municipal service company; he works the morning shift and spends the afternoons with his young child. After much deliberation, he has decided not to apply for the residence permit granted to parents of German citizens, because he does not want anyone to doubt that his son is a blessing in his own right, rather than for his potential to secure his father's legal status. Paul has instead applied for a residence permit for well-integrated youth under section 25a of German residence law, but has so far been unable to obtain the Guinean passport that is a prerequisite for the permit.

Like Paul, Idris lives in an apartment his caseworkers helped him find when his youth welfare support money ended. He works as a car mechanic, the profession he dreamed of since he was a little boy. He has been able to turn his *Ausbildungsduldung* into an *Aufenthaltserlaubnis* (residence title), and earns enough to send money home regularly to his family in Ethiopia and occasionally support charitable projects there. He even finally seems able to reconcile his religiosity with life in Europe's atheist capital.

On the face of it, everything has worked out for Idris. Yet he has said he needed my advice on a serious matter. For the past year or so, he rarely brought up his age, and instead only hinted at it through the occasional wink or innuendo. Now, however, he says he wants to leave the Ethiopian Muslim association that has been a major part of his social and spiritual life for the past several years. In a moment of carelessness, he told one of its members that he was twenty-eight, and he now worries that various members might realize he has told them different ages. "Can you help me find a lawyer?" he asked me. "I want to correct my age. Lying was the biggest mistake of my life."

Why does Idris consider his decision to claim being a minor—which, he readily concedes, was the gateway to his success in Europe—the biggest mistake of his life? The answer, I believe, lies in the fundamental dilemma of youth migrants like him: that merely to lead a decent life in Germany—to avoid Dublin, get an education, and live in private housing—they must temporarily give up on the independent and authentic life for which they have risked everything. They must play the European asylum game as though its outcome were open, while at the same time preparing for a likely defeat, their chance of winning so small that even just losing slowly becomes an achievement. Playing the game is as much of a liminal experience as is oscillating between the desire for an authentic self and the need for a pragmatic one. Let me recap the course of this losing game.

Minority as Springboard and Setback: A Dilemma

Like hundreds of thousands of young men, Idris, Paul, Samir, and the other protagonists of this book had believed that there was no worthwhile future for them in their countries of birth. Without saying goodbye to their families, they embarked on the infamous "Balkan route" from Turkey to Central Europe—or crossed the Sahara Desert to North Africa, a journey through heat, thirst, and hunger. With skin covered in sand dust, they were guarded by smugglers without patience for injuries, fatigue, or comradeship, past the bodies of people who had not survived the journey. After they had earned enough money in labor camps for the boat fare, or after their parents had paid smugglers the ransom they demanded over the phone, the young men traveled by boat from Egypt or Libya or Tunisia toward Greece or Italy or Malta. The crossing took a few days or a few weeks, but the stench, the sight of water from horizon to horizon, the faces of the other passengers, the sensation of incessant rocking, and the realization that their very lives had become a wager would stay with them. When they finally reached Europe in shock and exhaustion, they recalled the advice of friends who were already there: that to lead the kind of life they envisioned in the country of their choice—often Germany— they would have to say they were minors. Some were lucky and were immediately believed, or perhaps the local agencies responsible for them were simply overwhelmed in the wake of what came to be known in Germany as "the long summer of migration." Others were assessed in visual and forensic age determination exams, through which the German state increasingly sought to classify young migrants—who usually had no documentation and sometimes no knowledge of their birth dates—as either minors or adults.

While all asylum seekers tend to be received ambivalently with both care and suspicion, the image of unaccompanied minors is particularly ambiguous, as they are seen as both vulnerable and fraudulent. Old constructions of children as either "endangered little cherubs" or "dangerous little devils" (Ensor 2010, 30) continue to shape the reception of young migrants. Moreover, young asylum seekers in Europe often come from places where their identities were considered fluid or had not been documented, and this provides them with more ambiguity with which to construct their identity in Germany.

The migration of youth to Europe without identifying documents has therefore fueled an escalatory dynamic in which suspicion, deception, and punitive policy responses beget one another. Various places—including migration agencies, courts, youth welfare offices, and forensic labs—are involved in processing young asylum seekers' efforts to "get papers," both through the larger regulation of their asylum claims and through the specific process of determining their age. The German state even coined the legal term *hartnäckige Identitätsverweigerer* ("persistent identity resisters" or "persons refusing to have an identity") for migrants who lack passports or claim various identities. In 2019, the *hartnäckige Identitätsverweigerer* even became the basis of policy reforms intended to oblige migrants in Germany to identify themselves unequivocally, and to penalize those who did not do so. This curious legal concept symbolizes the escalation of ambiguity as well as the German state's attempts at disambiguation.

Although the German state ostensibly wants to establish the *truth* about migrants' identities, the actual bureaucratic practices installed to that end value precision over accuracy, aiming to uphold certain procedures and forms that fit bureaucratic conventions even at the expense of factual veracity. Asylum seekers and their helpers understand this and tell their personal truths in specific ways, turn their rich lives into thin stories, or even invent things that will make the truth more credible to state officials.

The frontline staff engaged in the German state's disambiguation practices are in a difficult bind. They must follow strict rules, regardless of whether those are workable or whether they align with their professional values; and they must balance demands for bureaucratic neutrality with their skeptical anticipation of asylum seekers' deceptions or, conversely, with sympathy for their plight. Other actors—particularly social workers, volunteers, and legal guardians—are not directly tasked with classifying or processing migrants, but are nonetheless involved in their reception. They advise, guide, and act as go-betweens. Just as the young men often manipulate and use their "helpers," these "helpers" also seek personal and professional validation from those they help, and in some ways even exploit young migrants for their own goals.

Idris, Paul, Samir and the others thus arrived in Europe at a time when their ambiguous presence was becoming a matter of great public concern. But that was only one part of the problem. While their friends in Europe had praised the legal advantages of minority age, they had mentioned neither how tedious was the process of gaining official recognition as a minor, nor how severe was the burden of living as one. After all, an official identity must be not simply attained, but maintained. You cannot merely perform a self; you have to live with that self—with yourself, as it were. If a migrant succeeds in gaining official recognition as a minor, they must deal with the attendant infantilization, which is even more painful as the migration to Europe has likely been intended as a rite of passage to adulthood. Young migrants thus try to pass as younger to eventually achieve their dreams of respectable adult lives. Unlike typical stories of passing "upward," in the direction of social power, they pass "downward," toward disempowerment, while hoping to become empowered in the long term. Ironically, the maturity and presence of mind required to delay the gratification of majority age and maintain an identity as a minor is perhaps the best proof of their adulthood.[1]

Most scholarship has focused more on how migrants frame their past experiences to qualify for asylum than on how they reconstruct their ongoing personal lives to that end. We also know little about the long-term consequences of invented memories and identities, or about how a "reverse passage" (Galli 2018), in particular, is experienced from day to day by those who go through it. In fact, the personal transformations that migrants undertake to improve their legal status can eventually have profound effects on their behaviors, outlooks, and selves which far outlast the need for residence papers and become meaningful in their own right. After one has lived for years with a legal category, the line between an authentic and a fake self becomes fuzzy as category, role, and self inevitably impinge on one another. Identities that begin as instrumental may sooner or later be experienced as authentic. Recall that Samir began referring to himself as a minor even when I was the only person around, and that Idris expressed his conviction that he actually *was* a minor, given that growing up in Ethiopia had not allowed him to mature to the level of a German in his mid-twenties. Changing one's behavior or identity in accordance with a real or imagined legal benefit, then, is not simply a "task" that is eventually accomplished. For better and worse, it can be the beginning of a durable transformation of the self.

On the other hand, when internalizing a strategic identity is impossible, it can lead to the feeling of being a liminal person, as when Ali said it did not matter to him whether someone was Christian or Muslim, as long as they were one thing fully. To say the Our Father each evening, only to ask Allah for forgiveness afterward—as did his friends who were waiting out their Dublin period in church asylum—could drive a person mad, Ali insisted.

For young men, life as minors may not only be experienced as either infantilizing, transformative, or liminal; lying also challenges their self-image of being good people. They often develop a ranking of lies from reprehensible to justifiable, in which whichever lie one tells tends to occupy the relatively innocent end of the spectrum, and the lie only told by others is deemed blameworthy. Potential legal pathways to residence similarly take on moral meaning. While asylum seekers see asylum applications and apprenticeships overall as righteous ways of securing one's residence in Germany, they generally view getting married or having a child for the sake of one's legal status as immoral and unacceptable.

A particularly sad consequence of living with a lie is the secrecy and suspicion it forces one to cultivate with others. Relationships between social workers, volunteers, and asylum seekers are often marked by a collective deliberate ignorance, comparable to the open secret in the folktale "The Emperor's New Clothes." Helpers are hurt when they must admit to themselves that they have been lied to, having apparently received as little trust as state officials, while asylum seekers are hurt when they realize that they are, first and foremost, *cases*. Perhaps most tragically, fabricated identities and the secrecy around them are an impediment to the real solidarity and community among asylum seekers that is often the silver lining of diaspora. The great potential for solidarity becomes obvious in the importance of the common experience of the boat journey to Europe, which—since it needs no fabrication or even embellishment—unites and bonds asylum seekers, finally allowing them to view themselves as part of a community of destiny.

While young migrants living as minors must cope with infantilization, remorse, and silence, young migrants classified as adults must live without the legal advantages and assistance available only to minors. When they arrive in Germany, they usually "have Dublin," meaning that Germany has six months and in some cases longer to return them to the country through which they first entered the European Union—usually a southern border state like Italy, or a country in which they have lived as minors before turning eighteen made them deportable, such as Switzerland or one of the Scandinavian countries. Unlike their slightly younger peers, young adults live in camps, with little privacy and only a handful of social workers for hundreds of residents. Some are lucky and, with the help of sympathetic bureaucrats, are able to enroll in regular schools. Others just move through unaspiring language classes.

The covid-19 pandemic brought to a peak the desperate situation of young adult asylum seekers, in the looking-glass way that crises can do.

Living in a camp was not exactly compatible with the recommended isolation and physical distancing. Whenever an occupant tested positive, the entire floor had to quarantine, which meant being stuck in a small room with others. While I was working on this book—safe, funded, and fully equipped—the young adult asylum seekers I was writing about were falling behind in school. After several months of trying to keep up with online classes and homework on their phones, the students in need finally received computer tablets distributed by Berlin's Senate Administration. A step in the right direction—except that asylum seekers living in camps still had no wi-fi. Some turned subway platforms, which offer free public wi-fi, into makeshift classrooms. For those not in school, the pandemic decimated the apprenticeships through which a rejected asylum seeker in Germany can receive an *Ausbildungsduldung* and eventually a residence permit. Many small businesses went bankrupt, leaving their apprentice asylum seekers in legal limbo. As courts and other public offices operated at reduced capacity, asylum case decisions were taking even longer than they had before the pandemic. The infrastructures many asylum seekers without caseworkers had relied on for support—such as volunteer-run events, tutoring, and counseling—closed down. In these myriad ways, then, young adult asylum seekers in Germany were among those most profoundly affected by the pandemic: stuck in crowded camps without the wi-fi needed for online classes, dependent on fewer and more fragile apprenticeships, and without formal support.

The extreme legal precariousness of young adults also sometimes necessitates other fabrications to make up for the lack of protection minors receive. For instance, young adults who have Dublin are sometimes able to convince parishes to grant them church asylum. Often this requires them to embellish their stories of persecution, and sometimes it can even mean converting to Christianity. Young adults whose real lives—however challenging and unjust they may have been—are unlikely to qualify them for asylum or refugee status, and who, not being minors, lack legal alternatives, sometimes feel compelled to claim different nationalities, illnesses that might serve as deportation impediments, or simply stories of persecution. Consequently, even if they do not live as minors, young adults are often pushed into inauthentic lives and selves.

Both minor and young adult asylum seekers thus often feel disappointed in their lives in Europe, a feeling compounded by their families' high hopes in them. So as not to be deviators from the European success story they imagine to be the norm among their peers, many begin circulating false information and kindling unrealistic expectations, lying to their families and friends about their prosperous lives in Europe in the hope of one day catching up with their own claims. When the accomplishments they have professed move too far out of reach, they sometimes break off contact. Unpredictable ages and temporary legal status, moreover, make imagining the future difficult. Young asylum seekers often resort to maintaining at least two futures, oscillating restlessly between the hope of making a life in Germany and the bitter resignation that they had better move elsewhere before they waste any more of their precious youth on an unrequited love—a country that doesn't want them.

A demand for a precise locating of the self, then, may paradoxically lead to abiding states of in-betweenness. Because young asylum seekers must choose unambiguous selves, they are caught between various selves that feel true and authentic, as well as between those authentic selves and the ones they choose only for pragmatic reasons. They cannot be officially vulnerable in one way and self-reliant in another, so, depending on how they are classified, they must either downplay their self-reliance in some areas of their lives in order to have their other needs met, or let their independence flourish at the cost of going without other much-needed kinds of support. Moreover, because state agencies are largely responsible for populations defined not qualitatively (say, as vulnerable) but quantitatively (as minors), complex selves, self-chosen or imposed, often seem to fall outside the responsibility of all agencies. Finally, because such complex selves forced into precise locations are highly precarious, so too is the future. It is safer to maintain multiple possible futures in the face of changeable and contested selves, but this comes at the cost of a sense of security and the will to more fully and confidently invest in a concrete future.

Of course, explanations for asylum seekers' divergent trajectories should account not only for structural factors like age classification, but for how individuals respond to such structural factors. Classification is not determinative, and much depends on how an individual uses the resources offered or compensates for those that are missing. I met young men who had learned German and mastered apprenticeships despite living in camps and with little or no support. Samir, on the other hand, did not—or could not—use the official minority age in which he had placed all his hopes. After all, the advantages of minority come with many drawbacks to endure—drawbacks so severe they caused Idris to regret having been a minor altogether, and to doubt whether his accomplishments had been worth their cost.

Age and Other Contested Categories

Despite the dilemma that age categorization presented for Idris, Paul, Samir, and the others, the legal distinction between minors and adults derives in principle from a laudable goal: to protect and support a group of society that particularly needs it. Because of its chronological facticity, age seems like a straightforward and fair way to distribute resources and afford rights: "Durational time can be scientifically measured and quantified in ways that appear objective and impartial, and ultimately even egalitarian" (Cohen 2018, 98). After all, everyone was born on a specific day and will live through the same ages of the same duration in the same order.

History suggests, however, that age categorization has been equitable only in theory. In practice, age "has been legislated and administered in ways that perpetuate inequality" (Field and Syrett 2020, 383), and has even been strategically manipulated to facilitate exploitation.[2] Chronological age, historians argue,[3] has never been a universally known fact or a transparent truth. Even in Europe, knowledge of one's birth date remained largely the privilege of the educated and wealthy until well into the twentieth century. Ages have always been contested, as states relied on legal distinctions between various age groups before they even began to record vital statistics like dates of birth. In Judith Treas's words, "age standards" (norms around age) predated "standards of age" (clear measurements of age; 2009, 82), and such standards remain contested today. There is disagreement, for instance, over the legal privileging of chronological age, and over the translation between different conceptions of age (somatic to calendric, for example) as well as from age as a medical category to a legal one, and ultimately to a social one.

Once we recognize that ages have always been contested with diverse understandings and negotiated with diverse intents, we cannot help but supplant the seemingly simple question of how old someone was with that of "who had the power to decide" (Field and Syrett 2020, 374), and to challenge taken-for-granted age brackets and boundaries, and the very category of age. We have come a long way in doing just that for the categories of race and gender, recognizing that they have only loose biological meaning, which the social category both reflects and imposes upon, distorting their earlier forms into expressions of power. This shift in discourse is reflected in laws and public attitudes, as well as in the fact that social scientists can no longer take race and gender "as a simple fact that can be used to frame other topics worthier of study" (Field and Syrett 2020, 371). Instead, race and gender themselves have become topics of study, social constructions to be explained.

Age still has a long way to go if it is to follow on a similar path, though migration scholars have already begun to examine the nexus between time and migration governance. Melanie Griffiths (2017), for instance, has coined the term "temporal governance" to capture the significance of time and temporality in the attempts of states to manage migration. I hope that a deeper look at the construction of youth in the particularly high-stakes context of unaccompanied youth migration—the approximate assignment of birth dates, and their subsequent treatment as biographical fact, even as a track switch for life in Europe—pushes us to at least question the legal line between child and adult, and to think of approaches that might more accurately capture the liminal, transitional life phase that adolescence really is. For nonmigrant Germans, adolescence has already begun to expand and fray around the edges—if not yet legally, then at least in cultural understandings and practices, through delays in social adulthood. No such comparably transitional phase exists for their migrant peers.

Upon closer inspection, much of the controversy about age determination is, in fact, not about the determination of age but about its definition. While forensic scientists, for instance, define age as biological and thus visible in X-ray images, social workers define it socially and thus deem it assessable only in conversation with the migrants. Young asylum seekers, for their part, view their age against its relative unimportance in their origin countries, and in light of their undeniable vulnerability and needs in the new country.

The fact that age is defined and experienced so differently, and that someone's subjective sense of their own age can be out of sync with their official or even natural age, shows that the number is merely a proxy for a diverse range of other things that in themselves are contested. Commensuration, as Elizabeth F. Cohen argues, "begins when something that is qualitative, and possibly intangible, is represented using a quantitative measure" (2018, 128). As clear and simple as the number seventeen is, it stands for properties much more complex, perhaps indeed intangible: vulnerability, innocence, dependence, and immaturity, but also openness and malleability, the capacity to transform oneself, the right to hope and joyful anticipation, and a jester's license to mess up and try again, to take more time and make detours. Aging means a narrowing of possibilities and solidifying of consequences.

The number seventeen, like other "single-moment fixed boundaries" (Cohen 2018, 54), cannot do justice to such complexity, but it is usually at least a governable quantity in a way that elusive qualities like vulnerability, openness, and hope are not. Without commensuration, we would have to make qualitative judgments every time we decided who was, for instance, a minor. Commensuration also allows for "compromise" in the face of "deep normative disagreement" (Cohen 2018, 14). Once we have agreed on a number, we no longer have to agree on what it stands for. All seventeen-year-olds are minors, even if one person believes it is because seventeen-year-olds are vulnerable, while another considers them

Does having passports mean conforming to western notions of bureaucracy?

malleable, and a third views them as something else altogether. Examples of such proxies abound in social and political life. For instance, a society only needs to agree that a certain crime warrants a corresponding number of years in prison, and does not necessarily have to agree on whether prison terms punish, rehabilitate, keep society safe, deter would-be criminals, or have some other objective. Cass R. Sunstein (2007) has termed such conventions 'incompletely theorized agreements.' The silence around what certain abstractions stand for, he argues, can be constructive and an important source of social stability and political efficiency.

Given that age is, in Sunstein's words, "incompletely theorized," it is unsurprising that forensic medical examiners and social workers approach their jobs so differently. What they have in common, however, is the impossibility of exact assessments. Both work with considerable uncertainties and unresolvable ambiguities, and must often rely on their own discretion and fallible judgments. This uncertainty, inherent in all age determination exams whether visual or forensic, stands in stark contrast to the matter-of-factness that dates thus determined later assume. Dates of birth that are initially rather arbitrary are treated as natural and real once printed on paper, thus creating tension between negotiated dates and their treatment as nonnegotiable.

The belief of migrants in minority age as a panacea thus finds its mirror image in the German state's own reductionist thinking about identity, which forces continuous and often ambiguous vulnerabilities into discrete, even binary protection categories. Although such binary conceptions of age are unrealistic, they are politically convenient. Just as Hamlin argues that the political distinction between forced and voluntary migrants "reassures publics in the Global North that they can support admitting and protecting refugees without having to support open borders or massively increased immigration" (2021, 74), treating minors as categorically different is another compromise in the politically overdetermined debate on migration. Critics can feel good about only admitting certain migrants, and supporters can avoid debates about how complicated the identities of refugees really are. Such "legal fictions" (Hamlin 2021) or "governmental contrivances" (De Genova 2018), then, are told by the state, which provides the narrative, and by young migrants, who make themselves its protagonists. These tales are not just oversimplifications of vulnerability, but they also do not engage with the fact that cultural conceptions and the bureaucratic management of identity differ greatly between the Global South and Global North, and that at the interface of different worlds, a distinction between honesty and deception is not always possible.

Thus, while binaries are meant to create clarity, they may just create the opposite: inbetweenness and uncertainty. When it turns out that a category system cannot capture everyone, some people end up as "residual categories" (Bowker and Star 2000, 39)—that is, outside categorization—or in perpetual liminality, classified as both adult and minor, or as neither, which amounts to the same state of inbetweenness. With a liminal age, no agency can be forced to assume responsibility, and a liminal identity only exacerbates what Menjívar (2006) has called "liminal legality," a state of chronified temporariness in which a migrant is repeatedly issued short-term, restrictive, or even punitive IDs with little hope of a legally secure future. The migrant's status, moreover, greatly depends on the discretion of individual bureaucrats, so that, although "choosing a country to settle in signifies creating a life for oneself and taking charge of one's destiny, [. . .] immigration difficulties can create just the opposite experience: a Kafka-esque nightmare that leaves us at the mercy of external circumstances" (Beltsiou 2016, 103).

Categorization is essential to migrants' context of reception, and age is not the only social category in which binary logic and a failure to either acknowledge or resolve the ambiguity behind the category yield far-reaching predicaments and frustrations. Particularly in the context of international migration, many similarly contested yet consequential categories are constructed by emphasizing trivial differences. David Fitz-Gerald (2019), for example, has shown how states manipulate space to decide where people can file for asylum. Such microdistinctions in space count centimeters to determine whether someone is in this country or the neighboring one. In Germany, microdistinctions in time, down to the day, serve to protect some and exclude others. The distinction between a minor and an adult, or between an Eritrean and an Ethiopian, may not seem micro; but the indicators that in the end have to stand in for that highly consequential difference are certainly micro: ossification lines or pronunciations of a word, for example. Such subtle differences, which are often hard to evaluate, assume a startling amount of clout once they have been determined.

Age shares another feature with other categories commonly used to draw lines between different groups of migrants: the fundamental dilemma of categories that protect as much as they oppress. By challenging a category, you give up the protection it might offer you. Conversely, by trying to benefit from a category, you at least implicitly help to maintain the categorization system of which it is a part, even if your need for protection arises precisely from the system's oversights. What does it do to a category when you imitate it? Does it delegitimize the boundaries the category is based on, or does it reify them? That immigrants engage in significant and durable changes of the self to fit into administratively available categories is at once testament to the power of state bureaucracies and official categories, and testament to migrants' agency despite—or, rather, within—those powerful sorting instruments. Migrants recognize the often destructive power of the law over their lives, "but they also recognize the empowering potential of the law" (Menjívar and Lakhani 2016, 1825). Young asylum seekers cannot change the fact that age matters so much—though they can be critical of it—but they can try to position themselves within that system in a way that allows them to use the resources it affords. In this way, they may inadvertently reproduce oppressive categories and help uphold the power of classification, as is often the case when "the possibility of resistance to norms [is located] within the structure of power itself" (Mahmood 2001, 212).

Tolerance as a Liminal Moral Commitment

Johann Wolfgang von Goethe, the exceptional German polymath, famously noted: "Tolerance should really only be a passing attitude: it must lead to recognition. To tolerate is to insult" (Goethe 1982, 385). Remarkably, in the German original, Goethe literally said that to *dulden* was to insult. Yet Germany's insistence on unrealistic binary categories and its emphasis on certain precise procedures of classification rather than truthful outcomes ultimately favor liminal categorizations, which in turn contribute to liminal legal statuses, such as that of being tolerated (*geduldet*), or even that of just being processed. Such liminal legal statuses reflect a liminal moral commitment from the German state.

Paradoxically, then, while Germany insists on asylum seekers' unambiguous identification, it has itself been unwilling to commit to them unambiguously. German state agencies issue short-term IDs to rejected asylum seekers, often including bans on employment, restrictions on movement, and other constraints. Yet Germany also usually does not deport asylum seekers, who continue to receive their state welfare—including housing, health insurance, and an allowance for food and other costs of living— long after their asylum applications have been rejected. They then live in Germany, where they get by but are largely prevented from prospering, knowing that they are as unlikely to be deported as they are to receive residence permits that would legalize their status. This state between in and out has been termed "liminal legality" (Menjívar 2006) for the US context, but it is perhaps particularly striking in Germany, where it combines formal exclusion from legal recognition with formal inclusion in the welfare state.

Germany's strategy of *dulden*—indefinitely tolerating—young migrants rather than truly welcoming or alternatively deporting them may surprise international readers, who may associate Germany with features that make other approaches appear more likely. On the one hand, Germany's decades of reluctance to even acknowledge being an immigration country (Triadafilopoulous and Schönwälder 2006) might make unlivable sanctions for rejected asylum seekers and hard enforcement of deportations seem like the most likely course of action. On the other hand, Chancellor Angela Merkel's decision in 2015 to open Germany's borders to refugees, to partially suspend the Dublin III agreement, and to insist that "we can do it," as well as the concurrent emergence of a vast *Willkommenskultur*, might have brought forth complementary, similarly inclusive, and committed policies and administrative practices. Finally, Germany—the land of Max Weber—is often associated with an elaborate and highly functional bureaucracy, unlike the bureaucratic whims and failings I have described throughout this book.

Germany's liminal moral commitment differs somewhat from the more determined US approach of admitting large numbers of immigrants but harshly punishing and expelling those who are unauthorized. Even so, debates on young asylum seekers in Germany are in many ways similar to those in the United States, where policy makers, academics, activists, affected migrants, and the general public likewise argue over unaccompanied minors and undocumented youths, the Development, Relief, and Education for Alien Minors (DREAM) Act, the DREAMers movement, and Deferred Action for Childhood Arrivals (DACA). As in Germany, these debates center notions of vulnerability, deservingness, accountability, and ultimately the question of where to draw the line.

The formation of a liminal group of people who are neither given secure, empowering legal status nor explicitly punished and deported is a compromise, even a cop-out. By allowing liminal categorizations and legal liminality to persist and grow, Germany makes neither a moral commitment to include young asylum seekers nor one to exclude them. The bitter irony is that this hurts not only those who are cast in perpetual legal and existential limbo, but also a country that is already extremely concerned about whether immigrants can ever truly belong to its society. After all, how can we expect young people to foster feelings of belonging, or to take concrete steps toward strengthening their societal membership, when we are unwilling to make a similar commitment to them?

Making It "Worth It": No Perfect Solutions, but Some Important Steps

Under the current laws, all young asylum seekers living in Germany are ultimately trapped in a quandary. They have come to Europe for the fulfilling, self-determined life that seemed inconceivable at home. Yet merely to be allowed to stay, and to qualify for the kind of schooling and housing without which a fulfilling, self-determined life is impossible, they have to relinquish their independence and often their truthfulness and integrity. Those officially recognized as minors and those classified as adults each have heavy burdens to bear. In contrast to their once keen hopes, their lives in Germany are marked by profound ambivalences. These include their belief that Europe might be, if not paradise, at least a place to work toward their dreams, versus the bitter reality of Aman and his roommates in their freezing apartment in Dessau—a town they did not choose to live in, and whose residents likely would not have chosen them as new neighbors. The ambivalences also include the narrow demands of the asylum system versus the trauma and hardship that asylum seekers have experienced, and the cordiality of open borders and *Willkommenskultur* versus the restrictive European asylum system. Finally, they include the rigidity of eligibilities and rights based on birth dates, versus the real complexity of age and youth; and the dangerous journey through which asylum seekers have proved their manhood, versus the boyhood to which it has ultimately led them.

After having risked their lives to come to Europe and having continuously made immense personal sacrifices, young asylum seekers often eventually wonder: Was it all worth it? At a poetry workshop Empower held for unaccompanied minors, a young Afghan simply wrote: "I am a stray arrow" [*Ich bin ein verschossener Pfeil*]." I thought of this image often throughout my fieldwork. An arrow shot at a target with purpose is just a waste of material and effort when it misses.

As more and more youths cross international borders unaccompanied by their parents, it is paramount that we understand their experiences. And how they answer the question of whether it was "all worth it" is not simply a matter of personal fortune; it will affect the societies in which those young people now live. Do we want thousands of youths among us who feel their life in Europe is a mistake? Or would we rather they feel encouraged by the rewarding of their past efforts, and hopeful that their future in Europe will be just as predictable and fair?

Policy interventions are particularly consequential for young adults, a volatile population with a highly contingent future. We expect children to adapt to a new country nearly automatically: to learn its language, to befriend locals, and to feel comfortable and eventually at home. With older adults, we sometimes simply write off this possibility. Yet with young adults, everything is somehow up in the air. That is why it pays to take a close look at how young asylum seekers fare, and why.

Some lessons are clear. To deny Guled youth welfare because he was eighteen when he applied, but keep Paul or Yakob in youth welfare well into their twenties, simply because they applied as seventeen-year-olds, makes as little sense as trying to pressure a mature teenager to make himself small. But what is the solution? I have asked this question of many of my interlocutors, and have usually received an answer along the lines of "You should be eligible for youth welfare until you're twenty-four," or "You should be able to attend regular schools until you're twenty-seven." But what if we were indeed to change a threshold from eighteen to twenty-one, or from twenty-one to twenty-seven? What would then become of the twenty-eight-year-old? Would he be forced to choose between passing as twenty-seven and being kept out of school, regardless of his needs, efforts, and ambition, as eighteen-year-olds are forced to choose between untruthfulness and exclusion today? Moving the boundaries doesn't change the basic problem: that if we extend special support to specific groups of migrants—for which there is often a very good reason—we will necessarily include some and exclude others, and we will need criteria and methods through which to do so consistently. States that have pledged particular concern for vulnerable groups can hardly avoid this problem. How can we begin to resolve it? Migration is an extremely polarizing issue, and that makes radical solutions unlikely. So instead of imagining an ideal-to-me world, I want to spend the last part of this chapter offering some pragmatic first steps in how the process of receiving and classifying unaccompanied asylum seekers could be reformed.

First, I think we should clearly separate immigration policies from policies that affect people who have already migrated. Here I follow Hiroshi Motomura, who distinguishes between immigration law ("government decisions to admit, bar, or expel noncitizens") and immigrants' rights ("the consequences of immigration status"; 2020, 460). The two are often conflated by governments arguing that giving immigrants more rights will increase future migration. Even if decreasing migration were a prudent objective, and curtailing immigrants' rights were a defensible means, the connection between the two is simply not clear. How my interlocutors were doing in Germany had little to no bearing on whether their friends at home expressed desires to come to Europe—not only because dreams are undeterred by reality, and indeed often feed upon a desire to beat the odds, but also because shame and hope turn migrants into dishonest communicators of policies and realities in their new country.

Second, we should continue to improve our methods of age verification, even just to ensure that no minor is classified as an adult. Germany, after all, has ratified international agreements on the special protection and rights of children. And there is another very good reason for reducing the number of true identity claims that get misevaluated as false. John Adams famously declared that it is preferable for guilty people to walk free than for innocent people to be punished. This stance of *in dubio pro reo*—giving someone the benefit of the doubt, in common parlance—reflects not just regard for an individual life, but concern for a functioning society. When law-abiding members of society can expect to be falsely convicted, they may decide not to bother adhering to the law at all, as their law-abiding behavior does little to guarantee their freedom. An asylum seeker whose truthful claims might be judged as false may reason that it does not pay to speak the truth, and may instead go with whatever story will yield the best outcome if believed.

Third, besides improving our means of identity verification, I think we ought to take a step back and debate the definition of vulnerability, rather than just its determination. For me, one of the most important insights of my research has been that the conflict over young asylum seekers' ages is primarily one not over the determination of age at all, but over its definition. When asylum seekers contest the assessment of their age, they are not saying that an examiner has misinterpreted the ossification of their bones or miscounted the wrinkles on their forehead. They are saying that they are vulnerable and deserving of support regardless of those assessment criteria. To them, their age is not a biological or chronological fact but a personal circumstance, even a relational one, as their needs differ from those of people in their home communities, or those of their German peers.

Such a contestation is more complex than simple deceit. We can take it as a reminder that a date of birth is a label. We do not care about birth dates because of some intrinsic obsession with calendar time—although the increased significance of birth dates certainly is related to the development of standardized time and its attendant economic, political, and social transformations. We care about dates of birth because we care about distributing resources fairly, assigning societal responsibilities realistically, and protecting the more vulnerable among us. These are important goals worth pursuing. But does a fixation on birth dates in the absence of birth certificates, for youths whose childhoods differed radically from the ones typical of the societies in which chronological age standards originated, serve those goals?

Because stability is not always beneficial and disagreement can be highly productive, it can actually be valuable to uncover an "incompletely theorized agreement." As long as a concept like minority—simple shorthand for more complex notions like vulnerability—works with little friction, its power is perpetuated without it ever having to justify itself by the sensibility of its underlying assumptions. Although this is necessary for a functional society to some extent—allowing us to protect all minors rather than make thousands of individual decisions, for instance—it also invites complacency. Even if a measure like minority will always remain a simplification, "incompletely theorized" and covering significant underlying disagreement about the complex characteristics it stands for, I think we ought to occasionally seek to theorize it anyway. We should remind ourselves what it is we disagree on, and ask whether this merits any amendments to our use of the concept. As Motomura puts it: "Responses to migration are badly hobbled if they start by relying on a sanguine belief that the line between refugees and other migrants is objective and immune to political sway, and then make that line hugely consequential. [. . .] It is essential to see a broad spectrum of migrants with many gray areas and hybrid categories that change over time" (2020, 495–96). As I have argued throughout this book, such critiques of the binary between forced and voluntary migrants can be extended to other binary distinctions, including the one between minors and adults. In other words, all laws that distinguish between different groups of migrants must account for complexity, ambiguity, and changeability.

In the specific case of young asylum seekers, we ought to remind ourselves of why we protect and support minors. Whether it is because of their vulnerability, their receptivity, their openness, or their special orientation toward the future, young migrants who display these traits ought to be protected and supported without their needing to go through official classification as minors. Conversely, no young migrant should feel that he has to downplay his strengths and accomplishments lest he be deemed too self-sufficient to merit assistance. Young people may be mature in one way and inexperienced or vulnerable in another, particularly after having moved between continents under traumatic circumstances. Our policies ought to be sophisticated enough to accommodate such entirely normal human complexities and not flag them as suspicious or use them to disqualify someone from help.

At the same time, while amending harsh cutoffs with more flexible policies that account for complex, ambiguous, and changeable selves, we must also grapple with the pitfalls of bureaucratic discretion. After all, we know—including from some of the stories told in this book—just how unjust discretion can be, and how adverse its outcomes. At the very least, we must be careful not to burden bureaucrats with unsolvable tasks, whose impossibilities they will inevitably seek to gloss over with discretion—not the responsive, judicious kind, but the one born of excessive demands and frustration. Frontline workers should also be well trained, and independent of the institutions to whom their classifications will make a financial or political difference.

Above all, we should be realistic and honest about what's possible. As it stands, we are asking nearly impossible things: of migrants, to be honest without expecting a reward for it; of age examiners, to uncover something that is undisputedly unknowable; and of front-line workers, to treat negotiated dates of birth as nonnegotiable. This is not, therefore, a book about good guys and bad guys—about blameless or insidious refugees, heroic or unscrupulous age examiners, diligent or cold-hearted bureaucrats. Age examiners and asylum seekers may seem like antagonists in my story, but I would say they are actually in a similar bind.

If we focus only on questions of determination, however, we might indeed find individuals at fault: examiners who produce incorrect estimates, asylum seekers who lie, or bureaucrats who apply dates of birth to an absurd degree of consistency. I take the fact that I found few blameworthy individuals but numerous people and institutions at their limits as a sign that our chronological legal definition of age is also at its limits. I therefore hope that this book can become a starting point for returning to questions of vulnerability instead of strict chronological age. Questions about defining vulnerability will be no less contested than questions about determining age—perhaps more so—but they will move us away from futile proxy debates about ossification lines, vocal pitch, and the authenticity of documents issued by unreliable bureaucracies. They will instead move us toward questions about individual needs, group vulnerabilities, national responsibilities, and global disparities. I suspect we will have to come to terms with the fact that the label of "minor"—for young migrants in Germany—no longer serves the goals it perhaps once advanced for native Germans. What is needed is a shift in the standards of both truth and deservedness away from the currently failing ones.

Finally, I believe it is crucial to give asylum seekers who have lived in Germany for some period of time and who meet basic requirements, such as that of recognizing the nation's liberal-democratic constitutional order, the option to obtain a more secure legal status, including a path to permanent residence and citizenship. The sheer duration of an asylum procedure and time spent in youth welfare mean that one has already made a life by the time one is denied asylum or ages out of youth welfare. Crucially, those who have given wrong ages or wrong nationalities and are now too fearful to obtain documents from their countries of origin should not be excluded from this path. We should grant amnesty to migrants who want to correct their age, nationality, or some other part of their identity or story but who are currently too afraid of the legal repercussions. This is in our own interest, as secrecy and fear hinder real integration. You cannot establish genuine relationships with locals that are built on trust and honesty, when you feel you must pretend indefinitely to be the person you once thought was the only version of yourself who would be given a chance in Europe.

If we followed these approaches—clearly separating immigration policies from those affecting people who have already migrated, ensuring that no minors are misidentified as adults, giving vulnerable young adults a chance, and allowing those who have given wrong identities to correct themselves—then surely no one would want to be *forever seventeen*. After all, migration is about mobility, not stasis. It has been likened to a "big gamble" (Belloni 2019) and to "running downhill without stumbling" (Lucht 2016, 155). Migration promises great fortune, but guarantees nothing. It entraps one in its flow in such a way that quitting eventually seems a more humiliating defeat than continuously losing.

About a month after our last prison visit, while Samir and I were watching TV, his phone rang and the caller's profile photo appeared on the phone's screen. It was Asim holding a British flag high and smiling triumphantly. I barely recognized the fragile, jittery boy from prison. This young man looked confident and hopeful, eager to finally explore a new country, a paradise that had been his childhood dream and which remained his ambition. Asim had once again spun the roulette wheel, once more launched into a downhill run. This book thus ends as it began: with the longing of young men for Europe,[4] where they hope finally to taste the sweetness of adulthood. Perhaps this has been the most remarkable manifestation of youth all along: unshakeable faith that new beginnings are possible, that hardships are worth it, and that no setback will last forever.

EPILOGUE * *The Difficulty of Studying Fabrications*

"*Kam omrak?* How old are you?" I asked Samir as we waited in a hospital aisle. We had discovered that practicing my Arabic was a fun and useful way to pass the many hours we spent together in waiting rooms. For me to be the one struggling with conjugations and pronunciations also created an important parity between us.

"*Wahid wa ashrin, tnen wa ashrin,*" he responded.

"Twenty-one, twenty-two?" I translated, perplexed. We had known each other about half a year, and until now he had always told me he was seventeen.

"*Wahid wa ashrin, tnen wa ashrin.* In German that means seventeen, you know?" he said with a sheepish smile.

I open the epilogue with this vignette because it encapsulates a crucial point of this book: that an age does not mean the same thing everywhere, or translate exactly from one country and context to another—and also because it hints at some of the issues I faced in my research: language and translation, power and privilege, thousands of hours of just "being there," and the critical question of how I could possibly assume I was being told the truth in a social world where lying was almost the default.

In this epilogue, then, I want to be more explicit about how I learned what I learned, and I want to discuss the above issues and others I faced. I hope this will allow readers to determine for themselves the validity of my findings, and provide points that may be useful to other ethnographers doing similar research. Perhaps the most important section of this epilogue is my discussion of trust and truthfulness—a crucial issue for any ethnographer, and one exceptionally explicit in my project, since my interlocutors were of interest precisely *because* of their uncertain and sometimes fabricated identities.

Entering and Moving through the Field

Germany turned out to be an ideal place to study the bureaucratic categorization of migrants, not only because it has been a major site of immigration and asylum seeking but because of its long sociological status as the quintessential high-functioning state bureaucracy. Yet, as is so typical of ethnographic projects, mine came about by chance. In the fall of 2015, when Germany and particularly my home city, Berlin, were quickly becoming the epicenter of a refugee crisis, I came across a newspaper article about the age determination exams being conducted in forensic institutes across Germany. Many young asylum seekers, I learned, were coming to Europe without documents to prove their dates of birth, so Germany was relying on X-ray images of their bones to determine whether their claims of minority were likely to be true or false. I was intrigued, and used the winter break of 2015–16—I had just started graduate school in the United States—to see whether I could get access to age examiners and perhaps do a lab ethnography of age determination.

My initial attempts were not successful at all. I contacted forensic scientists, who I assumed were working on age exams based on specialist journal articles they had published, but they had nothing to gain by talking to me about their increasingly controversial work. So they either declined my query or denied being involved in age exams altogether. In summer 2016 I decided to give the whole thing one more try. I had by now read everything I could find about age determination in forensic, pediatric, and generalist medical journals. I contacted several more age examiners, this time presumably writing more convincing emails, given the specialized knowledge I had acquired. I received several positive replies from forensic age examiners willing to be interviewed. One prominent age examiner invited me to the next AGFAD meeting and suggested more interview partners, among them Dr. Peters.

I immediately liked Dr. Peters's North German no-nonsense temperament. He spoke with a Frisian accent and seemed little concerned with the political and media feuds raging outside his institute. "I stopped fussing over stuff like this long ago," he said with a shrug. When, after our third interview, he asked me whether I was perhaps interested in observing the age exams he conducted, I could hardly contain my excitement and surprise. I had tried to content myself with the fact that age determination was simply too contentious an issue for me to actually observe, but Peters seemed, as usual, unfazed by all the reasons for which other age examiners did not want to be the subject of social research. So in summer 2016, winter and spring 2017, and throughout the summer of 2017, I spent Tuesdays—the day of the week when age exams were usually conducted—at the institute. During the exams, I began to wonder about the asylum seekers being examined, but I felt the exam room was not the right place to talk to them. They were quiet throughout the exams, and seemed unsure of how to respond to my occasional attempts at small talk. It was sheer coincidence that one of my main interlocutors, Ali, later turned out to have had his age exam with Dr. Peters and could tell me about it from his perspective.

I moved to Berlin in May 2017 and continued to talk to the social workers and pediatric opponents of age exams whom I had been interviewing since the summer of 2016. I met David, the social worker who conducts visual age exams, through a pediatrician who campaigns against age exams. Another social worker I had interviewed invited me to the summer party of the organization where she worked, and there I talked to someone who mentioned the founder of Empower—apparently a staunch opponent of age exams. I contacted and interviewed this woman, who asked if I would be willing to help out at Empower. I welcomed this opportunity to learn more about the context in which unaccompanied minors were received in Berlin, and agreed to manage the organization's email account, keep its website updated, and help organize some of the regular events it hosted to provide a networking space for legal guardians. Through Empower I met legal guardians and other volunteers, many of whom I interviewed formally. These interviews did not end up being cited in this book, but the things I learned in them certainly contributed to my understanding of the field. Through Empower, I met Paul, Franka (Paul's caseworker at the time), Ali, Samir, Michael, and Zeinab. Paul, Ali, and Michael had been referred to the organization by social workers from their camps, Samir by his German teacher, and Zeinab by her legal guardian. Paul introduced me to his friends Le Boss, Bouba, and others, as well as his classmates Guled and Leandre. I also met the young men who lived in the donation-based apartment for asylum seekers with uncertain identities, with whom Paul was living at the time. I met Idris and Yakob, at the time best friends, at an event to which Marie, an Empower volunteer, had invited me. I met more peripheral interlocutors through Empower events, in the waiting rooms of the Foreigner Registration Office, in other similar places, and, above all, through introductions by my main interlocutors, usually because someone needed help or had a question about their residence papers.

While I initially had only intended for my work at Empower to expand my knowledge of asylum politics and practice, I soon found that if I wanted to gain truly comprehensive knowledge of the significance of age, Dr. Peters's lab would not suffice. I began to take special note whenever conversations at Empower revolved around young asylum seekers' ages and identities, which they often did. And upon getting to know asylum seekers, I realized that these issues were truly central to their hopes and fears, their legal situation, and their everyday lives. Understanding that age was everywhere, and not just in the labs and courts that made its determination explicit, led me perhaps to what Mitchell Duneier has called an extended place method (1999, 345)—that is, to take the age exam lab only as a starting point, and to lay open connections by covering a range of sites. Beginning to see saturation in my field notes on age exams, I decided now to shift the focus of my study to the asylum seekers themselves.

Around this time, I also reduced my time spent volunteering at Empower and eventually stopped altogether, because I felt that my roles as a volunteer working for unaccompanied minors and as a researcher writing about them were increasingly difficult to reconcile. As a volunteer, for example, I was expected to tell the organization if I thought someone who was being supported financially through donations was using that money for alcohol or drugs. But as a researcher, I insisted that anything they told me would stay between us. This was as true for alcohol consumption or skipping school as it was for their identities and asylum cases. So, after an initial research phase studying age exams and a second one involved with Empower and talking to legal guardians, volunteers, and social workers, I spent every day and many nights between early fall 2017 and spring 2020—the outbreak of the covid-19 pandemic—with the young asylum seekers who had become my main interlocutors.

Many ethnographers study people who are close to each other: a group of regulars at a restaurant, residents of a neighborhood block, members of a youth gang, or students at a school. While some of the young men in my study know each other, they are not a bound group. Studying one group of befriended asylum seekers would have meant limiting my study to a certain nationality, official age group, or asylum status, among other things, as asylum seekers tend to know and befriend other asylum seekers who are similar to themselves in those respects. I wanted to include asylum seekers of various nationalities, of various ages, and at different stages of the asylum process. In hindsight, given how strongly even ostensibly intimate friendships among asylum seekers turned out to be marked by suspicion and secrecy, I now also believe that focusing on one group of friends would have made open conversations about their identity and legal status extremely unlikely, as interlocutors might have feared that my knowledge of them would reach other interlocutors and thus their own friends. In addition to information about my main interlocutors, my field notes contain information on about two hundred people who constitute an important foundation for my knowledge and make me confident that the experiences of my core interlocutors are not exceptions. I decided to exclude more peripheral individuals, however, so as to be able to develop certain stories in greater depth, and also because some did not want to be depicted in detail or had not been asked by me to be part of this project.

Of course, the process of migrating and pursuing an identity began before I met my interlocutors. Most migration scholars miss the beginnings of the processes they study (De León 2015), and my research shares this deficit, jumping in at a certain point in time after migration. The evidentiary value of observed behavior is naturally higher than that of recounted stories, yet I spoke extensively with my interlocutors about their past lives and choices, and they showed me pictures and videos. That material supplements my ethnographic data. Whenever I refer to events that took place in my interlocutors' home countries or during their earliest days in Europe, before I knew them, it should be clear that I did not observe those events but was told about them later. I generally witnessed the events I describe starting in 2017; if I was only told about something despite it occurring during the time of my fieldwork, I have tried to make that clear in my writing.

How I Spent My Days

Given my theoretical interest in identity negotiations and their repercussions in the lives of young asylum seekers—and my belief that this was where I could make the most meaningful contribution to the study of migration and categorization—I have focused the chapters of this book around those themes. However, for several years I spent every day and many nights "in the field." Naturally, most of this time was not spent watching asylum applications being decided, dates of birth changed, or youth welfare ended. Despite the omnipresence of issues of age, identity, and legal status in the lives of the young asylum seekers I came to know, they were also just young people who spent much of their time as many young people do: worried about the dramas of everyday life that occupy the minds of youth around the world. Besides clocking in countless hours in the waiting rooms of youth welfare offices, the BAMF, the LAF, the Foreigner Registration Office, and at police precincts, hospitals, and courts, I spent many more hours just hanging out with my interlocutors at parks and parties, grocery shopping and cooking, helping with homework and shopping for clothes, attending soccer matches and concerts, going to nightclubs and mosques, watching Netflix and smoking shisha, riding bicycles, swimming in lakes, playing table tennis, and listening to descriptions of the difficulties with parents, friends, school, and dreams for the future that young men coming of age grapple with under any circumstances. Sometimes I could almost forget what was at stake in these young men's lives—as when Paul, whose asylum application was rejected the same day as was his application to a professional soccer team, only wanted to talk about what that day meant for his soccer dreams, not for his residence in Germany. Or when Samir kept sending me pictures of various soccer jerseys the day before his asylum interview, as he pondered whether to get the white, the yellow, or the white one with black stripes, rather than worrying about the questions he would have to answer the following day.

Days in the field were erratic. While I usually knew of formal appointments in advance, most events could not be planned. During a typical day I might meet Ali for his ID renewal at the Foreigner Registration Office at 5 a.m., after a line had already begun forming outside the building. While we waited for the appointment, I would converse with him, write field notes as he dozed, or observe the other people in the waiting room. After the appointment I would go home and write about it, or sneak a nap. Then, I might pick Paul up from school. He would tell me about his day, and we would do homework together. In the evening I might have dinner with Guled and Idris, or accompany them to the mosque. At night, I often joined Samir at the park, where his work and our hanging out blended seamlessly. Occasionally, I continued directly from a night at the park to an early-morning appointment. Throughout the day I would receive messages and phone calls from interlocutors who wanted to share things that had happened, ask what letters they had received meant, or simply chat.

I would use my phone and scrap paper to jot down field notes right after something occurred, usually when I or the person I was with went to the bathroom or they were busy on their own phone. As soon as possible, I would type these notes up into detailed running texts, starting a new document each month. Even when I came home late at night or in the morning, I would write my field notes right then and there, save a handful of times. I had made a commitment to myself never to let more than twenty-four hours pass between an event and completing my notes on it, and I stuck to that. Between summer 2017 and spring 2020 I ended up with about 120 pages of typed notes for each month, and notebooks in which I scribbled ideas, tables, and diagrams, and also with the many pictures I took so as to aid my memory or capture details I felt would elude written description. After spring 2020 I continued to be in contact with my main interlocutors, but I was no longer doing daily fieldwork and only took field notes occasionally, when something particularly relevant occurred.

Language, Quoting, and Non-Ethnographic Data Sources

The lack of a common mother tongue between my interlocutors and me was less of a research impediment than one might think, and less than I had initially feared. My main interlocutors' native languages were Amharic, Arabic, Dari, English, French, Somali, Susu, and Tigrinya. Of these I only knew English and some French, though I gradually learned Arabic during my fieldwork. All of my interlocutors spoke German, and their German improved substantially throughout the years I knew them. Moreover, as is often the case when people spend a lot of time together, through sheer practice, necessity, and familiarity we learned to communicate with each other more easily than with people with whom we were in less frequent contact. In fact, my interlocutors often said that I understood them much better than other Germans did, and that only in my presence did they feel comfortable enough to talk without worrying about making mistakes. Our conversations occurred mainly in German, though those who spoke English, French, or Arabic often made use of those languages, particularly when they felt their German lacked expressiveness.

Duneier has advocated for the importance of exact quotes and the careful and deliberate use of quotation marks in ethnography, arguing that intended meanings are inseparable from the choice and order of words (1999, 339). The multiplicity of languages used in this study—from my interlocutors' native languages to German, the language in which our communication and their general lives in Germany occurred and in which my field notes were written, and English, the language in which I am now conveying my findings—makes it impossible for me to adhere to Duneier's standards for quoting in ethnography. I do, however, share his concerns. In my field notes I used quotation marks only for speech I was writing down soon after it had been said, so I could be relatively sure it had been said in that way. Wherever I use quotation marks in this book, they thus indicate that the original words were written down while they were still fresh in my mind—though of course I later had to translate them into English from German, and sometimes French or Arabic, for this book.

One might argue that the very fact that I had to translate everything people said makes it impossible for me to replicate what they meant without already infusing it with my own interpretation. As Walter Benjamin points out, "While content and language form a certain unity in the original, like a fruit and its skin, the language of the translation envelops its content like a royal robe with ample folds" (1968, 75). This unity may explain why Samir told me his true age—or what I assume was his true age—when I asked him for it in Arabic, but insisted he was seventeen in German. Perhaps speaking and being spoken to in one's own language makes one let one's guard down a bit, and opens a wider door to the self than a foreign language can, especially the language of bureaucratic scrutiny. I am aware of this caveat; but the distance and artificiality created by communication in a foreign language, as well as the interpretation that precedes and shapes translation, were issues impossible to avoid in a study of a diverse group of asylum seekers.

It is also unfortunately in the nature of the topic that I cannot verify my ethnographic data against other types of data. Statistics can only ever approximate the scope and nature of the asylum seeker population in Germany, and they obscure the ambiguity of categories. They do not show the often merely provisional belonging to categories such as nationality or age. Most importantly, statistics conceal the negotiations between migrants and state bureaucrats over who will be admitted to which identity category. Interviews, on the other hand, lack the long duration and the relationship between researcher and interlocutor that are necessary when examining the issue of migrants' contested identities. My own dissatisfying interviews from the beginning of my fieldwork attest to this.

I conducted some interviews with young asylum seekers I met through Empower in summer 2017, but stopped because, frankly, these interviews had not gone very well. It was simply impossible not to feel intrusive and insensitive, or to learn anything worthwhile, by sitting down with young men I had seen only a few times and asking them prepared questions about their residence papers, identities, and dreams. I cringe now when I hear the recordings of those interviews. For example, I scheduled my interview with Mustafa, a young man from Afghanistan, during his summer vacation, thinking it would be a more relaxed time for him. But by sheer bad luck, he ended up having his asylum interview just two days before our scheduled interview. When I heard about this, I offered to postpone our meeting; but generously, Mustafa insisted we keep it. During our interview, I could not shake the feeling that I was asking him the same questions he had had to answer only two days before. He told me how emotionally draining it had been for him to answer the asylum interviewer's questions about his childhood and flight. But then he said, "It's over now. No more interviews." The irony was palpable, and I decided to take a hint: no more interviews.

Becoming Comfortable with Ambiguity

Without at least some trust in our interlocutors, we could not do ethnography. But wouldn't it have contradicted my own research findings for me to simply believe the stories I heard, the identities I was presented with, and the introductions I received—namely, that the young men I wrote about felt that to fabricate parts of their identities and withhold others was nearly inevitable in a world where the boundaries between authenticity and falsehood were fuzzy in any case? The line between trusting my interlocutors and taking my own arguments about the ubiquity of fabrication seriously was at times difficult to tread. It meant reconciling the personal closeness I felt with many of them with the admission that I too was a member of the world in which they felt they could not be honest. Although over time I developed my own hunches about what was true and what less so, I needed to get comfortable in the ambiguity and indeterminacy of their identities. As Jay MacLeod (1987) has argued, ethnographic research itself becomes a microcosm for the topic under study. Naturally, I was confronted with the very fabrications I had set out to study. In a twisted bit of logic, this was what successful research would look like. The following two examples, I hope, will each illustrate a different aspect of the role of trust and truthfulness in my research.

Guled had asked whether I could help a Somali woman he knew with some paperwork. Nimco was in her early thirties and had spent her entire adult life in Norway with her Somali husband. At twenty-nine, not long after the birth of her first son, she ran away to Germany. There, she and her young son lived in a camp, where she met Guled. Shortly afterward, Nimco was pregnant again, and the LAF offered her an apartment so that she and her two small children would not have to live in the camp. Because Nimco only spoke Somali, I asked Idris, whose German was much better than Guled's, to join me and translate. Guled, Idris, and I had a pleasant evening at Nimco's, drinking sweet tea, eating samosas, and going through all the official mail regarding the birth of her baby daughter that Nimco had received but not understood. We played with her then three-year-old son, and admired and cuddled the newborn. When Idris and I finally left later that night, Guled said he would stay a bit longer and catch a later train. On our way down the stairs, Idris and I looked at each other evocatively, but kept quiet, as our words would have echoed through the stairway.

As we stepped onto the street, Idris blurted out: "Is that Guled's baby?"

I'd had the same thought, and, reinforced by each other's hunches, we began exchanging bits of "evidence" we had noticed. The timing indicated that the baby girl could not have been conceived in Norway. Idris said that Somalis do not befriend people of the opposite sex, and that it would be inappropriate for Guled to stay with Nimco after Idris and I had left, unless they were Islamically married. Nimco had been wearing a golden band on her ring finger, and Idris told me that the baby girl's name meant "secret" in Somali. When I had asked to see little Secret's birth certificate to double-check that I had filled in the forms correctly, Nimco had claimed there was no birth certificate, which was highly unlikely for a baby born in a German hospital. Surely, Guled and Nimco did not want us to see the father's name. Had I noticed the glances they had exchanged when I asked about the birth certificate? I now thought I remembered them looking at each other. But why, I asked Idris, would they keep the baby a secret? Maybe they thought it would be bad for Guled's papers, Idris speculated. Or maybe they were just embarrassed.

I initially drew one lesson from the evening: namely, the humbling reminder that we do not know as much about our interlocutors as we perhaps think we do. They have lives of which we know nothing—relationships, even babies. They alone decide what to disclose of themselves and what to conceal. When I was doing my first research project as an undergraduate student—an oral history of public housing in St. Louis—one of my interlocutors recited part of a Nikki Giovanni poem to me: "and my windows might be dirty / but it's my house / and if I can't see out sometimes / they can't see in either." I am not sure this is how Giovanni meant it, but I have since seen the dirty windows as a metaphor for the impossibility of ever truly knowing what goes on in someone else's life, even if they seem to have opened the curtains.

I started visiting Nimco and her children a couple of times a month, with Guled, with Idris, or with both. As I got to know her better, the lesson I drew from our encounter changed. Idris and I had convinced ourselves that Secret's father was Guled. But the more time we spent with them, the more we observed Guled with the children, and when we eventually met Secret's actual father, we had to admit to ourselves that we had merely worked ourselves up and seen evidence in coincidence. We had defaulted to thinking that Guled was lying, because that was what Idris—and perhaps increasingly I—assumed of everyone.

Another enlightening incident occurred one Saturday night. Samir and I were on our way to the place of one of his friends who lived in the southern outskirts of Berlin and had promised to finish dreading Samir's hair. We had taken the subway to the last stop, from which we had another ten minutes or so to walk. Samir led the way. From a previous visit I remembered where the friend lived, and I was almost certain we were taking the wrong path, or at least a big detour. But I followed Samir anyway on his zigzag through the dark and quiet streets. Abruptly, he stopped and pointed at a plastic bag hanging from an iron fence in front of an apartment building. "That's my friend's," he said. "He lost it, and it has all his documents in it. He'll be so glad I found it." He walked over to the fence, took the bag down, and, as if to corroborate his story, opened it for me to look inside. It contained several manila folders which indeed could have held documents.

Later that night, after his friend had finished dreading Samir's hair and I was about to head home, Samir said he would spend the night there at his friend's place, since he had an appointment in the area early the next morning. I asked what appointment he could possibly have in the outskirts of the city on a Sunday morning, and he said he needed to return the plastic bag to the friend who had lost it. The whole thing seemed odd to me. How could his friend have lost a plastic bag with his papers in a neighborhood in which he did not live, and how had Samir happened upon the bag and been able to identify it? Why did his friend need his documents back on a Sunday morning?

In many ways, I fully trusted my interlocutors. Guled sat my cat whenever I had to go to the United States. I was at ease around Samir even when he was high. Yet I could never be sure that what they had told me about themselves was the true, complete, final version of their identity. And that was OK. I did not believe that the plastic bag contained Samir's friend's papers, or that Samir had happened upon the bag by chance, but I decided not to pry. Just because he allowed me to write about his life did not mean I was entitled to know everything about it. Whenever an interlocutor asked me to leave the room for part of an appointment with a doctor, therapist, or lawyer, I always did so—of course.

Respecting the privacy of interlocutors is especially important in a field site where failing to do so might amount to mirroring the extreme scrutiny they are already being put under by the state. Belloni has argued that it is important to consider the "preterrain" of research—that is, "the preexisting structural relationships that underlie, and possibly shape, research settings and interactions" (2019, 21). Asylum seekers are an overly interrogated population even without additional attention by researchers. The only way to avoid mirroring the role of BAMF and other state agencies was to not view their lives through a lens of truth.

Whether refugees are speaking the truth may in any case simply be the wrong question to ask. I am, unsurprisingly, not the first researcher to encounter lies in my fieldwork. Todd Meyers, for instance, noted the omnipresence of "lies, half-truths, and distortions" (2014, 192) among the adolescents whose drug addiction treatment he studied. Meyers shows how the system of addiction treatment is actually set up for both patients and doctors to lie: "What the patient-subject represents under the therapeutic activity of opioid replacement therapy is [. . .] a figure who has always already failed to live up to therapeutic expectation, and whose failure is anticipated but always, in the end, remains disappointing. The tragedy here is not the failure of the patient-subject, but rather that pharmacy requires a subject to personify failure (which in turn to reject) as a precondition of therapeutics" (2014, 192). Similarly, the question of whether refugees lie belies the fact that the asylum system—through its stratification along markers that cannot be verified; through the performance of exams and procedures that ostensibly verify; and through the silent agreement of refugees, social workers, and bureaucrats to treat a determined date of birth as fact—already expects them to lie. And in a bizarre way, it depends on the fulfillment of that expectation for its own vindication. There is a paradox when asylum seekers are asked to be something (young, for example, or persecuted), but to not *try* to be that. The nature of "living in prognosis" (Jain 2007) is that one is asked to refrain from doing what is already statistically expected of one. Early sociologists like Georg Simmel (1950) and Émile Durkheim (2005) already recognized the important role that lying and other acts of deviance play in functional societies. Lies throw not sand into the system's gears, but oil.

Lies, rumors, inventions, denials, evasions, and silences are thus data (Salamone 1977; Nachman 1984; Bleek 1987; Fujii 2010), and they provide valuable insight into the social world in which they are deemed necessary, justified, or even just possible. They can actually serve as entry points into sensitive subjects. While retests, comparisons to multiple forms of evidence, and cross-checking of accounts (Obligacion 1994) may be useful approaches to data that can be meaningfully evaluated for its veracity, I found another path to be more fitting: that of redefining the object of study and the limits of knowledge, an ontological shift inspired by the work of the anthropologist Amira Mittermaier. Mittermaier (2010) writes about the role of dreams in Cairo's religious and political landscapes, participating in the spaces where Cairenes experience, relate, and interpret their dreams. In a manner wonderfully wry for a book titled *Dreams That Matter*, Mittermaier concludes that dreams as such cannot be studied. In being remembered and shared, the dream has already been transformed. Mittermaier herself admits that she is actually studying not dreams, but how people relate their dreams, what they make of them, how dreams are used to form group memberships, and the waking-life consequences dreams can have. Similarly, I am studying not identities but stories, narratives, reflections, and claims about identities, because identities—like dreams—cannot be seen. I never took the state's stance that how old someone is or where he is from must be discoverable if only examined in the right way. When an interlocutor claimed to be from Eritrea and the state workers charged with verifying his identity insisted he was from Ethiopia, I did not take sides when it came to the facts. Rather, I examined why his nationality mattered, how each side argued for one citizenship or the other, and what consequences those negotiations had.

Just as I did not think it was my job to discover the "truth" about my interlocutors' identities, I also do not believe it should be the ethnographer's goal to somehow recreate her interlocutors' situation for herself—a goal whose fulfillment would be impossible merely because it stems from a goal. Idris, for example, knew three Somalis who were stranded in Turkey and were trying to get to Greece. Stupidly, I asked him if he thought they would mind me coming to Turkey and perhaps joining them on their journey to Greece. I wanted to see what it was like. Idris said that was much too dangerous, and could not understand why anyone would voluntarily make that trip. He was right, and I felt embarrassed by what I had mistaken as ethnographic zeal, but really had to take as a lesson on something fundamental I clearly had not yet understood:[1] You cannot imitate another human's experience. In fact, by attempting to imitate another's experience, you run the risk of trivializing it. If you think that as a researcher you are getting closer to understanding migrants' lifeworlds by traveling on a dinghy or crossing the desert, you have not understood that the real crux of that journey is not the physicality of it, but its why and its how, and the fact that there are people in the world—hundreds of thousands of them—who decide to take it despite the dangers and the odds. Taking that same journey for another reason and with other means—not in ignorance or spite of its risks, not for lack of knowledge or alternatives, but precisely because of the danger, and in full expectation of its horror—makes a mockery of the real suffering of clandestine migration.

Being a Woman in the Field

A male friend of mine was also doing fieldwork with male refugees in Berlin, and we were initially surprised to learn from each other that while women were a main topic of conversation in his fieldwork, they came up as a topic only occasionally in mine. Surely, my gender has to account for the fact that conversations with and among young men rarely turned to the subject of love and sex in my presence. Perhaps the men feared making me uncomfortable or were themselves embarrassed, or maybe they simply did not think I was interested in hearing about their sexual experiences or their opinions of girls. This is one way in which my gender limited my research.

Particularly during the first few months of my research, I was also anxious that my male interlocutors might mistake my interest in them as romantic. Early on, I decided against writing about two young men who did not seem to accept my rejection of their advances. Unlike me, my interlocutors had largely not been brought up to view friendships between women and men as normal; and the intense commitment of time and sympathetic attention ethnographers make to their interlocutors is easily misunderstood by anyone. But I believe that over time, both my interlocutors and I became more sure and comfortable in our relationship. From my perspective, they seemed to better understand my intention of writing about them and helping them with their residence papers in the process. As a result of having lived in Germany for a while, they probably also recognized that friendships between women and men were nothing out of the ordinary there; and they also were beginning to form other friendships or even romantic relationships with Germans, so that I was no longer their primary point of contact.

I was rarely uncomfortable or uneasy when I was the only woman in a group of men, but my interlocutors sometimes assumed I was apprehensive for my safety, or thought I ought to be. Paul would sometimes whisper, "*Tu as peur?* Are you scared?" when we were in a group of male asylum seekers. He seemed surprised when I responded, completely genuinely, "Why? Not at all." When I asked him to take me with him to the camp where he had lived before he became a minor, and where he still went to get his hair cut by one of the residents, he hemmed and hawed before finally saying that he did not feel comfortable taking me there since I was a woman. Samir similarly told me I could not come to the all-male parties he sometimes held with friends, as that was inappropriate "in Africa." He also always told me to leave when he sensed that there would be a feud between drug dealers, one time literally shoving me into a nearby convenience store just before the eruption of a street fight. Another time, after I tried to break up a fight between dealers, Samir scolded me for putting myself in danger. He made me promise never to intervene on his behalf again, and said that otherwise he would stop taking me along.

After having felt such limitations of being a female researcher, I considered it almost a badge of honor when, one day, Samir called me a man. As we waited for our train back to Berlin after having visited Asim in his Bavarian prison, Samir said, "You're like a man." He added, presumably because of the displeased look on my face, "It's a good thing. I didn't think a woman could be strong and reliable and come to prison with me, and be there no matter what." In that moment, I felt a camaraderie between us that defied gender.

For their lives in Germany, however, my interlocutors' gender mattered greatly. Young male asylum seekers epitomize societal fears, and these fears grow with their—however rare—actualization, as they did after the mass sexual assaults in Cologne on New Year's Eve 2015.[2] "Young healthy men" are also a category of people BAMF and administrative courts evoke to reject asylum applications and appeals. "As a young healthy man," a rejection letter typically concludes, "the applicant would survive a return to his country of origin. Even without family support, he is working-age and healthy and can provide for himself. In fact, he has proven his self-sufficiency before, during previous difficult times in his country of origin and during flight." Young male asylum seekers, then, are a group of people whose virility not only provokes fear but also seems to disqualify them from protection.

This widespread public perception of male asylum seekers, among other factors, makes their experience quite different from that of female asylum seekers, which is why I decided, for the most part, not to write about the girls and women I met. While male asylum seekers evoke fear, seem too self-sufficient for youth welfare, and are purported to be just fine if they were to be returned to their countries of origin, female asylum seekers are often automatically perceived as victims of the very societies the men had ostensibly made unlivable. Having accompanied female asylum seekers to dozens of appointments, I can say that the street-level bureaucrats in charge often seemed more sympathetic to their requests than to those of young men.[3] Empower and other organizations for legal guardians kept long lists of young male asylum seekers waiting to be assigned volunteer guardians; and, at least during the peak of arrivals in 2015–16, there simply were not enough volunteers. Yet on the rare occasion when a female asylum seeker needed a legal guardian, there would always be multiple interested volunteers. One organization seeking to recruit volunteer guardians posted advertisements around Berlin that included a picture of a German woman rock climbing with a young female refugee. When I asked the organization's director why it had chosen that picture, even though only a handful of female asylum seekers passed through the organization each year, she responded that it was simply easier to pique the interest of Germans by suggesting that the volunteers would be helping girls.

Similarly, whenever I was helping a female asylum seeker with something, especially female-specific issues, I found it easy to get support from other volunteers and professionals. Nimco, for example, told me that her younger sister, who still lived in Mogadishu, had contacted her because her family was planning her FGM procedure, which she did not want. I asked a social worker for help in finding local organizations and women's houses in Mogadishu to which Nimco's sister could turn, and within hours we got an overwhelming number of responses from people wanting to help. I want to be clear: female genital mutilation and other forms of violence inflicted on women are horrific, and deserve the kind of outrage and offers of help they drew. But male asylum seekers, who also experience horrific things and are in desperate situations, rarely garner as much sympathy.

Helping as a Research Strategy

The notion of science as mere observation of a world presumed pure and easily altered by researchers' interference clashes with the often immense need for help that ethnographers encounter in the field. Philippe

Bourgois and Jeffrey Schonberg write: "It is imperative to link theory to practice. Otherwise, we would be merely intellectual voyeurs" (2009, 297). But how can we offer help to our interlocutors without compromising standards of scientific inquiry? I believe few fieldworkers, when confronted with opportunities to help their interlocutors, would decline on the grounds of noninterfering science. So the challenge is not so much the researcher's decision as it is that of convincing our readers that our interference in the field does not diminish the scientific validity of our findings. One approach, I believe, lies in recognizing that helping is often much more revealing about a problem than is idly looking on.

Helping my interlocutors through my German language skills and familiarity with German bureaucracy, then, was the way I tried to give back; but it was also a research strategy. One learns a lot about a problem by trying to solve it, or about a mistake by trying to rectify it. When the hospital where Samir had received surgery would not remove his stitches because the problem did not qualify as an emergency and asylum seekers' insurance did not cover it, I learned a bizarre fact. What more could I have learned by seeing what would happen without proper medical care? Could I have learned whether the nurse would make good on her promise that if the stitches were to get infected, she would be happy to treat him? After attempting to pull the threads myself, I took Samir to a doctor who I knew treated every patient in need, insured or not.

In the summer before he became a minor and entered youth welfare, Samir missed an appointment at LAF during which he should have received his cash payment for the month. He went to LAF the next day, apologized for the missed appointment, and asked for his money, but was told he would have to wait for the following month's appointment. Exasperated, he called me, said he did not know what to live on for the next month, and asked rhetorically whether LAF wanted him to deal drugs to make ends meet. The following day, we went to LAF together. I explained the situation to the woman at the front desk and stressed that Samir had no savings to tide him over. The woman was friendly and understanding, and scolded Samir almost affectionately, saying he should get a calendar to keep his appointments straight in the future. She also said she had assigned us a fast number so that we would not have to wait the usual three to six hours, but that it would have to stay between us. She winked.

Samir could hardly believe it. "I swear," he said, "when you're here, everything works out. By myself, I would have waited five hours and not gotten any money." The man who eventually attended to us was, according to Samir, the same one he had talked to the day before, but now he was friendly, and without objection he handed us the card with which to retrieve the money. We went to the cash machine and put the card in the slot. The bills and coins fell into the receptacle one by one. "Come on, give me another cent," Samir yelled at the machine enthusiastically, as coin after coin clanked against the plastic. On our way to the subway Samir laughed, evidently happy that everything had gone smoothly, but also indignant over how different the treatment, waiting times, and outcomes were at LAF and other agencies when he went alone as opposed to when I accompanied him. Clearly, then, I sometimes did change the outcome of events. That in itself is a research finding.

Researching a "Hot" Topic

Colleagues have sometimes expressed concerns that my research could foment anti-immigrant sentiments and even help the state clamp down on asylum seekers by revealing their strategies for attaining and passing with certain identities. I care deeply not only about the individuals in this study, but about the future of other migrants. My aim is obviously not to expose them. The state already knows the strategies of migrants anyway. Ever since the introduction of ID cards, people have sought to influence their official identities. Valentin Groebner, for instance, describes in impressive detail the methods through which medieval states tried to identify the people crossing their borders: the classification schemes they applied, the danger they faced of creating an "illusory world of self-confirming registration systems and files" (2007, 193), and the public anxieties over impostors, impersonators, proxy persons, and doppelgängers who used "their appearances, testimonies, and particularly their papers to substantiate their claims" (2007, 214). New forms of identity documentation and verification inevitably beget corresponding techniques for manipulating them. Denying that today's migrants sometimes fabricate their identities would imply an odd break from a historical constancy. Researchers working with refugees cannot help but admit that "to be a refugee means to learn to lie" (Voutira and Harrel-Bond 1995, 216), and that "fraud is an inevitable part of any study of identity documents" (Dhupelia-Mesthrie 2014, 18). This is particularly true during exceptional times when conventional methods of identity verification are unavailable, such as during the 2015–16 refugee crisis. Historically, there have been other similarly exceptional times. Burgard, for instance, describes how the Second World War "dramatically disrupted the system for knowing age" (2021, 180) by "simultaneously weaken[ing] legal identities and blur[ring] the boundaries between childhood and adulthood" (181). Identity documents were lost, the horrors of the war changed children both physically and psychologically, and youths often learned to misrepresent their ages merely to survive.

So we know that migrants sometimes lie—as uncomfortable a truth as that may be. What we know less about are migrants' complex motivations, and the practical and emotional costs of lying to a state that rigidly applies old categories even in a new context in which they no longer work smoothly. It is here, in giving context to something that is empirically undeniable, that I see the contribution of—and justification for—my research. Leaving the discussion of false identities to ideologically motivated politicians (from both sides)—or to sensationalized media stories on criminal offenders who also happened to have false identities, or upstanding asylum seekers whose lives were allegedly ruined by misclassification—impedes a realistic approach to migration.

Fabricated identities among asylum seekers are more widespread than the political left admits. And how could they not be, given that the German welfare and asylum systems offer very different treatments and resources for people who just barely fall to one side or the other of some legally defined threshold? Given such extreme stratification by age and nationality, for example, it is hardly surprising that people try to compensate for disadvantageous aspects of their identities in strategic ways. Yet such identity "frauds" or "compensations" are also more benign than the political right alleges. And identity is not always as clear-cut as Germans with known birth dates, citizenship, official spellings of their names, and so on might think. "Fraud" is often more of a grey zone than the term suggests.

Acknowledging that fleeing one country and being excited to move to another are not mutually exclusive is similarly double-edged. As Belloni writes: "When stating the continuity between forced and voluntary migration and the space for choice in migration dynamics, researchers may face a major ethical dilemma. On the one hand, we are afraid to undermine the system of categories that protect research interlocutors. On the other hand, we feel the need, as Thomas Faist puts it, 'to challenge the power of categorization which oppresses the subjects we talk about'" (2018, 8). Similarly, I do not want to add to the blanket suspicion of migrants' accounts. But I *do* want to spark a conversation that questions the rigidity and salience of official identity categories, not to mention while staying true to my empirical findings. Moreover, most asylum seekers who tinker with aspects of their identities do so not out of some malicious wish to cheat the system or conceal their true identities, but out of a sincere ambition to pursue what has been denied them for their entire lives: education, health care, adequate housing, and a self-determined safe existence.

Besides, the fact that asylum seekers sometimes fabricate parts of their identities does not in itself support particular political claims. To consider a debate in a very different discipline,[4] evolutionary biologists whose empirical research has shown that natural selection is not the only mechanism in evolution have hesitated to publish their findings for fear of "strengthening the wrong side in politically contentious debates with latter-day creationists promoting intelligent design," and are even warned by their own colleagues that "everything [they] will say will be used against science" (Milo 2019, 15). This closely echoes my own colleagues' concerns about which political stances might be undergirded by my research.

However, the empirical fact that natural selection does not exhaust all of evolution doesn't support a particular side of the evolution debate. Likewise, the fact that migrants don't always speak the truth doesn't support a particular side of the debate on migration. Questioning the prevalence of natural selection does not deny its reality, and none of the alternative explanations put forth by evolutionary biologists necessitate intelligent design. Analogously, the empirical observation that asylum seekers respond predictably to the rigid, unrealistic stratification systems in which they are trapped does not reflect badly on them as people, or justify more restrictive immigration policies.

It was ultimately my interlocutors' decision to be part of my research. Still, I have sometimes wondered why they wanted to participate in such a sensitive study. One reason, I believe, is that people on either side of the age question—the examiners and the examined—feel guilty for their particular roles, and want to atone for their involvement in what they see as an impossible quandary. For instance, when I thanked David, the social worker and age examiner, for opening up to me despite the risks, he told me he wanted to "come clean" out of conviction. Idris, the asylum seeker, told me he thought being a part of my book would mean he had used his experience for good, to promote understanding for the intractable situation he and other asylum seekers were in.

The fact that refugees sometimes lie about their identities nonetheless remains an uncomfortable truth—even for me. I certainly did not set out looking for it. But what do you do with uncomfortable truths that are in front of you? Do you leave them to others, for whom telling them with as little context as possible would conveniently help in confirming and propagating their unkind view of the world? To ignore uncomfortable truths is to ignore the plight of people who live them, and to be oblivious to possible solutions. What such uncomfortable truths need is not disregard or disavowal, but nuance and contextualization. It is only the lack of either that makes them uncomfortable in the first place.

ACKNOWLEDGMENTS

It should go without saying that, above all, I am grateful to my refugee interlocutors, who made my fieldwork fun and inspired me by stubbornly fighting against all odds for the life they knew they deserved. I am also grateful to the medical examiners, social workers, and volunteers who shared their vast and impressive knowledge with me.

At different phases of research and writing, there were people who had great impact on my project. Janet Vertesi first introduced me to science and technology studies and to three particularly stimulating works: Lorraine Daston and Peter Galison's *Objectivity*, Susan Leigh Star and Martha Lampland's *Standards and Their Stories*, and Stefan Timmermans's *Postmortem*. I managed to stay optimistic despite setbacks during my early fieldwork, largely because of Janet's mantra: "It's all data!" Jagat Sohail has supported my work every step of the way—literally, during the long walks during which we discussed all the questions I could not have worked through without his brilliance and patience. Finally, Stefan Timmermans's guidance during my writing of this book cannot be overstated. He read the manuscript with a careful eye and an open mind, being firm about what would improve it while empowering me to write the book I wanted to write. I cannot imagine another editor as conscientious and supportive as him.

I am grateful to Mitchell Duneier, William B. Helmreich, and Kathleen A. Montgomery for their upliftment and support. To Mitch I am particularly grateful for trusting in my research from the beginning and urging me to do the same. Thank you to Richard Alba, Dalton Conley, and Douglas Massey for their constructive feedback. Thank you to Parijat Chakrabarti and Sarah Reibstein for their care and companionship in graduate school, something I will always cherish.

For their generous comments and encouragement I thank Elizabeth F. Cohen, Ángel A. Escamilla García, David FitzGerald, and Ryan Parsons, as well as Elizabeth Branch Dyson of the University of Chicago Press, John

Mollenkopf, and another anonymous reviewer of the book proposal and manuscript. Thank you to Renaldo Migaldi for his careful copyediting.

Thank you to Princeton University, particularly the Department of Sociology and the Princeton Institute for International and Regional Studies (PIIRS), for their very generous financial support, which gave me an unusual amount of time and freedom to do fieldwork.

The Max Planck Institute for the Study of Religious and Ethnic Diversity in Göttingen has been the perfect workplace for finishing this book, and I am indebted to Karen Schönwälder and Steven Vertovec for letting me be a part of it. At the institute, I am particularly grateful to Megha Amrith, Johanna Lukate, and Farhan Samanani for their feedback.

Besides these people who directly shaped my research, I want to thank those who made sure I also had a life apart from research—or at least one to return to afterward.

NOTES

Preface

1. This is also why I usually use male pronouns when referring to asylum seekers.

Chapter 1

1. As Rawan Arar and David FitzGerald (2023) argue, the term "Global South" describes a concept rather than a region, and should thus not be used unmindfully. I use the term in the context of bureaucratic misrecognition and incompatibility—precisely to denote a concept rather than a region.

2. Because only those asylum seekers are counted as minors who submit their asylum applications with legal guardians before turning eighteen—not those who wait to submit their asylum applications themselves upon turning eighteen—the actual number of minor asylum seekers is likely much higher.

3. I use the term "refugee crisis" for readability, but want to provide the caveat that this term tends to highlight the crisis experienced by receiving countries like Germany while obscuring crises transpiring in sending countries and in the lives of individual migrants.

4. In November 2020, almost two years after Aman and his roommates lamented Ethiopia's new democratic face, the war in Tigray seriously tarnished Abiy Ahmed's international image. Yet while BAMF (2021) acknowledged Ethiopia's violent conflict and conceivable disintegration in its updated country report, Ethiopian asylum seekers' chances of protection are unlikely to increase, as BAMF tends to argue that localized conflicts still leave the possibility of domestic migration.

5. Belloni (2019, 116) points out that smugglers may also be described or even remembered as more violent in hindsight, because this helps asylum seekers position themselves as victims.

6. The improved treatment of minors—more costly than that of adults—also incentivized the German state to keep this population small, however. When an unprecedented number of young people filed for asylum starting in 2015 (BAMF 2020), Germany increasingly relied on age exams to winnow out those classified as adults (Mansour et al. 2017).

7. Notably, in March 2022 Ukrainian refugees were offered accommodation by volunteers in much the same way.

8. Six years later, when thousands of Ukrainian refugees came to Berlin, the same church helped readily, and even became an emergency shelter.

9. As Fran Meissner (2018) points out, rules regarding migrants' entry and residence in Europe are subject to frequent change. The ones mentioned in this book reflect the time of my fieldwork, unless noted otherwise.

10. Between 2014 and 2016, only 13 percent of asylum applications in the EU were submitted in southern Europe, and 76 percent in western or northern Europe (Fernández Huertas Moraga 2021).

11. For a history of the concepts of asylum and refugees, see Hamlin (2021). As Hamlin convincingly shows, while ideas like "asylum, protection, and hospitality" (36) are ancient, the idea that an individual "is" a refugee did not exist before the modern period, perhaps not until World War I. Early conceptions of refugees were much less essentialist than today's binary logic. They focused on the consequences of displacement, not its causes, so that poor migrants and political refugees were not considered distinct. The International Committee on Refugees (ICR) only began to focus on why particular people were being displaced in 1938, thus leading to what has been called the "individualization" of refugee law. Yet scholars, according to Hamlin, often tell the story of the 1951 Refugee Convention, whose definition of refugees built directly on the individualized IRC definition, as though "an essentially unique group of people who have existed since ancient times were finally recognized as being particularly in need of protection" (41).

12. In 2019, for instance, Germany deported about 10 percent of those who could have been legally deported (Deutscher Bundestag 2020b).

13. In July 2022 the federal government of Germany proposed the so-called *Chancen-Aufenthaltsrecht* (opportunities residence law). It stipulates that anyone who on January 1, 2022, had been living in Germany for five years (or three, for those under the age of twenty-seven) will have the chance to obtain permanent residence. The law aims to end the cycle of *Kettenduldungen* (chain tolerations), and has the potential to truly change the lives of rejected asylum seekers like my interlocutors.

14. The *Ausbildungsduldung* is somewhat of an exception, as it can, after successful completion of the apprenticeship, lead to an *Aufenthaltserlaubnis* (residence permit).

Chapter 2

1. During the covid-19 pandemic, for instance, more girls in the United States were experiencing early puberty, providing, as journalist Jessica Winter argues in the *New Yorker*, "a chance to rethink puberty: to see it not as a gateway into adulthood but as another stage of childhood—one that is highly variable from kid to kid." Even the pediatric endocrinologist James Tanner, after whom the Tanner stages of pubertal development are named, insisted that puberty was "a spectrum, not a strict schedule," and that "every child's progress through puberty had its own rhythms and tempo." In fact, teenagers' physical development may be spurred by stress, lending support to the idea that young refugees mature faster than do their peers who have not had traumatic experiences of flight (Winter 2022).

2. In its asylum application rejections, BAMF actually argues that young, healthy men can survive in their home countries without familial support, and the realization by migrants that being an orphan is irrelevant to asylum has "resurrected many a parent," as one social worker put it. She told me about young men who had described the deaths of their parents in detail during asylum interviews—and who had later applied for family reunification.

3. It is also possible that my interlocutors were downplaying their own knowledge of their age. I thank Tinashe Chimbidzikai for pointing this out.

4. Asylum seekers like Idris thus also place their age claims on a different imagined trajectory (Tavory and Eliasoph 2013) than the German state does. When I see lying about my age as happening on a trajectory of years of unfulfilled youth, and in a context of extreme global inequality, its moral implications become quite different from when I start the trajectory with showing up at a German registration center and making false claims.

5. BAMF also cooperates with national delegations, especially from West African countries like Guinea, which are supposed to determine whether migrants are indeed nationals from their respective countries (Deutscher Bundestag 2020a).

6. Since many migrants' rights organizations depend on the goodwill of funders—be they governmental or private—they may also feel obligated to instruct their clients to tell the truth, even if they are personally sympathetic to fabrications.

Chapter 3

1. The fact that methods of age determination had not originally been developed to categorize refugees irritated many critics of age exams. An age examiner, however, put it this way: "Sildenafil wasn't developed for heart disease, but it works!"

2. The guidelines instruct social workers to assess voice pitch, hair, forehead and neck wrinkles, facial features, body build, hands, and facial and body hair; and also to select from personality traits like shy, reserved, scared, nervous, sad, polite, aggressive, stable, impulsive, naive, confident, or spiteful.

3. This could also be related to the so-called "own-race bias" (Lindsay et al. 1991): people usually find it easier to recognize and differentiate faces of their own race than those of other races. I thank Johanna Lukate for pointing this out.

4. When David describes shirking guidelines, he often uses the subjunctive.

5. While this is technically true, an asylum seeker determined to be underage does not have to file for asylum until he is eighteen. This gives him time to prepare for the interview or secure his residence through an apprenticeship. The Dublin III agreement also does not apply to minors, so they can file for asylum in Germany rather than live in fear of being returned to the EU country they first entered. Various alternative paths to residence, such as section 25a of the German Residence Act, are also closed to those classified as adults. Finally, an asylum seeker's allegedly false age claim can cast doubt on his entire story, decreasing his chances of receiving asylum.

6. In July 2016 I attended a meeting of maybe two hundred social workers from across Germany. They met to discuss their profession's role in the refugee crisis "between managing asylum and solidarity." The organizers made clear that the meeting's premise was unconditional solidarity with refugees. The attendants agreed—or at least none openly disagreed—that social work meant "reflexive partisanship" and "positioned working." They described their everyday work as a constant balancing of their personal and professional values against administrative guidelines that contradict those values.

7. For a problematization of defining the "typical" in science, particularly in atlases of natural phenomena, see Daston and Galison 2007.

8. "Empirical value" is comparable to what Lorraine Daston and Peter Galison have called trained judgment, "the necessity of seeing scientifically through an

interpretive eye" (2007, 311). Starting in the early twentieth century, notions of objectivity as inherent in machine-produced images were supplemented by a novel celebration of the skill and intuition crucial to their interpretation. Dr. Peters says he "just has a feeling," and that he "just knows." Accuracy began to be seen as more important than objectivity, and the new scientific self was more intellectual than algorithmic. Some scientists even began to perceive mechanical objectivity as a threat to their expertise and authority. Resorting to the language of instinct when justifying decisions is also typical in street-level bureaucratic work (Zacka 2017, 70).

9. It is perhaps important to note that pregnancy can actually affect a woman's bones (Naylor et al. 2000), which the exam did not take into account. I thank Johanna Lukate for pointing this out.

10. Of course, medical examiners' judgments are always consequential in some way. For example, Timmermans (2007) shows how medical examiners' classification of a death as a suicide affects family members, who may try to pressure them to opt for a less stigmatized cause of death. But these consequences, however traumatic they may be for individual families, are not political in the way a global migration crisis is.

Chapter 4

1. Young men from the Global South often intend for their migration to Europe to be a rite of passage—that is, an event that transitions them from membership in one group to another (Turner 1967; van Gennep [1909] 2019), and most importantly from childhood to adulthood and manhood (Massey et al. 1999; Kandel and Massey 2002).

2. This aspiration has been documented across diverse regional contexts, including West Africa (Vigh 2009; Gaibazzi 2010; Dougnon 2013; Drotbohm 2017; Suso 2019), East Africa (Grabska and Fanjoy 2015; Belloni 2019), Central Africa (Jua 2003; Ungruhe 2010), Southeast Asia (Aguilar 1999; Osella and Osella 2000; Ali 2007), the greater Middle East (Monsutti 2007), and Eastern Europe (Horváth 2008).

3. Each Berlin district has its own youth welfare office, and each has a reputation as permissive or strict.

4. Studies from the United States have also shown that Black boys (Goff et al. 2014) as well as Black girls (Epstein et al. 2017) tend to be seen as more mature and less childlike than their white peers. Similar biases may affect youth welfare employees' stance toward young male asylum seekers.

5. From other contexts, we know that socioeconomically disadvantaged men find alternative ways to assert their masculinity—as, for example, through promiscuity, illicit business, or risky alcohol and drug consumption (Bourgois 1995).

6. Jaeeun Kim (2022) similarly found that people who convert to a different religion for the sake of their legal residence status often internalize the new religion.

7. I would not have done this anyway. In line with Clifford Geertz's aphorism that to be an ethnographer is to learn to tell the difference between a wink and a blink, I had by now learned not to mistake a date of birth for a birthday.

8. I include his comments only to show how suspicion is practiced not only by the state but by asylum seekers with each other. It is not intended as commentary on people's identities.

9. Ravi Kohli similarly found that social workers often deliberately suspend their disbelief, taking a "vague approach to facts" (2007, 174), and taking the person they work with at face value.

10. It has been argued in the case of the Soviet Union (Yurchak 2005), the Eastern Bloc (Havel 2018), and Assad's Syria (Wedeen 2015), for example, that, rather than false consciousness, these countries' citizens had what Peter Sloterdijk has called an "enlightened false consciousness" (1993): they knew better, but deliberately pretended "as if" they did not.

11. The boat journey is a notable exception to this secrecy. As I argue in chapter 1, this is probably because its horror does not need to be embellished.

Chapter 5

1. Ali's recollection of his age exam serves as an important reminder of how different the ethnographer's perception can be from that of the people she studies. While I found Dr. Peters to be jovial and the atmosphere during the exams calm, Ali remembered a "loud, unfriendly man" and an "angry atmosphere." While I eagerly completed my field notes on the train home to Berlin in the afternoons following age exams, Ali returned to his youth shelter after his exam, only to learn that he was now eighteen and would have to leave immediately: "They told me to pack my things. I couldn't even have lunch."

2. In 2019, 1,003 asylum seekers were deported from Berlin (Abgeordnetenhaus Berlin 2020).

3. Thanks to vaccinations and improved living conditions, tuberculosis was extremely rare in Germany before 2015. Many asylum seekers from Africa, however, have tested positive for tuberculosis (Ärzteblatt 2017), fomenting fears about a resurgence of this infectious disease. Local newspapers even published the photograph of an asylum seeker with tuberculosis, who, like Samir, had refused treatment and thus was wanted by the police.

Chapter 6

1. Mustafa Emirbayer and Ann Mische define projectivity as "the imaginative generation by actors of possible future trajectories of action, in which received structures of thought and action may be creatively reconfigured in relation to actors' hopes, fears, and desires for the future" (1998, 971).

2. Similarly, Paolo Gaibazzi (2012) found that young Gambians, whose plans to migrate failed or were delayed, consoled themselves by proclaiming that it must not have been "God's time."

3. Interestingly, Idris's analogy mirrors critiques by migration scholars such as Rogier Van Reekum and Willem Schinkel (2017), who have pointed out the striking visual similarity between flowcharts of human and bird migration, in spite of which we tend to think of birds as belonging everywhere while humans belong to nation-states.

4. It bears repeating that I am not denying that many—perhaps most—of my interlocutors left their home countries for very understandable reasons. It is also true, however, that in the wake of the 2015–16 crisis, migrants' rights and legal counseling organizations in Germany became so fixed—as well as financially dependent, in some cases—on "refugees" that they labeled and treated every migrant who entered their offices as a refugee. I once witnessed a particularly jarring conversation between a well-meaning counselor and a young man from Moldova. Having come to Germany to find work, he was visibly confused by the counselor urging him to file for asylum, and her unrelenting attempt to identify hardships in his past beyond poverty and

unemployment: "But something bad must have happened to you! Otherwise you wouldn't be here," she exclaimed, despite his insistence that he had been absolutely fine.

5. Only two years later, such "worries" would turn out to have been unfounded, as the war in Tigray fueled fears over a looming Balkanization of Ethiopia, and thwarted international hopes in Abiy's presidency.

6. Valentina Mazzucato (2011) points out that in focusing only on the perspectives of migrants, we might get an impression of their families back home as being more demanding and less understanding than they actually are.

7. In January 2020, 1,700 unaccompanied minor asylum seekers were reported missing in Germany—comprising 20 percent of all missing persons in Germany (*Tagesspiegel* 2020).

8. I am not aware of statistics on the likelihood of surviving the journey from France to England, but UNHCR estimates the likelihood of dying while crossing from Africa to Italy to be 1:23 (Asserate 2018, 38).

9. Mische (2009) identifies various cognitive dimensions of future projection, among them reach (the degree to which a future is imagined in the long term or short term), contingency (the degree to which future scenarios are imagined as fixed or open), expandability (the degree to which future possibilities are seen as becoming greater or fewer), and volition (the level of influence someone has over the future).

Chapter 7

1. I thank Andrey Shlyakhter for this observation.

2. Sojourner Truth, for example, recounts how her age was adjusted to enable her sale as a slave: "When too old I was made younger, and when too young I was made older" (Ciafone and McGeehan Muchmore 2021, 4). In 2022, Japan lowered the legal majority age from twenty to eighteen—in an attempt, critics say, to expand the population that can be capitalized upon through credits and contracts.

3. See, for example, the roundtable "Chronological Age: A Useful Category of Historical Analysis," *American Historical Review* 125, no. 2 (2020).

4. For a critique of the "legal fiction" that only forced migrants are vulnerable, see Hamlin 2021; and for the converse critique of our tendency to overlook the desires of forced migrants, see Belloni 2019.

Epilogue

1. Various scholars of migration have made different decisions in this regard. While Seth Holmes (2013) crossed the US-Mexican border in order to "witness" this journey, Jason de León (2019) instead turned down his interlocutors' invitations to that end, because it would have put them in greater danger, exacerbated hierarchies between the "documented observer" and undocumented migrants, made the crossing anything but ordinary, and put the focus on the ethnographer rather than the interlocutors. I completely agree with de León's stance, and am glad not to have embarked on such a trip—from which, I believe, I would have learned nothing ethically justifiable.

2. On New Year's Eve 2015, about a thousand men—mostly from North African and Middle Eastern countries—assaulted, and in some cases raped, more than one thousand women gathering near Cologne Central Station. The events ignited a public

debate on whether young male migrants' alleged cultural values, frustration, and loneliness in Germany, as well as their propensity for aggression and violence, were putting German women at risk.

3. Lidwina Gundacker, Yuliya Kosyakova, and Gerald Schneider (2021) have found that for applicants from "free" countries, being male is indeed negatively associated with a positively decided asylum case.

4. I thank Eric Mazelis for pointing me to this debate.

SOURCES

Abbott, Andrew. 1981. "Status and Status Strain in the Professions." *American Journal of Sociology* 86, no. 4: 819–35.

Abdi, Cawo M. 2015. *Elusive Jannah: The Somali Diaspora and a Borderless Muslim Identity.* Minneapolis: University of Minnesota Press.

Abgeordnetenhaus Berlin. 2020. "Drucksache 18/22059 [Printed matter 18/22059]." https://pardok.parlament-berlin.de/starweb/adis/citat/VT/18/SchrAnfr/s18 -22058.pdf. Accessed June 4, 2021.

Adichie, Chimamanda Ngozi. 2013. *Americanah.* London: Harper Collins.

Aguilar Jr., Filomeno V. 1999. "Ritual Passage and the Reconstruction of Selfhood in International Labour Migration." *Sojourn: Journal of Social Issues in Southeast Asia* 33, no. S: 87–130.

Ali, Syed. 2007. "'Go West Young Man': The Culture of Migration among Muslims in Hyderabad, India." *Journal of Ethnic and Migration Studies* 33, no. 1: 37–58.

Arar, Rawan, and David Scott FitzGerald. 2023. *The Refugee System: A Sociological Approach.* Cambridge, UK: Polity.

Ariès, Philippe. 1973. *Centuries of Childhood.* Harmondsworth, UK: Penguin.

Ärzteblatt. 2017. "Tuberkulose: Häufige Erkrankung unter Asylbewerbern—geringes Risiko für Einheimische [Tuberculosis: Common among asylum seekers—low risk for natives]." https://www.aerzteblatt.de/nachrichten/83194/Tuberkulose -Haeufige-Erkrankung-unter-Asylbewerbern-geringes-Risiko-fuer-Einheimische. Accessed April 21, 2022.

Asserate, Asfa-Wossen. 2018. *Die neue Völkerwanderung: Wer Europa bewahren will, muss Afrika retten* [The new migration: To preserve Europe, we have to save Africa]. Berlin: Ullstein.

Asyl in der Kirche. 2022. "Aktuelle Zahlen: Kirchenasyle Bundesweit [Current numbers: Church asylums nationwide]." https://www.kirchenasyl.de/aktuelles/. Accessed April 21, 2022.

Bal, Ellen, and Roos Willems. 2014. "Introduction: Aspiring Migrants, Local Crises and the Imagination of Futures 'Away from Home.'" *Identities* 21, no. 3: 249–58.

Balibar, Étienne. 2015. "Borderland Europe and the Challenge of Migration." https:// www.opendemocracy.net/en/can-europe-make-it/borderland-europe-and -challenge-of-migration/. Accessed May 22, 2021.

BAMF. 2015. "Das Bundesamt in Zahlen [The Federal Ministry in numbers]." https:// www.bamf.de/SharedDocs/Anlagen/DE/Statistik/BundesamtinZahlen/bundesamt -in-zahlen-2015.html?nn=284738. Accessed May 22, 2021.

BAMF. 2016. "Das Bundesamt in Zahlen [The Federal Ministry in numbers]." https://www.bamf.de/SharedDocs/Anlagen/DE/Statistik/BundesamtinZahlen/bundesamt-in-zahlen-2016.html?nn=284738. Accessed May 22, 2021.

BAMF. 2017. "Das Bundesamt in Zahlen [The Federal Ministry in numbers]." https://www.bamf.de/SharedDocs/Anlagen/DE/Statistik/BundesamtinZahlen/bundesamt-in-zahlen-2017.html?nn=284738. Accessed May 22, 2021.

BAMF. 2018. "Das Bundesamt in Zahlen [The Federal Ministry in numbers]." https://www.bamf.de/SharedDocs/Anlagen/DE/Statistik/BundesamtinZahlen/bundesamt-in-zahlen-2018.html?nn=284738. Accessed May 22, 2021.

BAMF. 2019. "Das Bundesamt in Zahlen [The Federal Ministry in numbers]." https://www.bamf.de/SharedDocs/Anlagen/DE/Statistik/BundesamtinZahlen/bundesamt-in-zahlen-2019.html?nn=284738. Accessed May 22, 2021.

BAMF. 2020. "Das Bundesamt in Zahlen [The Federal Ministry in numbers]." https://www.bamf.de/SharedDocs/Anlagen/DE/Statistik/BundesamtinZahlen/bundesamt-in-zahlen-2020-asyl.html. Accessed May 22, 2021.

BAMF. 2021. "Länderreport 33: Äthiopien [Country report 33: Ethiopia]." https://www.bamf.de/SharedDocs/Anlagen/DE/Behoerde/Informationszentrum/Laenderreporte/2021/laenderreport-33-Aethiopien.pdf?_blob=publicationFile&v=2. Accessed August 1, 2021.

Barnett, Michael N., ed. 2017. *Paternalism beyond Borders*. Cambridge, UK: Cambridge University Press.

Bayerische Staatskanzlei. 2016. "Zuerkennung der Flüchtlingseigenschaft aufgrund von Verfolgung in Afghanistan [Granting refugee status because of persecution in Afghanistan]." https://www.gesetze-bayern.de/Content/Document/Y-300-Z-BECKRS-B-2016-N-53689?hl=true&AspxAutoDetectCookieSupport=1. Accessed June 3, 2021.

BBC. 2015. "Denmark Places Anti-Migrant Adverts in Lebanon Newspapers." https://www.bbc.com/news/world-europe-34173542. Accessed May 28, 2021.

Belloni, Milena. 2019. *The Big Gamble: The Migration of Eritreans to Europe*. Oakland: University of California Press.

Belloni, Milena. 2020. "When the Phone Stops Ringing: On the Meanings and Causes of Disruptions in Communication between Eritrean Refugees and Their Families Back Home." *Global Networks* 20, no. 2: 256–73.

Beltsiou, Julia. 2016. *Immigration in Psychoanalysis*. London: Routledge.

Beneduce, Roberto. 2015. "The Moral Economy of Lying: Subjectcraft, Narrative Capital, and Uncertainty in the Politics of Asylum." *Medical Anthropology* 34:551–71.

Benjamin, Walter. 1968. *Illuminations*. New York: Schocken.

Berger, Peter L., and Thomas Luckmann. 1967. *The Social Construction of Reality: A Treatise in the Sociology of Knowledge*. New York: Anchor.

Bhabha, Jacqueline. 2019. "Governing Adolescent Mobility: The Elusive Role of Children's Rights Principles in Contemporary Migration Practice." *Childhood* 26, no. 3: 369–85.

Bleek, Wolf. 1987. "Lying Informants: A Fieldwork Experience from Ghana." *Population and Development Review* 13, no. 2: 314–22.

Blommaert, Jan. 2009. "Language, Asylum, and the National Order." *Current Anthropology* 50, no. 4: 415–41.

Boehm, Deborah A. 2012. *Intimate Migrations: Gender, Family, and Illegality among Transnational Mexicans*. New York: NYU Press.

Bohm, Simon. 2021. *Kirchenasyl unter der BAMF-Kirchen-Vereinbarung: Zur Verrecht-lichung des Kirchenasyls in Folge der Flüchtlingskrise* [Church Asylum under the BAMF-Church Agreement: On the Legalization of Church Asylum as a Result of the Refugee Crisis]. Göttingen, Germany: Universitätsverlag Göttingen.

Bourdieu, Pierre. 1998. *Practical Reason: On the Theory of Action.* Redwood City, CA: Stanford University Press.

Bourdieu, Pierre. 2000. *Pascalian Meditations.* Redwood City, CA: Stanford University Press.

Bourgois, Philippe. 1995. *In Search of Respect: Selling Crack in El Barrio.* Cambridge, UK: Cambridge University Press.

Bourgois, Philippe, and Jeffrey Schonberg. 2009. *Righteous Dopefiend.* Oakland: University of California Press.

Bowker, Geoffrey C., and Susan Leigh Star. 2000. *Sorting Things Out: Classification and Its Consequences.* Cambridge, MA: MIT press.

Brigden, Noelle, and Ćetta Mainwaring. 2016. "Matryoshka Journeys: Im/mobility during Migration." *Geopolitics* 21, no. 2: 407–34.

Brubaker, Rogers. 2016. *Trans: Gender and Race in an Age of Unsettled Identities.* Princeton, NJ: Princeton University Press.

Buchmann, Marlis C., and Irene Kriesi. 2011. "Transition to Adulthood in Europe." *Annual Review of Sociology* 37:481–503.

Burgard, Antoine. 2021. "Contested Childhood: Assessing the Age of Young Refugees in the Aftermath of the Second World War." *History Workshop Journal* 92:174–93.

Butler, Judith. 1993. *Bodies That Matter: On the Discursive Limits of "Sex."* London: Routledge.

Campbell, John R. 2011. "The Enduring Problem of Statelessness in the Horn of Africa: How Nation-States and Western Courts (Re)Define Nationality." *International Journal of Refugee Law* 23, no. 4: 656–79.

Certeau, Michel de. 1984. *The Practice of Everyday Life.* Berkeley: University of California Press.

Chang, Aurora. 2016. "Undocumented Intelligence: Laying Low by Achieving High; An 'Illegal Alien's' Co-option of School and Citizenship." *Race Ethnicity and Education* 19, no. 6: 1164–76.

Chudacoff, Howard P. 1992. *How Old Are You? Age Consciousness in American Culture.* Princeton, NJ: Princeton University Press.

Ciafone, Amanda, and Devin McGeehan Muchmore. 2021. "Old Age and Radical History: Editors' Introduction." *Radical History Review* 139:1–12.

Cohen, Elizabeth F. 2018. *The Political Value of Time: Citizenship, Duration, and Democratic Justice.* Cambridge, UK: Cambridge University Press.

Crosnoe, Robert, and Monica Kirkpatrick Johnson. 2011. "Research on Adolescence in the Twenty-First Century." *Annual Review of Sociology* 37:439–60.

Daston, Lorraine, and Peter Galison. 2007. *Objectivity.* New York: Zone Books.

De Genova, Nicholas P. 2002. "Migrant 'Illegality' and Deportability in Everyday Life." *Annual Review of Anthropology* 31, no. 1: 419–47.

De Genova, Nicholas P. 2018. "'Crises,' Convulsions, Concurrences: Human Mobility, the European Geography of 'Exclusion,' and the Postcolonial Dialectics of Subordinate Inclusion. *Parse Journal* 8 (autumn).

De León, Jason. 2015. *The Land of Open Graves: Living and Dying on the Migrant Trail.* Oakland: University of California Press.

Desroche, Henri. 1979. *The Sociology of Hope*. London: Routledge & Kegan Paul.

Deutscher Bundestag. 2020a. "Drucksache 19/25290 [Printed matter 19/25290]." http://dipbt.bundestag.de/dip21/btd/19/252/1925290.pdf. Accessed May 26, 2021.

Deutscher Bundestag. 2020b. "Drucksache 19/18201 [Printed matter 19/18201]." https://berlin-hilft.com/wp-content/uploads/2020/08/1918201-3.pdf. Accessed July 3, 2022.

Deutscher Bundestag. 2021. "Drucksache 19/28109 [Printed matter 19/28109]." https://dip21.bundestag.de/dip21/btd/19/281/1928109.pdf. Accessed May 26, 2021.

Deutscher Bundestag. 2022. "Drucksache 20/1048 [Printed matter 20/1048]." https://dserver.bundestag.de/btd/20/010/2001048.pdf. Accessed July 5, 2022.

Dhupelia-Mesthrie, Uma. 2014. "Paper Regimes." *Kronos* 40, no. 1: 10–22.

Die Welt. 2018. "Organisierter Widerstand gegen die Altersfeststellung [Organized resistance against age determination]." https://www.welt.de/politik/deutschland /article172253669/Altersfeststellung-bei-Fluechtlingen-Diese-Lobby-organisiert -Widerstand.html. Accessed May 23, 2021.

Die Zeit. 2015. "Flüchtlinge: Das Ende der Verwöhntheit [Refugees: The end of fastidi-ousness]." https://www.zeit.de/2015/51/fluechtlinge-krieg-probleme-wohlstand -europa. Accessed May 22, 2021.

Die Zeit. 2019. "Für uns ist Migration eine natürliche Bewegung [Migration is a natu-ral movement for us]." https://www.zeit.de/politik/ausland/2019-09/eric-chinje -migration-fluechtlinge-mittelmeer-solidaritaet-afrika. Accessed May 22, 2021.

Diop, Mati, dir. 2019. *Atlantique*. ARTE France Cinéma.

Dougnon, Isaie. 2013. "Migration as Coping with Risk and State Barriers: Malian Migrants' Conception of Being Far from Home." In *African Migrations: Patterns and Perspectives*, edited by Abdoulaye Kane and Todd H. Leedy, 35–58. Bloomington: Indiana University Press.

Drotbohm, Heike. 2017. "How to Extract Hope from Papers? Classificatory Perfor-mances and Social Networking in Cape Verdean Visa Applications." In *Hope and Uncertainty in Contemporary African Migration*, edited by Nauja Kleist and Dorte Thorsen, 35–53. New York: Routledge.

Duneier, Mitchell. 1999. *Sidewalk*. New York: Macmillan.

Durkheim, Émile. 2005. *Suicide: A Study in Sociology*. New York: Routledge.

Emirbayer, Mustafa, and Ann Mische. 1998. "What Is Agency?" *American Journal of Sociology* 103, no. 4: 962–1023.

Ensor, Marisa O. 2010. "Understanding Migrant Children: Conceptualizations, Ap-proaches, and Issues." In *Children and Migration: At the Crossroads of Resiliency and Vulnerability*, edited by Marisa O. Ensor and Elżbieta Goździak, 15–35. New York: Palgrave Macmillan.

Epstein, Rebecca, Jamilia J. Blake, and Thalia González. 2017. "Girlhood Interrupted: The Erasure of Black Girls' Childhood." https://genderjusticeandopportunity .georgetown.edu/wp-content/uploads/2020/06/girlhood-interrupted.pdf. Accessed November 2, 2022.

Espeland, Wendy Nelson, and Mitchell L. Stevens. 2008. "A Sociology of Quantifica-tion." *European Journal of Sociology* 49, no. 3: 401–36.

Eule, Tobias G. 2016. *Inside Immigration Law: Migration Management and Policy Appli-cation in Germany*. London: Routledge.

Faist, Thomas. 2018. "The Moral Polity of Forced Migration." *Ethnic and Racial Studies* 41, no. 3: 412–23.

Fassin, Didier. 2018. *Life: A Critical User's Manual*. Cambridge, UK: Polity.

Faus, Rainer, and Simon Storks. 2019. "Das pragmatische Einwanderungsland: Was die Deutschen über Migration denken [The pragmatic immigration country: What Germans think about migration]." https://library.fes.de/pdf-files/fes/15213–2019 0402.pdf. Accessed July 12, 2022.

Fernández Huertas Moraga, Jesús. 2021. "Asylum Policies and the Distribution of Refugees across European Countries." Keynote address at IAB-ECSR interdisciplinary conference, May 27, 2021.

Field, Corinne T., and Nicholas L. Syrett. 2020. "Introduction." *American Historical Review* 125, no. 2: 371–84.

FitzGerald, David Scott. 2019. *Refuge beyond Reach: How Rich Democracies Repel Asylum Seekers*. Oxford, UK: Oxford University Press.

FitzGerald, David Scott, and Rawan Arar. 2018. "The Sociology of Refugee Migration." *Annual Review of Sociology* 44:387–406.

Fujii, Lee Ann. 2010. "Shades of Truth and Lies: Interpreting Testimonies of War and Violence." *Journal of Peace Research* 47, no. 2: 231–41.

Gaibazzi, Paolo. 2010. "Migration, Soninke Young Men and the Dynamics of Staying Behind (the Gambia)." PhD dissertation, University of Milano-Bicocca.

Gaibazzi, Paolo. 2012. "'God's Time is the Best': Religious Imagination and the Wait for Emigration in the Gambia." In *The Global Horizon: Expectations of Migration in Africa and the Middle East*, edited by Knut Graw and Samuli Schielke, 121–35. Leuven, Belgium: Leuven University Press.

Galli, Chiara. 2018. "A Rite of Reverse Passage: The Construction of Youth Migration in the US Asylum Process." *Ethnic and Racial Studies* 41, no. 9: 1651–71.

Galli, Chiara. 2020. "The Ambivalent US Context of Reception and the Dichotomous Legal Consciousness of Unaccompanied Minors." *Social Problems* 67, no. 4: 763–81.

Galonnier, Juliette. 2017. "Choosing Faith and Facing Race: Converting to Islam in France and the United States." PhD dissertation, Northwestern University and Institut d'études politiques de Paris.

Gamson, Joshua. 1995. "Must Identity Movements Self-Destruct? A Queer Dilemma." *Social Problems* 42, no. 3: 390–407.

Goethe, Johann Wolfgang von. 1982. *Maximen und Reflektionen* [*Maxims and Reflections*]. Hamburger Ausgabe Band 12. Munich: Dtv.

Goff, Phillip Atiba, Matthew Christian Jackson, Brooke Allison Lewis Di Leone, Carmen Marie Culotta, and Natalie Ann DiTomasso. 2014. "The Essence of Innocence: Consequences of Dehumanizing Black Children." *Journal of Personality and Social Psychology* 106, no. 4: 526.

Goffman, Alice. 2014. *On the Run: Fugitive Life in an American City*. Chicago: University of Chicago Press.

Goffman, Erving. 1959. *The Presentation of Self in Everyday Life*. New York: Anchor Books.

Goffman, Erving. 1967. *Interaction Ritual: Essays on Face-to-Face Interaction*. New York: Anchor Books.

Gonzales, Roberto G. 2011. "Learning to be Illegal: Undocumented Youth and Shifting Legal Contexts in the Transition to Adulthood." *American Sociological Review* 76, no. 4: 602–19.

Goodman, Adam. 2020. *The Deportation Machine: America's Long History of Expelling Immigrants*. Princeton, NJ: Princeton University Press.

Grabska, Katarzyna, and Martha Fanjoy. 2015. "'And When I Become a Man': Translocal Coping with Precariousness and Uncertainty among Returnee Men in South Sudan." *Social Analysis* 59, no. 1: 76–95.

Griffiths, Melanie. 2017. "The Changing Politics of Time in the UK's Immigration System." In *Timespace and International Migration*, edited by Elizabeth Mavroudi, Ben Page, and Anastasia Christou, 48–60. Cheltenham, UK: Edward Elgar Publishing.

Groebner, Valentin. 2007. *Who Are You? Identification, Deception, and Surveillance in Early Modern Europe*. Princeton, NJ: Princeton University Press.

Gundacker, Lidwina, Yuliya Kosyakova, and Gerald Schneider. 2021. "Global Norms, Regional Practices: Taste-Based and Statistical Discrimination in German Asylum Decision-Making." Working Paper Series, no. 05.

Gusterson, Hugh. 1996. *Nuclear Rites: A Weapons Laboratory at the End of the Cold War*. Oakland: University of California Press.

Hacking, Ian. 1986. "Making Up People." In *Reconstructing Individualism: Autonomy, Individuality, and the Self in Western Thought*, edited by Thomas C. Heller, Morton Sosna, and David E. Wellbery, 222–36. Redwood City, CA: Stanford University Press.

Hage, Ghassan. 2009. "Waiting Out the Crisis: On Stuckedness and Governmentality." *Anthropological Theory* 5:463–75.

Hamlin, Rebecca. 2021. *Crossing: How We Label and React to People on the Move*. Redwood City, CA: Stanford University Press.

Harpaz, Yossi. 2019. *Citizenship 2.0: Dual Nationality as a Global Asset*. Princeton, NJ: Princeton University Press.

Havel, Václav. 2018. "The Power of the Powerless." *East European Politics and Societies* 32, no. 2: 353–408.

Hegde, Radha Sarma. 2016. *Mediating Migration*. Hoboken, NJ: John Wiley & Sons.

Holmes, Seth. 2013. *Fresh Fruit, Broken Bodies*. Oakland: University of California Press.

Hopkins, Peter E., and Malcolm Hill. 2008. "Pre-Flight Experiences and Migration Stories: The Accounts of Unaccompanied Asylum-Seeking Children." *Children's Geographies* 6, no. 3: 257–68.

Horst, Cindy. 2006. "Buufis amongst Somalis in Dadaab: The Transnational and Historical Logics behind Resettlement Dreams." *Journal of Refugee Studies* 19, no. 2: 143–57.

Horváth, István. 2008. "The Culture of Migration of Rural Romanian Youth." *Journal of Ethnic and Migration Studies* 34, no. 5: 771–86.

Jain, Sarah Lochlann. 2007. "Living in Prognosis: Toward an Elegiac Politics." *Representations* 98, no. 1: 77–92.

Joppke, Christian. 2019. "The Instrumental Turn of Citizenship." *Journal of Ethnic and Migration Studies* 45, no. 6: 858–78.

Jua, Nantang. 2003. "Differential Responses to Disappearing Transitional Pathways: Redefining Possibility among Cameroonian Youths." *African Studies Review* 46, no. 2: 13–36.

Juárez, Fatima, and Cecilia Gayet. 2014. "Transitions to Adulthood in Developing Countries." *Annual Review of Sociology* 40:521–38.

Kandel, William, and Douglas Massey. 2002. "The Culture of Mexican Migration: A Theoretical and Empirical Analysis." *Social Forces* 80, no. 3: 981–1004.

Katz, Jack. 2012. "Ethnography's Expanding Warrants." *Annals of the American Academy of Political and Social Science* 642, no. 1: 258–75.

Kibreab, Gaim. 2004. "Pulling the Wool over the Eyes of the Strangers: Refugee Deceit and Trickery in Institutionalized Settings." *Journal of Refugee Studies* 17, no. 1: 1–26.

Kim, Jaeeun. 2015. "Seeking Asylum, Finding God: Religious Conversion for Immigration Purposes and the Politics of Deservingness in Contemporary America." Presented at the Law and Society Association Annual Meeting, Seattle, May 28–31.

Kim, Jaeeun. 2022. "Between Sacred Gift and Profane Exchange: Identity Craft and Relational Work in Asylum Claims-Making on Religious Grounds." *Theory and Society* 51, no. 2: 303–33.

Köhler, Horst. 2017. "Jung, dynamisch, afrikanisch sucht . . . [Young, dynamic, African and searching . . .]" https://www.tagesspiegel.de/politik/afrika-jung-dyna misch-afrikanisch-sucht-/20691654-all.html. Accessed May 22, 2021.

Kohli, Ravi. 2007. *Social Work with Unaccompanied Asylum-Seeking Children*. London: Palgrave Macmillan.

Lakhani, Sarah Morando. 2013. "Producing Immigrant Victims' 'Right' to Legal Status and the Management of Legal Uncertainty." *Law & Social Inquiry* 38, no. 2: 442–73.

Lamont, Michèle, and Virág Molnár. 2002. "The Study of Boundaries in the Social Sciences." *Annual Review of Sociology* 28:167–95.

Lampland, Martha, and Susan Leigh Star. 2008. *Standards and Their Stories: How Quantifying, Classifying and Formalizing Practices Shape Everyday Life*. Ithaca, NY: Cornell University Press.

Lawrance, Benjamin N., and Jacqueline Stevens, eds. 2017. *Citizenship in Question: Evidentiary Birthright and Statelessness*. Durham, NC: Duke University Press.

Le Courant, Stefan. 2020. "Expulsion or Differential Inclusion? Governing Undocumented Migrants in France." In *Digesting Difference*, edited by Kelly McKowen and John Borneman, 209–26. London: Palgrave Macmillan.

Lems, Annika, Kathrin Oester, and Sabine Strasser. 2020. "Children of the Crisis: Ethnographic Perspectives on Unaccompanied Refugee Youth in and En Route to Europe." *Journal of Ethnic and Migration Studies* 46, no. 2: 315–35.

Lindsay, D. Stephen, Philip C. Jack, and Marcus A. Christian. 1991. "Other-Race Face Perception." *Journal of Applied Psychology* 76, no. 4: 587.

Lipsky, Michael. 1980. *Street-Level Bureaucracy: Dilemmas of the Individual in Public Services*. New York: Russell Sage.

MacLeod, Jay. 1987. *Ain't No Makin' It: Aspirations and Attainment in a Low-Income Neighborhood*. London: Routledge.

Mahmood, Saba. 2001. "Feminist Theory, Embodiment, and the Docile Agent: Some Reflections on the Egyptian Islamic Revival." *Cultural Anthropology* 16, no. 2: 202–36.

Mahmood, Saba. 2005. *Politics of Piety: The Islamic Revival and the Feminist Subject*. Princeton, NJ: Princeton University Press.

Mansour, Hussam, Andreas Fuhrmann, Ilona Paradowski, Eilin Jopp van Well, and Klaus Püschel. 2017. "The Role of Forensic Medicine and Forensic Dentistry in

Estimating the Chronological Age of Living Individuals in Hamburg, Germany." *International Journal of Legal Medicine* 131, no. 2: 593–601.

Marfleet, Philip. 2011. "Understanding 'Sanctuary': Faith and Traditions of Asylum." *Journal of Refugee Studies* 24, no. 3: 440–55.

Marwick, Alice E., and danah boyd. 2010. "I Tweet Honestly, I Tweet Passionately: Twitter Users, Context Collapse, and the Imagined Audience." *New Media & Society* 13, no. 1: 114–33.

Massey, Douglas S. 2007. *Categorically Unequal: The American Stratification System.* New York: Russell Sage Foundation.

Massey, Douglas S., Joaquín Arango, Graeme Hugo, Ali Kouaouci, Adela Pellegrino, and J. Edward Taylor. 1999. *Worlds in Motion: Understanding International Migration at the End of the Millennium.* Oxford, UK: Clarendon Press.

Mazzucato, Valentina. 2011. "Reverse Remittances in the Migration-Development Nexus: Two-Way Flows between Ghana and the Netherlands." *Population, Space and Place* 17, no. 5: 454–68.

McKinsey Global Institute. 2016. "Lions on the Move II: Realizing the Potential of Africa's Economies." https://www.mckinsey.com/~/media/McKinsey/Featured%20 Insights/Middle%20East%20and%20Africa/Realizing%20the%20potential%20 of%20Africas%20economies/MGI-Lions-on-the-Move-2-Full-report-September -2016v2.pdf. Accessed May 22, 2021.

Meissner, Fran. 2018. "Legal Status Diversity: Regulating to Control and Everyday Contingencies." *Journal of Ethnic and Migration Studies* 44, no. 2: 287–306.

Menjívar, Cecilia. 2006. "Liminal Legality: Salvadoran and Guatemalan Immigrants' Lives in the United States." *American Journal of Sociology* 111, no. 4: 999–1037.

Menjívar, Cecilia. 2023. "State Categories, Bureaucracies of Displacement, and Possibilities from the Margins." *American Sociological Review* 88, no. 1: 1–23.

Menjívar, Cecilia, and Sarah M. Lakhani. 2016. "Transformative Effects of Immigration Law: Immigrants' Personal and Social Metamorphoses through Regularization." *American Journal of Sociology* 121, no 6; 1818–55.

Merton, Robert K. 1987. "Three Fragments from a Sociologist's Notebooks: Establishing the Phenomenon, Specified Ignorance, and Strategic Research Materials." *Annual Review of Sociology* 13:1–29.

Meyers, Todd. 2014. "Promise and Deceit: Pharmakos, Drug Replacement Therapy, and the Perils of Experience." *Culture, Medicine, and Psychiatry* 38, no. 2: 182–96.

Mezlekia, Nega. 2000. *Notes from the Hyena's Belly: An Ethiopian Boyhood.* New York: Picador USA.

Milo, Daniel S. *Good Enough: The Tolerance for Mediocrity in Nature and Society.* Cambridge, MA: Harvard University Press.

Mische, Ann. 2009. "Projects and Possibilities: Researching Futures in Action." *Sociological Forum* 24, no. 3: 694–704.

Mische, Ann. 2014. "Measuring Futures in Action: Projective Grammars in the Rio + 20 Debates." *Theory and Society* 43, no. 3: 437–64.

Mittermaier, Amira. 2010. *Dreams That Matter: Egyptian Landscapes of the Imagination.* Oakland: University of California Press.

Monk, Ellis P., Jr. 2015. "The Cost of Color: Skin Color, Discrimination, and Health among African-Americans." *American Journal of Sociology* 121, no. 2: 396–444.

Monsutti, Alessandro. 2007. "Migration as a Rite of Passage: Young Afghans Building Masculinity and Adulthood in Iran." *Iranian Studies* 40, no. 2: 167–85.

Motomura, Hiroshi. 2020. "The New Migration Law: Migrants, Refugees, and Citizens in an Anxious Age." *Cornell Law Review* 105:457–548.

Nachman, Steven R. 1984. "Lies My Informants Told Me." *Journal of Anthropological Research* 40, no. 4: 536–55.

Naylor, K. E., P. Iqbal, C. Fledelius, R. B. Fraser, and R. Eastell. 2000. "The Effect of Pregnancy on Bone Density and Bone Turnover." *Journal of Bone and Mineral Research* 15, no. 1: 129–37.

Obligacion, Freddie R. 1994. "Managing Perceived Deception among Respondents: A Traveler's Tale." *Journal of Contemporary Ethnography* 23, no. 1: 29–50.

Osella, Filippo, and Caroline Osella. 2000. "Migration, Money and Masculinity in Kerala." *Journal of the Royal Anthropological Institute* 6, no. 1: 117–33.

Partridge, Damani James. 2008. "We Were Dancing in the Club, Not on the Berlin Wall: Black Bodies, Street Bureaucrats, and Exclusionary Incorporation into the New Europe." *Cultural Anthropology* 23, no. 4: 660–87.

Pew Research Center. 2018. "At Least a Million Sub-Saharan Africans Moved to Europe since 2010." https://www.pewresearch.org/global/2018/03/22/at-least -a-million-sub-saharan-africans-moved-to-europe-since-2010/. Accessed May 22, 2021.

Pro Asyl. 2018. "Pressemitteilung: Einwanderungsgesetz; Geduldete Schüler/innen, Studierende und Alleinerziehende dürfen nicht vergessen werden [Press Release: Immigration Law; Tolerated Students, College Students, and Single Parents Must Not Be Forgotten]. https://www.proasyl.de/pressemitteilung/einwanderung sgesetz-geduldete-schueler-innen-studierende-und-alleinerziehende-duerfen-nicht -vergessen-werden/. Accessed June 4, 2021.

RöV. 1987. "Verordnung über den Schutz vor Schäden durch Röntgenstrahlen (Röntgenverordnung) [Decree for the Protection against Damage from Radiation (X-Ray Ordinance)]."

Salamone, Frank A. 1977. "The Methodological Significance of the Lying Informant." *Anthropological Quartlerly* 50, no. 3: 117–24.

Sassen, Saskia. 2014. *Expulsions: Brutality and Complexity in the Global Economy.* Cambridge, MA: Harvard University Press.

Sassen, Saskia. 2016. "Three Emergent Migrations: An Epochal Change." *SUR: International Journal on Human Rights* 23:29.

Schmeling, Andreas, Walter Reisinger, Dieter Loreck, Klaus Vendura, Markus Wohlschläger, and Gunther Geserick. 2000. "Effects of Ethnicity on Skeletal Maturation: Consequences for Forensic Age Estimations." *International Journal of Legal Medicine* 113:253–58.

Schuster, Liza. 2005. "The Continuing Mobility of Migrants in Italy: Shifting between Places and Statuses." *Journal of Ethnic and Migration Studies* 31, no. 4: 757–74.

Schutz, Alfred. 1967. *The Phenomenology of the Social World.* Evanston, IL: Northwestern University Press.

Scott, James C. 1998. *Seeing Like a State.* New Haven, CT: Yale University Press.

Sheridan, Lynnaire Maria. 2009. *"I Know It's Dangerous": Why Mexicans Risk Their Lives to Cross the Border.* Tucson: University of Arizona Press.

Simmel, Georg. 1950. *The Sociology of Georg Simmel.* New York: The Free Press.

Skiba, Melanie. 2017. "Was ist eigentlich . . . eine Tazkira? [What is . . . a Tazkira?]" Rundbrief 01/2017 des Flüchtlingsrat Baden-Württemberg [Newsletter 01/2017 of the Baden-Württemberg Refugee Council].

Sloterdijk, Peter. 1993. *Critique of Cynical Reason*. Minneapolis: University of Minnesota Press.

Smith, Stephen. 2018. *Nach Europa! Das junge Afrika auf dem Weg zum alten Kontinent*. Berlin: Edition.fotoTAPETA. Published in English as *The Scramble for Europe: Young Africa on Its Way to the Old Continent*. Cambridge, UK, and Medford, MA: Polity, 2019.

Star, Susan Leigh. 2010. "This Is Not a Boundary Object: Reflections on the Origin of a Concept." *Science, Technology, & Human Values* 35, no. 5: 601–17.

Star, Susan Leigh, and Geoffrey Bowker. 2007. "Enacting Silence: Residual Categories as a Challenge for Ethics, Information Systems, and Communication." *Ethics and Information Technology* 9:273–80.

Stevens, Jacqueline. 2017. "Introduction" and "The Alien Who Is a Citizen." In *Citizenship in Question: Evidentiary Birthright and Statelessness*, edited by Benjamin N. Lawrance and Jacqueline Stevens, 1–24 and 217–39. Durham, NC: Duke University Press.

Süddeutsche Zeitung. 2019. "Kirchenasyl: Bundesamt agiert immer restriktiver [Church asylum: Federal ministry becomes ever more restrictive]." https://www.sueddeutsche.de/politik/fluechtlinge-kirchenasyl-1.4629036. Accessed June 3, 2021.

Sunstein, Cass R. 2007. "Incompletely Theorized Agreements in Constitutional Law." *Social Research: An International Quarterly* 74, no. 1: 1–24.

Suso, Catherine T. Conrad. 2019. "Involuntary Immobility and the Unfulfilled Rite of Passage: The Implications for Migration Management in the Gambia, West Africa." *International Migration* 58, no. 4: 184–94.

Tagesspiegel. 2020. "Auf der Suche nach den verschwundenen Flüchtlingskindern [In search of the disappeared refugee children]." https://interaktiv.tagesspiegel.de/lab/wo-die-meisten-gefluechteten-jugendlichen-vermisst-werden/. Accessed June 4, 2021.

Tangermann, Julian. 2017. "Documenting and Establishing Identity in the Migration Process. Challenges and Practices in the German Context. Focused study by the German National Contact Point for the European Migration Network (EMN)." Working paper 76, Federal Office for Migration and Refugees.

Tavory, Iddo, and Nina Eliasoph. 2013. "Coordinating Futures: Toward a Theory of Anticipation." *American Journal of Sociology* 118, no. 4: 908–42.

Thorsen, Dorte. 2006. "Child Migrants in Transit: Strategies to Assert New Identities in Rural Burkina Faso." In *Navigating Youth, Generating Adulthood: Social Becoming in an African Context*, edited by Catrine Christiansen, Mats Utas, and Henrik E. Vigh, 88–114. Uppsala, Sweden: Nordiska Afrikainstitutet.

Ticktin, Miriam I. 2011. *Casualties of Care: Immigration and the Politics of Humanitarianism in France*. Oakland: University of California Press.

Tilly, Charles. 1998. *Durable Inequality*. Berkeley: University of California Press.

Timmermans, Stefan. 2007. *Postmortem: How Medical Examiners Explain Suspicious Deaths*. Chicago: University of Chicago Press.

Timmermans, Stefan, and Steven Epstein. 2010. "A World of Standards but Not a Standard World: Toward a Sociology of Standards and Standardization." *Annual Review of Sociology* 36:69–89.

Torpey, John. 1999. *The Invention of the Passport: Surveillance, Citizenship and the State*. Cambridge, UK: Cambridge University Press.

Treas, Judith. 2009. "Age in Standards and Standards for Age: Institutionalizing Chronological Age as Biographical Necessity." In *Standards and Their Stories*, edited by Martha Lampland and Susan Leigh Star, 65–87. Ithaca, NY: Cornell University Press.

Triadafilopoulos, Triadafilos, and Karen Schönwälder. 2006. "How the Federal Republic Became an Immigration Country: Norms, Politics and the Failure of West Germany's Guest Worker System." *German Politics & Society* 80, no. 24/3: 1–19.

Turner, Victor. 1967. *The Forest of Symbols: Aspects of Ndembu Ritual*. Ithaca, NY: Cornell University Press.

UN. 1990. "Convention on the Rights of the Child." https://www.ohchr.org/en/pro fessionalinterest/pages/crc.aspx. Accessed December 21, 2020.

UNHCR. 2010. "Convention and Protocol Relating to the Status of Refugees." https:// www.unhcr.org/3b66c2aa10. Accessed December 21, 2020.

UNHCR. 1997. "Guidelines on Policies and Procedures in Dealing with Unaccompanied Children Seeking Asylum." https://www.unhcr.org/3d4f91cf4.pdf. Accessed June 3, 2021.

Ungruhe, Christian. 2010. "Symbols of Success: Youth, Peer Pressure and the Role of Adulthood among Juvenile Male Return Migrants in Ghana." *Childhood* 17, no. 2: 259–71.

Van Gennep, Arnold. [1909] 2019. *The Rites of Passage*. Chicago: University of Chicago Press.

Van Reekum, Rogier, and Willem Schinkel. 2017. "Drawing Lines, Enacting Migration: Visual Prostheses of Bordering Europe." *Public Culture* 29, no. 1: 27–51.

Vertovec, Steven. 2023. *Superdiversity: Migration and Social Complexity*. New York: Routledge.

Vigh, Henrik. 2009. "Wayward Migration: On Imagined Futures and Technological Voids." *Ethnos* 74, no. 1: 91–109.

Voutira, Eftihia, and Barbara Harrell-Bond. 1995. "In Search of the Locus of Trust: The Social World of the Refugee Camp." In *Mistrusting Refugees*, edited by E. Valentine Daniel and John Chr. Knudsen, 207–24. Oakland: University of California Press.

Waage, Trond. 2006. "Coping with Unpredictability: 'Preparing for Life' in Ngaoundéré, Cameroon." In *Navigating Youth, Generating Adulthood: Social Becoming in an African Context*, edited by Catrine Christiansen, Mats Utas, and Henrik E. Vigh, 61–87. Uppsala, Sweden: Nordiska Afrikainstitutet.

Wedeen, Lisa. 2015. *Ambiguities of Domination: Politics, Rhetoric, and Symbols in Contemporary Syria*. Chicago: University of Chicago Press.

Wiesinger, Irmela. 2018. "Integration und Identitätsbildung junger Geflüchteter in der Jugendhilfe: Ein Drahtseilakt ohne Sicherung [Integration and identity formation of young refugees in youth welfare: A balancing act without safety net]." *Jugendamt* 10:426–36.

Winter, Jessica. 2022. "Why More and More Girls Are Hitting Puberty Early: A Pandemic-Era Rise in Early Puberty May Help Physicians to Better Understand Its Causes." https://www.newyorker.com/science/annals-of-medicine/why-more -and-more-girls-are-hitting-puberty-early. Accessed November 2, 2022.

Yurchak, Alexei. 2005. *Everything Was Forever until It Was No More: The Last Soviet Generation*. Princeton, NJ: Princeton University Press.

Zacka, Bernardo. 2017. *When the State Meets the Street.* Cambridge, MA: Harvard University Press.

Zelizer, Viviana A. 1994. *Pricing the Priceless Child: The Changing Social Value of Children.* Princeton, NJ: Princeton University Press.

Zerubavel, Eviatar. 2006. *The Elephant in the Room: Silence and Denial in Everyday Life.* Oxford, UK: Oxford University Press.

INDEX